PIRATES
PUNKS
& POLITICS

PIRATES
PUNKS
& POLITICS

NICK DAVIDSON

In memory of Helen and Elijah
YNWA

Also by Nick Davidson
Team Shirts to Ticket Stubs:
A Visual History of Watford Football Club 1977–2002

By Nick Davidson & Shaun Hunt
Modern Football is Rubbish
Modern Football is Still Rubbish

CONTENTS

They're not a team, we are a club
Sankt Pauli 'til I die, Sankt Pauli 'til I die,
The Totenkopf's the flag I fly,
Sankt Pauli 'til I die, Sankt Pauli 'til I die,
And when I dream:
I'm wearing brown and white,
standing under Millerntor lights,
singin': Sankt Pauli 'til I die

Swearing At Motorists

FOREWORD

I WILL NEVER forget the moment I first stepped foot into the Millerntor; I just knew that I belonged to this club. Everything about the place was special: the green grass, the towering floodlights, the intimidating Totenkopf hoodies being worn by almost everyone inside but more importantly the incredible atmosphere. I'm sure that is a feeling recognisable to those people reading this who have visited our club.

As a player, the first thing you do when you sign to play for FC St. Pauli is take a tour around the district. It is a tradition that will live with the club forever, so that every player who is lucky enough to wear that shirt knows that you don't just represent a football club, you represent a community, a political movement, a religion. The walk around St. Pauli made me proud to be a KiezKicker because I knew that if I could help our club have success we could give our fans the opportunity on a national level to have their voice heard and they did not disappoint. Being part of the squad that won promotion from the wilderness of the Regionalliga back to 2. Bundesliga in 2006–07 was one of the highlights of my professional career.

The fight against racism, homophobia, sexism, discrimination and other political movements is a world issue that fans of FC St. Pauli will forever stand up for and it makes me proud to represent FC St. Pauli for the rest of my life.

This book explains why FC St. Pauli is a special club to support; it is also a very special club to play for. Whether you are a player or supporter, there is no better feeling than being at the Millerntor when it is full to the brim, floodlights on, Hamburger Dom whirring and spinning in the background as the opening clang of *Hells Bells* kicks in. Even now it makes me want to pull on that Number 3 shirt and get on the pitch.

I hope you enjoy the book and it helps you to understand the unique atmosphere and culture of St. Pauli.

Forza!

Ian Joy
FC St. Pauli 2005–06 to 2007–08

Ian Joy grew up in Scotland and spent time on the books of Manchester United and Tranmere Rovers as a youngster. He made his professional debut for Montrose in a career that also took in clubs in England, Germany and the United States. Joy arrived in Hamburg for the 2004–05 season playing for Hambuger SV's reserve team. A year later, he journeyed across town to join FC St. Pauli. His time at the Millerntor saw him play 87 times for the club, scoring one goal. He slotted into the side at left back and quickly became a popular figure both in the dressing-room and on the terraces, where his no-nonsense tackling was particularly appreciated by the fans.

Joy helped the club escape from the Regionalliga, winning promotion to 2. Bundesliga in 2007. He went on to play for Real Salt Lake in the MLS and captained the Portland Timbers in the USSF Division 2 Professional League. Since retiring from professional foootball in 2010, Joy has worked as sports presenter on US television. Ian's time at FC St. Pauli left a mark on him in more ways than one: he has an enormous Totenkopf (skull and crossbones) tattooed across his back. He remains a huge fan of the club and all it stands for.

MATCH

...AND I KNOW WHY I STAND HERE

FC St. Pauli 1 Bayer Leverkusen 0
DFB Pokal first round
Saturday 4 August 2007, 3.30pm, Millerntor Stadion

A SWELTERING HOT afternoon in August. Whatever the weather the football season has always started this way. My old man and I find ourselves in a tightly packed crowd, edging our way closer to the narrow stadium entrance. It takes ages to get into the ground, but no one is complaining, after all, there is still an hour and a half until kick-off. The sun is beating down and has turned the neck of the bloke in front of us lobster pink, but the weather only adds to the mood and the crowd around us has that air of optimism that the first Saturday of a new season always brings.

We've started so many seasons this way, a father–son bond stretching back over a quarter of a century to 1982, when my Dad took me to my first ever match at Vicarage Road. Only this season is slightly different. We've not parked the car in our usual spot at the bottom of Whippendell Road, or made the familiar trek through the streets of west Watford. We've not stopped at our regular newsagent, round the corner from the ground, to buy our chewing-gum (for the tension) and the Mars Bars (for half-time sustenance). And, unusually, we can't understand more than the odd word uttered by the crowd that surrounds us. We are a long way from Vicarage Road. A long way from Watford FC.

We are at the Millerntor Stadium in Hamburg to watch FC St. Pauli play Bayer Leverkusen in the first round of the German cup. FC St. Pauli are on a high, having secured promotion back to the second division after four seasons in the relative wilderness of the Regionalliga (the regionalised third tier of German football) but Leverkusen are formidable opposition and will provide a real test.

Over the last few years things have changed for my Dad and me. We stopped our Watford season tickets a couple of years back and, as each season passed, we found ourselves going to fewer and fewer games. There were reasons: we'd both moved further away; I've got young kids and couldn't afford – or justify – the time or expense of watching football every other Saturday; and, on top of all that, my old man beat cancer although he lost a kidney in the process. But truth be told, the real reason I packed it in was because I fell out of love with English football. Watford's season in the Premier League in 1999–2000 was the beginning of the end. It wasn't the 1980s any more. Watford simply couldn't compete. In 1982–83 we'd marked our debut season in the top flight with a runners' up spot behind Liverpool. Seventeen years later we finished bottom with 24 points and a paltry six wins. So, by the time Gianluca Vialli replaced Graham Taylor as manager and the fall-out from the ITV Digital debacle began to bite, I'd lost faith. Football had sold itself down the river. The Premiership had distorted everything. Salaries and admission prices had gone through the roof, kick-off times were at the mercy of television executives and the very soul of football had been sold to the highest bidder.

There's nothing unique about my disillusionment. I'm sure many of you who have picked up this book have been on a similar journey. The specific club and time frame may be different, but the feelings of despondency are pretty universal. However, like most football fans, I found kicking a lifetime's habit wasn't easy. I might have found it surprisingly painless to quit following Watford, but I still needed a fix of football. I'm a fairly all-or-nothing type person, and once I'd got out of the routine of going every other Saturday, I found it easy to completely switch off from Watford – I know that sounds awful; a football club is supposed to be for life, but it was true. Once I'd broken the habit, following the scores on *5Live* or the internet left me cold.

Yet, I couldn't kick football altogether. I tried our local non-league club for a couple of seasons, even doing a stint on the committee. I enjoyed the total lack of pretension that I found in the lower reaches of the football pyramid. I was a sucker for the romanticism of it all and loved travelling to the windswept outposts of the United Counties League, occasionally taking my Dad with me – he got to Ford Sports Daventry but, quite rightly, drew the line at a cross-country trip to St. Neots on a Tuesday night. So, often I went on my own, just enjoying the relative solitude of a midweek away game at Step 5 of the non-league pyramid. I got onto the committee which had its advantages: sandwiches and cups of tea at away games (a flash of a dog-eared pass marked 'Committee Member' gets you past an old bloke in a blazer and into the inner sanctum of Northampton Spencer FC). Non-league also threw up unusual opportunities: I got to run the line in a friendly against Kettering Town (pre-Gazza) but, sadly, these curios were totally offset by the *politics* – relentless, petty, small-town politics. For me, a relative outsider, the club was riven with fissures: long-running feuds went head-to-head with daily squabbles, making the atmosphere at committee meetings unbearable.

I'm pretty sure I didn't know the half of what was going on, but I knew enough to realise that being a committee member wasn't for me, something that came to a head when at one particularly prickly meeting, the club captain – also a police officer – was stationed at the door to act as a deterrent to trouble-makers. I stopped enjoying the football and took to sneaking into the ground just before kick-off in the hope of not being spotted and drawn back in to that week's instalment of the club soap opera – not easy when the average attendance for the season was 46.

Perhaps, too, this lack of a crowd played a bigger part than I imagined. There's something to be said for the intimacy of non-league, being close to the pitch, marvelling at your centre-forward's ability to construct a sentence entirely out of swearwords, but after a while I began to miss the atmosphere, the sense of belonging that I used to have standing on a terrace and singing my heart out. But, more than anything, it was the incessant politics and infighting that put me off – after 20 years of following Watford, my dalliance with non-league football lasted, all told, about 18 months.

In a roundabout way, this is how I ended up queuing to get into St. Pauli's ramshackle Millerntor stadium on the first Saturday of the 2007–08 season. At about the same time my enthusiasm for the local non-league scene was waning, I read an article in *FourFourTwo* magazine about the German 'Kult club' FC St. Pauli.

Ironically, just as politics drove me away from non-league football, it was politics that attracted me to FC St. Pauli. The article described St. Pauli fans as staunchly left-wing, fighting (metaphorically, but sometimes physically) against racism, fascism and homophobia in football. They were also opposed to the continued commercialisation of the game. As an old-school socialist, I was fascinated. Could football and The Left really flourish? I had my doubts. Aside from a photocopied *'Reclaim the Game'* pamphlet produced by the Socialist Party, I'd picked up in the early 1990s from the sadly defunct *Sportspages* bookshop on Charing Cross Road, I'd never seen any real evidence of a collective left-wing interest in football. The pamphlet itself was a bit of a disappointment – it seemed more like an ill-conceived attempt to appeal to football fans, rather than something written by supporters genuinely concerned about the ills of the game. Perhaps, the fanzine movement of the late 1980s and '90s was as political as things got? True, when it started it did feel like it was a reaction to the ludicrous policies of the Tory government on ID cards and all-seater stadia, but – in the main – the fanzine movement was never overtly political; cheap political points instead were scored with the aid of satire, wit and sarcasm. Fanzines tended to rally around club specific issues rather than coming together to look at the bigger picture. As a result, while we were worrying about problems with club chairmen, ground moves or rubbish pies, Sky TV and the Premier League crept up on our blindside and changed the game forever. Magazines such as *When Saturday Comes* documented the upheaval, but no organised opposition to these sweeping changes took root. In Britain, politics in football usually boiled down to the pathetic attempts of the National Front to recruit on the terraces. Undoubtedly, the far right were a real problem in football grounds in the 1970s and '80s, and they still reared their ugly heads in more recent times under the guises of the British National Party and the English Defence League. Supporting Watford, I'd been lucky. Only once had I come into contact with the far-right at football, when in the autumn of 1994, the BNP tried their luck setting up a stall on Vicarage Road on matchday. They were given short shrift and were never seen again. Much to my delight, Watford fans did their bit when needed to rid the club of the BNP, but any link to politics stopped there. Of course, there are British clubs considered slightly more left-wing than others – AFC Wimbledon, and Celtic spring to mind – but these links never seemed to be based on much more than a 'feeling' or as opposition to the politics of rival fans. So, to discover FC St. Pauli and their proud tradition of left-wing support was something of a revelation. Fortuitously, it also came at a time when I'd started to become interested in German football.

The 2006 World Cup had proved a tremendous showcase for the country and its football. Not so much the national team's run to the semi-finals, more the excellence of their stadiums and the passion of the supporters. I loved the fact that many of the state-of-the-art stadiums used for that summer's World Cup could be converted back and forth from all-seater to a mix of seats and terracing, and I loved the fact that ticket prices appeared to be so ridiculously cheap.

I also loved the fact that I knew so little about the Bundesliga. A mate of mine, with whom I'd regularly gone to Watford games, had regaled me with stories of trips to Schalke 04 and had baulked when I'd suggested a trip to watch their arch rivals Borussia Dortmund – a game I'd fancied making just because I'd read about the terrace that could accommodate 25,000 fans at their Westfalenstadion stadium home. I knew nothing of the rivalry with Schalke, only that, after a decade of watching football in increasingly uniform and passionless all-seater stadia, I wanted to witness Dortmund's 'Yellow Wall' first hand. My only other knowledge of German club football was rooted firmly in the past: Keegan signing for Hamburger SV; Tony Woodcock playing for 1FC Köln (and later, Fortuna Köln); memories of Borussia Mönchengladbach competing in Europe via snatches of Ron Jones' radio commentaries on *Midweek Sports Special* on a crappy radio while doing my homework; or Watford's one foray into Europe in the 1983–84 UEFA cup that paired us with Kaiserslautern. How I'd longed to be in the Fritz-Walter stadium in Kaiserslautern for Watford's European debut. I'd not even dared ask my Dad if we could go, there was no way we could have afforded it, or got it past my Mum. In the days before budget airlines a select few Hornets fans had paid to fly on the same plane as the players, while the bulk of the travelling supporters had gone on a three-day round coach trip to the Rhineland. Mum would never have let me bunk three days off school so, again, I relied on the radio (I still have a cassette recording of Mike Vince's commentary of the game for Chiltern Radio in the loft somewhere) and waited patiently for the return leg at Vicarage Road. I often wonder if the fact that the second leg and Watford's remarkable 3-0 win (overturning a 3-1 deficit from the first game) had some subconscious impact on my interest in German football. But if so, it was a long time coming, waiting nearly a quarter of a century to manifest itself.

Of course, I'd come across West Germany (and later a reunified Germany) watching international football. I knew all the stereotypes but I'd never been much of a follower of the England team, so managed to side-step the rivalry with the Germans and the predictable references to the war, 'ruthless German efficiency' and the endless renditions of 'The Great Escape'. In fact, my only real prejudice against the Germans came as a result of Harald 'Toni' Schumacher's brutal challenge on Patrick Battiston in the semi-final of the 1982 World Cup. I was only ten, but had fallen head-over-heels in love with the French, their *Carré Magique* of Platini, Giresse, Genghini and Tigana and the free-flowing locks of striker Dominique Rocheteau. I watched in horror as Schumacher clattered into Battiston, sending teeth flying and knocking him unconscious. I couldn't believe that Schumacher was still on the pitch let alone the nonchalant way he took the resultant goal kick without a second thought for the opponent he had injured. Then, of course, in true pantomime villain style, he saved Max Bossis' penalty after clearly moving off his line, leaving Hamburger SV's Horst Hrubesch to convert the spot-kick that sent West Germany to the World Cup final. I even read Schumacher's autobiography *Blowing The Whistle* on its release in 1987 to try to see if he showed any remorse, but as far as I can recall (I really wish I still had my copy) he dealt with the Battiston incident fairly swiftly before moving on to make some sensational allegations against his fellow professionals that ended up costing him his place in the German national side.

So, as you can see, my knowledge of German football was pretty threadbare, although in a way, this only helped to fuel my obsession. It is far too easy these days to be a font of all knowledge about the Premier League; the news coverage is all-encompassing, available 24 hours a day via the internet or *Sky Sports News* (well, at least until they pulled it from Freeview). There's something quite refreshing about diving headlong into the unknown and trying to accumulate knowledge about a football club in a language you can't decipher, especially when that club is playing in the third, regionalised, tier of German football.

The article in *FourFourTwo* pricked my conscience. It sketched an outline of FC St. Pauli as a club at one with its fans, fans who took a firm stance against the far-right extremists that had allied themselves to other clubs in the 1980s and 1990's. It was only a couple of pages (and just as with Schumacher's book, I've long since thrown the article away) but it had me hooked. I needed to find out more about this club that seemed at odds with the conventions of modern football; where left-wing politics and football went hand-in-hand.

I guess, from there on in, I was lucky. I Googled FC St. Pauli and found some great clips on YouTube that convinced me even more that I'd found something special. Then, I stumbled across the FC St. Pauli UK Messageboard, a fans forum – *in English* – that provided a wealth of background information on the club and the district, but more importantly was buzzing with like-minded individuals, who contributed regular reports on trips to the Millerntor stadium. The message board is also blessed with regular news updates and match reports from fans living in Hamburg. As a result, I found myself checking its pages daily and after a short period of lurking, towards the end of October 2006, I took the plunge and started posting various rambling contributions of my own. I was also lucky to get hold of an old video called *'And I Know Why I Stand Here'* – a documentary made in 1991 and dubbed into English, that explained in detail the birth of the club's fan culture. Put together by those involved with the influential fanzine, *Millerntor Roar!* it explained how the unique supporter culture was born out of the changes happening in the wider St. Pauli district and through opposition to plans to transform the Millerntor stadium into a 'Sport-Dome' complete with underground parking and a shopping mall. I found it fascinating that back at the tailend of the 1980s, when many supporters were getting into the fanzine scene in the UK, motivated by the treatment of football fans by clubs and the authorities and the police and government's shameful response to the Hillsborough disaster, that much the same thing was happening in Germany. Of course, despite the boom in football fanzines, English football took a very different path with the birth of the Premier League and distortion of the game by TV money. But, as I was becoming increasingly aware, German fans in general and FC St. Pauli fans in particular didn't give up that easily.

I had started following FC St. Pauli at an opportune moment. The club had been relegated to the Regionalliga Nord (the regionalised third tier of German football, akin to the old Third Division North–South set up in the UK) in 2003, and had finished eighth, seventh and sixth in the following three seasons. Despite another mid-table finish, the 2005–06 campaign had been augmented by a memorable run to the semi-finals of the German Cup, beating Bundesliga sides Hertha Berlin and Werder Bremen before falling to a 3-0 defeat at the hands of Bayern Munich. Perhaps more significantly, the club had almost gone out of existence in 2003 and was only saved by a remarkable, fan-led, 'Retter' (saviour) campaign that saw thousands of T-shirts sold to fans across Germany; a beer kick-back scheme that had fans literally downing Astra beer to raise funds for the club; and a friendly game against Bayern.

In the autumn of 2006, as my obsession intensified, FC St. Pauli were their usual inconsistent selves. Going into the winter break, they had won only one of their previous eight matches, drawing four. FC St. Pauli sat 12th out of 19 teams; another season in the Regionalliga beckoned. However, something had changed. After a disappointing home draw against Rot-Weiss Erfurt, the club parted company with Andreas Bergmann, the suave-looking architect of the previous season's cup run – a man with more than a hint of José Mourinho about him (in appearance, if not in demeanour). He was replaced by former Millerntor defensive stalwarts Holger Stanislawski and André Trulsen. When the season restarted in February 2007, the team seemed to have found the knack of converting those earlier draws into wins, and went on an impressive run that saw them top the table with six games to go, hanging on to claim promotion in the penultimate game of the season against Dynamo Dresden.

By this stage, I had given up looking up the results the following day on the internet and had taken to following the dramatic climax to the season on a 'live-ticker' service – real-time website updates, that could possibly be described as the internet generation's equivalent of watching matches on Ceefax.

For the final game against Dresden, I even managed to find a live-stream from a Hamburg radio station and was at least able to get a feel for what was happening on the pitch via my extremely limited German and the inflection of the commentator's voice. In Hamburg, the game was a complete sell-out, and thousands more watched the action unfold on giant screens on the Reeperbahn. The match itself was a nervy affair. FC St. Pauli needed a draw to secure promotion back to the second division and, true to their early season form, went ahead twice before being pegged back in stoppage time of both halves. The game finished 2-2 and FC St. Pauli were up. Although I wasn't entirely sure what had happened as, with the last kick of the game, I was convinced from the hysteria in the stadium that Michél Mazingu-Dinzey, who had been put clean through on goal with seconds to play, had fired home the winner for FC St. Pauli (he hadn't; somehow his shot had careered back off the post). Not that anyone inside the ground or on the surrounding streets cared; the club was back in the Bundesliga 2 after four long seasons in the regional wilderness. I carried on listening to the radio stream for an hour or so after the final whistle as they seemingly interviewed half of Hamburg. The party on the Reeperbahn continued until the following morning.

Now, three months on from the victory over Dynamo Dresden, my Dad and I slowly edge closer to the turnstiles. The mood is still jovial and we strike up a conversation with the bloke in front of us in the queue (the one with the sunburnt neck). Naturally he speaks fabulous English, and was extremely impressed that we have travelled to watch the game. I give him a stripped down version of the story above, and he and his mate seem genuinely pleased that the club have such a following in the UK. He wants us to stand with him in the middle of the Gegengerade, the crumbling terrace that runs down one side of the pitch (literal translation 'the back straight') but I am already a bit worried about my Dad going the distance in the heat, and he suggests that once inside the ground we make our way to the North end of the terrace, where we might still bag a spot behind a crush barrier.

As we finally make our way through the security check – it turns out there were no turnstiles as such, just some makeshift barriers funnelling fans through into the stadium – I have to admit I've not felt so excited about a match since I was a kid. But I am nervous too. Nervous that the experience wouldn't be as good as what I'd been led to believe from various recounts or YouTube video clips. We then find ourselves in the concourse underneath the seated upper section of the Gegengerade. The seats were installed as a temporary measure in 1988. They are supported by what looks like rusting metal pillars, giving the structure the look of an elongated Meccano stand at Northampton Town's old County Ground. It is anything but modern, but I love it. Already, the underbelly of the Gegengerade was a complete antidote to the pre-cast concrete uniformity of most modern English league grounds.

There is still about 50 minutes to go until kick-off, but we decide we'd better take our place on the terrace. As I walk up the shallow steps, between the makeshift metal struts supporting the 'temporary' seating above, I really feel as if I am ten years old again, sensing the expectation of the crowd and being almost blinded by the brilliant green of the playing surface. It really is like stepping back in time: no taking your seat five minutes before kick-off, here the terrace is already heaving. We decide to heed the advice of our friend in the queue and head for the far end, where there are still a few spaces left. We are not early enough to bag a crush barrier, but we get a fairly decent spot halfway up next to the fence that separates the home fans on the Gegengerade from their comrades on the Nordkurve. It seems perfect until we realise that we are right in the middle of the thoroughfare to the beer kiosk at the back of the terrace. Never mind, 'when on a terrace in Germany' and all that: we decide to get a couple of beers to quench our thirst. Only towards the end of the game do we realise that we are in the middle of a fabulously ingenious beer distribution system that sees cups being handed down then along the rows to their intended recipients, with the person due to buy the next round shuffling into position on the end of the row.

As kick-off approaches, there is no space left, except right down the front at pitch level, where the view is pretty much obscured by kids clinging gallantly to their premium spot on the fence. The game is a sell-out, as you'd expect of a cup-tie against Bundesliga opposition, and tickets are at even more of a premium due to the demolition of the

Südkurve terrace towards the end of the previous season. Slowly, and only after a lot of wrangling, the club got the go-ahead and the funds to start modernising the stadium – an upgrade that was required by the German FA in order for the club to retain their licence. Then, out of nowhere, comes the moment I'm waiting for: the clang of the bells at the start of AC/DC's *Hell's Bells* rings out over the loudspeakers. It is a moment I'd watched countless times on YouTube, but witnessing it live sends shivers down my spine. As the teams emerge from the tunnel at the other end of the Gegengerade, I strain to get a better view, and as I do I am showered in confetti – not ripped-up bits of yellow pages like at home but a storm of what look like paper drinks coasters. The noise and the atmosphere are incredible; craning my neck I can see that much of the terrace has been covered in huge red, white and brown stripes, and an enormous banner proclaiming 'You'll Never Walk Alone'.

It is like nothing I've seen before, not even at cup semi-finals or vital promotion–relegation fixtures. I try to drink in as much of it as I can. The match hasn't kicked off yet, but I am pretty sure that I won't go home disappointed that the experience hadn't matched up to my expectations. Even my Dad, who doesn't know too much about St. Pauli but was keen to experience something new, appears impressed (although this might be down to being allowed to have a pint and a smoke on the terrace, in full view of the pitch!).

The game eventually starts and is pretty scrappy with few clear-cut chances. We are sweltering on a terrace totally devoid of shade, so it is no surprise that as the game wears on the players start to tire. But if I'm honest, I'm watching the crowd as much as the players; the nature of the support seems very different to back home. Maybe some things are lost in translation, but I see or hear very little goading of opposition players or fans and the majority of the noise is devoted to supporting the team. We are right by the corner flag and there is none of the moronic gesticulating at opponents when they come over to take a throw or a corner. Indeed, we go an entire 90 minutes without anyone making the 'wanker' hand gesture that's so ubiquitous among British football fans. The chanting is also, pretty much, non-stop. True, not everyone joins in all the time, but for almost the entire game there is noise coming from some part of the ground.

The other thing that is noticeably different to anything I've experienced at football in recent years is that virtually everyone around us is smoking: usually tobacco, but there are also several sweet-smelling spliffs being passed around. The vibe is definitely a party one and, anyway, my Dad is just pleased to be able to have a puff on his pipe – tobacco only, I presume – without being made to feel like a social pariah.

The first half ends scoreless, and after much deliberation we decide against getting another beer from the kiosk behind us. But as we are debating this, a woman in her twenties with blonde dreadlocked hair held in place by a skull and crossbones headscarf, asks us politely if we are English. She, too, is intrigued to find out that we have come from the UK to watch St. Pauli. She tells her group of friends about us, and everyone is keen to say hello and shake our hands. They, too, are impressed by the fact that FC St. Pauli has a sizeable following back in Britain. My Dad spends the second half chatting to the group and trying to follow the action, and as usual the language barrier is only one way – as everyone speaks excellent English.

The second half continues in much the same vein as the first, although as time goes on, the game starts to open up. Suddenly, the St. Pauli number five, Björn Brunnemann, identifiable by his shock of punk-rock peroxide hair, bursts through the middle only to shoot straight at the keeper. Then, Charles Takyi releases fellow midfielder Timo Schultz, who collides with the keeper, as the ball spills to the on-rushing Ralph Gunesch. Everyone around us holds their breath, but Gunesch blazes his shot high, wide and into the Nordkurve. Even so, Bayer look rattled. As the action on the pitch intensifies – St. Pauli are attacking the Nordkurve with which we are standing roughly in line – so does the noise. It's interesting to note that songs are not just sung in German, but also in English and French. As the pressure builds on the Leverkusen goal, I pick up on another curio, the jangling of car keys as St. Pauli take a corner – I've no idea what it signifies, but it is strangely effective.

Then on 87 minutes it happens. Takyi – very much the playmaker in the St. Pauli side – floats a free-kick into the box, it is half cleared but is headed back across the area by René Schnitzler. The ball bounces through a crowd of players but the St. Pauli number 17, a part-time policeman, Fabian Boll slides in and fires the ball into the back of the net. It isn't a classic goal, but it is a vital one. The terrace around us goes absolutely mental. It is literally raining beer as every plastic cup is thrown into the air in pure joy. We hug everyone around us. I look up to see my Dad being mobbed by his new friends. Somewhere in the bedlam, Blur's *Song 2* is being played, and I vaguely remember 'Whoo-whooing' along to the chorus. No one can quite believe it, we are 1-0 up against Bayer Leverkusen with under three minutes to go. There's isn't even time for the obligatory last, heart-in-mouth, chance for the visitors, or if there is we didn't notice. Our German friends are convinced my Dad is a lucky mascot and are already trying to persuade him to come back for the next round. I am covered in beer and as high as a kite on the pure adrenalin of a last-gasp winner. At some point the final whistle blows and the celebrations start up again. I realise that I haven't felt like this for years.

What happens after the final whistle is just as remarkable as the 90 minutes that preceded it. Back home, there'd be a bit of a celebration, the players would wander half-heartedly over to the home end to applaud the fans (although there's always one or two in every team that scurry off down the tunnel at the earliest opportunity, however historic the result). Then the fans would start the slow process of shuffling out of the stadium. Not here. Instead, people are getting more drinks in, perhaps to replace those lost in the beer storm that had greeted the winning goal, but also to extend the party. One thing is for sure, no one around us is leaving. The team, too, are still on the pitch. They emerge from a post-match huddle and head over to the fans on the Gegengerade. The team form a long line and hold hands. Suddenly, the crowd and the team are as one, lifting their hands together in unison, accompanied by a guttural, 'Waaay! Waaay! Waaay!' from the fans. Some of the team come to the fence in front of us and 'high-five' the hands reaching through the railings. Timo Schultz spends a couple of minutes chatting to fans on the terrace. Then, the team moves on and goes through the same procedure with the fans on the Nordkurve and the seated Haupttribüne on the opposite side of the pitch to us. We ask the girl with the dreadlocks if this prolonged celebration with the fans is due to the nature of the win over Bundesliga opposition. She seems puzzled, and replies: 'No, it is like this every time we win a game.'

Finally, after what seems like a good quarter-of-an-hour after the final whistle, the players leave the pitch. Again, I imagine that people will start to head home. Maybe our close proximity to the beer kiosk had something to do with it, but nobody around us looks like they are ready to leave just yet. With the football over, I take the opportunity to talk to the girl and her boyfriend in more depth. I explain my disillusionment with English football, and my affinity with the politics and fan culture of St. Pauli. Again they seem a little surprised, not that English football has no St. Pauli equivalent, but that English supporters in general are so passive. They are more shocked, however, when I explain that we got to Hamburg by train, and have to catch the overnight sleeper back to Köln, then get back to London via Brussels. The shock isn't particularly down to the time or distance of such a rail trip (Germany is rather fond of its railways) but because we aren't staying in Hamburg to continue the party that night.

It is now about 40 minutes after the final whistle, and most people are finally starting to exit the stadium. We consider following suit. Our hosts don't want to see us go, but the sun has taken its toll and we both need to get something to eat and to sit down somewhere and take stock. Before we leave, we exchange more hugs and kisses with those around us – which leads to the surreal situation of seeing my old man hugged, first, by our dreadlocked translator, then by a man with more piercings and tattoos than seems humanly possible, and finally by a six-foot Rastafarian. To the casual observer – or cliché-seeking journalist – it represents the perfect stereotypical cross-section of St. Pauli's supporter base, but I've not made any of it up. It's exactly how it happens.

We say our goodbyes – promising to return for the second round of the cup – and make our way through the debris of confetti and scrunched-up plastic beer glasses that litter the Gegengerade. As we get to the top of the gently shelving terrace, we turn and lean on a crush barrier. Pockets of fans are milling about, deep in conversation, finishing their drinks. The August sun is still warm, but hazy clouds are starting to gather high in the sky above. I think back to the video produced by the *Millerntor Roar!* fanzine, and consider that now I too know exactly why they stand here. I also know that I want to stand here again – soon. After an afternoon spent with the fans of St. Pauli on the Gegengerade, no other football experience would feel quite the same.

As we leave the ground, exiting underneath those rusty girders supporting the 'temporary' Gegentribune seating above, there are fans everywhere, loitering outside the stadium drinking more beer. A sound system is blasting out something akin to industrial house from what looks like a freight container that has migrated the short distance from the docks (later I find out that this is the legendary AFM supporters 'container' that lets a different group of fans provide the music for each game. The AFM is the 'Abteilung Fördernde Mitglieder', of which more later). It looks like the party is about to get in full swing – just like our friends in the ground said it would. Sadly, we have to get our bags from the hotel, find some food and think about getting ourselves to the central station to start the long journey back to London. On the plus side, we are both absolutely buzzing. I am relieved that the Millerntor really was as mind-blowing as other fans had described it. And I am really glad that I'd experienced it with my old man. After all, I'm forever grateful to him for taking me to my first football match all those years ago – now it feels like I've returned the favour.

Chapter 1
PIRATES, PUNKS & POLITICS

The mythos of St. Pauli

THE WORKING TITLE for this book was *Pirates, Punks and Prostitutes*. The idea being it might attract a bit of media attention and would stand out on the shelf in the sport section of Waterstones, or catch the eye of thrill seekers searching Amazon. The hope was that it might help shift a few more copies and, thus, raise more money for St. Pauli's Fanladen (the independent supporters' organisation that works tirelessly to help fans, run social projects and maintain links with the local community). But, more than that, it is a reflection of the way the club is usually portrayed when written about in the English press (and sometimes the German media too). In the end – and despite the fact the media image of the club will always be simply and intrinsically linked with the Reeperbahn red-light district, and by implication prostitution – I felt that politics played a far more important role in defining the identify of the club and its supporters.

There are plenty of English language references to FC St. Pauli on the internet, although in-depth, reliable sources of information can be hard to come by. Google FC St. Pauli and one of the first links you'll come across, after the official club website and the Wikipedia entry, is a report from CNN entitled: *Punks, Prostitutes and St. Pauli: Inside soccer's coolest club*. If we leave aside the reference to 'soccer' and not football (it is CNN after all) then we have, in the title alone, the makings of a generic piece about FC St. Pauli.

The article – and it's a pretty good one all told – brings together all the ingredients that help to sustain the myth of St. Pauli. There's reference to the skull and crossbones flag, or Totenkopf, which occasionally gets linked back to Hamburg's seafaring past but is more correctly associated with the district's squatter movement of the mid-1980s. Then, there's the Reeperbahn, the world-famous street with the surrounding red-light district that is a mere stone's throw from the Millerntor stadium. The Beatles' stint in Hamburg is usually thrown in at this point, especially now that sculptures of the group can be found on *Beatles-Platz* at the junction of the Reeperbahn and Große Freiheit. Then there's a reference to the arrival of punks, squatters and anarchists on the terraces in the late 1980s, and how this changed the club forever, bringing left-wing idealism into the stadium as well as creating a vibrant atmosphere.

Cross-town rivals, Hamburger SV also get a mention, and it is worth considering that during the late 1980s the atmosphere developing at the Millerntor stadium was in sharp contrast to what was found at HSV's Volksparkstadion and, indeed, most other football stadiums in Germany. The article goes on to mention the progressive stance FC St. Pauli took against racism, fascism and homophobia in football at a time when few others were brave enough to stand up and be counted.

The CNN piece, like countless others written about FC St. Pauli, also mentions that the club has in Corny Littmann an 'openly gay' chairman – or to be precise 'had'; he stood down shortly after the club achieved promotion to the top flight in May 2010. Many other newspaper or magazine articles go on to claim, embellishing the myth of St. Pauli even further, that Littmann is allegedly a transvestite. Corny Littmann, born in 1952 in Münster, is an entrepreneur, businessman and entertainer who owns the Schmidt group of theatres in the St. Pauli district. He was the chairman of his local football club for eight years between 2002 and 2010. He is 'openly' gay (itself an interesting choice of adverb, in as much as you don't often hear other football club chairman as 'openly' heterosexual), but he is not a transvestite. The misunderstanding is believed to have come from the fact that, in his role as a theatre impresario, Littmann has from time to time come on stage dressed as a woman. This discrepancy between fact and legend is all part of the growing media myth surrounding FC St. Pauli. Of course, it wouldn't matter one jot if Littmann *was* a transvestite; after all the club and its fans pride themselves on their inclusivity, and would, quite rightly, hate to see people discriminated against on such grounds. And in many ways, if this were the case it would make the story more titillating – which is probably why so many editors run with it. As we shall see during the course of this book, Corny Littmann was a controversial and divisive figure among many fans, but this had absolutely nothing to do with his sexuality or the way he was supposed to have dressed. I once found myself sharing a train platform in Aachen with Littmann at 6.45am in the morning. He looked as tired and emotionally drained as the rest of us who had witnessed the previous night's 5-0 away victory against Alemannia Aachen – a victory marred by a serious injury to a St. Pauli fan inside the stadium – he was wearing the same white away shirt as me, but had chosen to offset it with a suit jacket and jeans, just in case you were wondering.

Of course, the myth of St. Pauli gets built upon with each new article. Here's a short extract from a piece that appeared in the weekly UK 'lads' mag' *Nuts:* 'Punks, hippies, bikers, freaks, anarchists, drop-outs, plus the odd pimp and transvestite are the core audience for this German side based on the edge of Hamburg's Reeperbahn red-light district.' Now, having stood, reasonably regularly, on two of the three terraced areas inside the Millerntor stadium, I don't doubt that the punks are fairly easy to spot, and some (but not all) of the anarchists help you out a bit by waving big flags with the anarchist symbol emblazoned on them, but so far I have yet to readily identify the pimps or transvestites that supposedly contribute to the club's core audience. However, like most myths, this one is constructed from a kernel of truth. As I described in the opening chapter, while many of the Millerntor faithful are regular football fans (and there is, of course, room for a wide-ranging debate about how you would define a 'regular' football fan) the terraces of St. Pauli *are* very different in composition from any football ground in the UK, and with a few exceptions – SV Babelsberg 03, Tennis Borussia Berlin in Germany, Cadiz in Spain, Sampdoria and AS Livorno in Italy – very different from the rest of Europe.

Britain's flagship lads' mag, *Loaded*, published a similar article in January 2008 entitled: *'Never mind the Ballacks, here's St. Pauli...'* It, too, went through the usual tick-list, but instead of pimps and prostitutes discovered that 'skins, punks and ultras drink booze on the terraces.' The *Loaded* boys produced a flag bearing the legend *Loaded loves St. Pauli,* which they displayed proudly on the Südkurve during their time in Hamburg. It would have been interesting to see what would have happened had they decided to hand out copies of their magazine – a publication bursting at the seams with scantily clad women – on a section of terracing occupied by the club's Ultras, a group of fans passionately opposed to sexism and the derogatory depiction of women. For one weekend only, and to facilitate a story, *Loaded* might have actually loved St. Pauli, but it seems unlikely that the feeling would have been mutual.

And here's the conundrum that, for me, lies at the heart of wanting to write this book. Aside from those British fans whose links with St. Pauli go back decades, established via family connections, mutual friends or time spent in Hamburg, most of us (myself included) stumbled across FC St. Pauli via one of these articles. And, as a result, it would be churlish and a little bit elitist to dismiss them totally as ill-conceived myth making. After all, it was this promise of something different, something aligned with our left-wing political viewpoint and our desire to watch football among passionate fellow believers that made us delve further. Without that initial article in *FourFourTwo* magazine back in 2006, I may never have discovered FC St. Pauli. Without it I would never have known that watching football could be so different, so close to what I had always wanted it to be when I was young and angry at the way ordinary fans were treated at football matches. Back in the late 1980s, as I mucked about excitedly with fanzines, hoping they would change the world (or football at the very least), real progress was occurring in a quarter of Hamburg – real changes were being made. In England, we had lost our battle – not to the Tory government and their ludicrous ID card scheme, but to the unstoppable commercial juggernaut that was the Premier League. By the time I found that article in *FourFourTwo*, I'd all but given up on English football, but after a bit of internet research and a trip out to Germany my faith in the game was on its way to being restored.

So, although these snapshots and slightly clichéd articles about FC St. Pauli tend to grate a little with the more devoted fan, they represent the myth that we all bought into at the start. Quite rightly, there is the very real and on going concern that these articles trivialise the St. Pauli cause, making the Millerntor a minor diversion from the Reeperbahn for the plane loads of stag parties that descend on the city.

Though, fortunately, they don't tend to have much luck getting their hands on the coveted terrace tickets. On one trip I witnessed a group of English blokes dressed up in pirate costumes (they had clearly done their research: the skull and crossbones = pirates, right?) outside the stadium, only to pick them out taking their places in the posh (and very pricey) seats while I, thanks to the Fanladen, was able to take my place on the terracing below. But in all probability, these blokes will never return to the Millerntor, and in one sense that's fair enough; we are all different, not everyone is going to commit to travelling 800-odd miles to watch a game of football on a fairly regular basis. For others, though, a similar magazine or internet article is the start of something special – the opportunity to fall in love with football all over again. The start of a whole new era of watching matches among like-minded individuals, fans who care about ideals as much as results. Fans who don't want models wandering round in bikinis advertising tat, or who object to selling the name of *their* stadium to the highest bidder.

For some, discovering St. Pauli is like a breath of fresh air. Stories of transvestite chairmen, a stadium full of punks and anarchists and a fan base that is massively left-wing were the hooks that reeled us in. What I hope to do in this book is to add some detail and context to these stories, fill in some of the blanks and perhaps dispel a few of the myths along the way.

The reason I chose the CNN article about the club as a reference point at the start of this chapter is because it dug a little deeper. James Montague, the journalist responsible, recognised that the club, far from living in an idealistic vacuum, faced fresh challenges from the creeping commercialism in professional sport. He looked beyond the cliché and understood that the club is being pulled in different directions. It is not just in the English Premier League that money rules; even in Germany with the stringent '50+1' rule that prevents German clubs being snapped up by powerful individuals like Roman Abramovich or Sheikh Mansour bin Zayed bin Sultan Al Nahyan, money still talks and that means bigger clubs like Bayern Munich, or those bankrolled by large organisations, like Wolfsburg or Hoffenheim, can afford to pay much higher wages than the likes of FC St. Pauli. Montague took the time to interview the FC St. Pauli manager, Holger Stanislawski, who was only too aware of the problems the club faced, and which it continues to face: 'Some fans don't like it, merchandising [and other commercial considerations] and want us to play in the third league,' he told CNN. 'But if you want to play in the Bundesliga you must go this way, you must build a new stadium. We have €50 million for this season, everyone else has €80 million. But you must be St. Pauli too. And that's the difficult thing here.'

This is, perhaps, the biggest issue facing the club today. Promotion to the Bundesliga at the start of the 2010–11 season was an incredible achievement – especially coming as it did during the club's centenary – but it also represented real challenges. Could the club maintain its top-flight status without selling out the values so many of its fans hold dear? The very same values that define FC St. Pauli to the outside world? It remains a double-edged sword.

I mentioned at the start of this chapter that English language source material about the club is relatively thin on the ground. There are, however, a couple of notable exceptions. Firstly, a great debt of gratitude is owed to Chris Sanderson who made his excellent masters' dissertation, *'Nie wieder Faschismus, Nie wieder Krieg, Nie wieder 3. Liga!' A Social History of FC St. Pauli, 1986–1991*, available to read online. It is a truly remarkable piece of work that I have used as a constant reference point throughout the writing of this book. René Martens' *Here to Stay with St. Pauli*, published in *Hooligan Wars: Causes And Effects Of Football Violence* and edited by Mark Perryman, is another excellent English language article about the club. In addition, there are many nuggets of information about St. Pauli hidden away on the internet, but I have also referred back to the plethora of books and articles about the club written in German while speaking at length to fellow fans and officials, drawing on their collective experiences of supporting or working for the club.

I hope that, for the remainder of this book, I can add a little more detail to the *'mythos of St. Pauli'* and provide a half-decent English language account of the club and its significance that goes a little further than the usual pirates, punks and prostitutes. I decided to mix an historical account of the club's transformation into a 'Kult' with my personal experiences following St. Pauli. I did this because I felt the 'personal' perspective of an English fan falling in love with the club would make more interesting reading than a straightforward historical retelling. At the start of the book, the personal and the historical are more distinct, but by the final chapters I found that I was actually emotionally involved in some of the events shaping the future direction of the club and, as a result, the boundaries between the personal and factual accounts begin to blur. I also hope that this is just the first English language book about the club. There are other fans out there that have been supporting St. Pauli far longer than I have, and I for one would be intrigued to hear their stories.

Chapter 2
OUTSIDERS, LOOKING IN

A brief history of the district of St. Pauli

THOUGH NINE YEARS older, FC St. Pauli has spent most of its history in the shadow of its more illustrious neighbour, Hamburger Sport-Verein (Hamburger SV, or simply HSV). The contrast between the two clubs could not be greater. At the time of writing HSV holds the distinction of being the only club to play continuously in the Bundesliga since its inception in 1963–64. On the other hand, FC St. Pauli has managed just eight seasons in the top tier of German football in that time. HSV has three Bundesliga titles to its name as well as three previous Deutsche Meisterschaften, has appeared in five European finals, winning the Cup Winners' Cup in 1977 and then the European Cup six years later, beating Juventus 1-0 in Athens. FC St. Pauli's trophy cabinet is a little less crammed – the club has several regional league titles to its name but has never come close to winning the Bundesliga.

Hamburger SV made six appearances in the German cup final, winning the DFB Pokal on three occasions, while FC St. Pauli doesn't have a solitary cup final appearance to its name – although an exhilarating cup run in 2006 saw them reach the semi-final stage where they crashed 3-0 at home to Bayern Munich. On top of all this, it wasn't until September 2010 that FC St. Pauli was able to host HSV at the Millerntor in a Bundesliga match – the last time the two sides had met in a league fixture at the Millerntor stadium was in 1962 in the Oberliga Nord. On the seven previous occasions the sides had met in the top flight St. Pauli had ceded advantage and switched the 'home' fixture (partly on the grounds of safety) to the Volksparkstadion.

If HSV has the pedigree, and the blue blood of Bundesliga aristocracy running through its veins, then FC St. Pauli is the down-at-heel sibling cast out into the world and left to fend for itself, only occasionally turning up at family gatherings, dressed inappropriately, behaving raucously, just to remind its 'bigger' brother that they still exist.

In many ways, the relationship between HSV and FC St. Pauli is similar to that of the district of St. Pauli and the city of Hamburg itself.

Today, Hamburg is a modern, prosperous place ranked in the top ten European cities according to GDP per capita (2001). With a population of around 1.8 million people it is Germany's second largest city. The St. Pauli district, one of its 105 'quarters', has a population nearing 28,000. The economic contrast is dramatic: despite the creeping gentrification of the area and an influx of businesses, restaurants and renovated apartments, the St. Pauli quarter – once the poorest district in all of West Germany – is still beset with social and economic hardships. Despite being among the richest cities in Europe, Hamburg has an unemployment rate of 7.6 per cent (January 2013) compared with 7.4 per cent nationally. Unemployment is significantly higher in districts such as St. Pauli where over 17 per cent of the population are forced to rely on social security.

This discrepancy in wealth between the St. Pauli quarter and the city as a whole is not a new phenomenon – it is not even a product of the industrial age. The history of the St. Pauli quarter is synonymous with deprivation and struggle. The history of St. Pauli is the history of the outsider, and, in some senses, that is meant quite literally.

Situated on high ground on the north bank of the Elbe, the district of St. Pauli, originally known as *Hamburger Berg* (Hamburg mountain), remained relatively scarcely populated for hundreds of years, situated, as it was, outside the protective walls of both the city of Hamburg and the Danish-controlled city of Altona. In 1616, during the 30 Years' War, the Hamburg Senate reinforced the city walls using sand and clay from the Hamburger Berg, which also had the effect of flattening the raised area, probably giving the city's artillery battalions a clearer line of fire to the west of the city. The prospect of live artillery fire and, what is more, the lack of protection outside the city walls may have contributed to the relatively limited settlement of the area but, as the 17th century continued, the Hamburger Berg had about 2,000 inhabitants.

Many of them had decided to move to the area as they found life inside the city walls too expensive; typically the inhabitants were small-time craftsmen and peddlers, and day labourers. Also, trades and businesses that were considered antisocial because of noise, pollution or smell were encouraged to relocate to the Hamburger Berg, such as whale oil refineries producing lamp oil and similar products. Rope for ships was in heavy demand in Hamburg's bustling port, and the city's rope makers – who required long, straight stretches of land – relocated to the Hamburger Berg during this period. These workers gave St. Pauli's most famous street its name: the Reeperbahn, which translates literally as 'Rope Walk.' The street that later became known as the 'sinful mile', due to the profusion of sex shops, brothels and strip joints, originally played host to the long lines of maritime rope destined for the docks of Hamburg and the world beyond. Access to the city was regulated through several gates in the city wall. The Millerntor ('millern gate') used to be one of them – its earliest mention reaching back as far as 1246, its name probably owing to the fact that it used to be the middle one (in old German 'Milderdor' or 'Middele-Thor') of three gates at that time. The Millerntor gate was relocated several times to follow expansions of the city walls, moving ever closer to the location of the Millerntor stadium today. Here the German language provides an amusing curio, 'tor' meaning gate, archway or portal as well as 'goal', giving a wry twist to the popular terrace chant of 'Tor! Tor! Millerntor!'

Despite the existence of the Millerntor gate (quite steep tolls had to be paid for imports), residents of the Hamburger Berg were still very much on the outside looking in and were not afforded the same protection as those living inside the city walls. By the end of the 17th century, the Hamburg Senate had moved workhouses and the *Pesthof* (a quarantine hospital) out of the city and into the area now known as St. Pauli. A pattern was emerging: when the city of Hamburg wanted to sanitise its surroundings, the undesirables – be they tradesmen, the poor or the ill – were sent in the direction of St. Pauli. By 1682 a church dedicated to St. Paul had been built in the area; it didn't last long: when the Danes besieged Hamburg in 1686, the church was destroyed after only four years of existence – ironically, not by the Danes, but by the bullets and cannonballs fired by Hamburg's soldiers from the city walls – 'collateral damage', as they say today. Although the resilient people of the Hamburger Berg rebuilt it right away, the church became a casualty again in 1814, this time of Napoleon's army. However, in 1833, the quarter would be officially renamed St. Pauli in its honour, and another rebuilt church by the same name stands on the site of the original.

As trade in Hamburg continued to grow during the 19th century, St. Pauli's proximity to the Elbe made it an ideal additional landing point for ships wanting to offload their cargo. The city's port authority was also concerned about the potential fire risk posed by new coal-powered steam ships, and as a result many sought alternative moorings away from the main port. Then, it was decreed that from 1 January 1861, the Millerntor gate was to be left open, providing permanent access to the city.

The mid-19th century saw a period of massive expansion in the St. Pauli quarter. The Great Fire of 1842 that devastated much of central Hamburg left many people homeless and it was estimated that up to 20,000 people moved into the St. Pauli district as a result. Entertainment in the district grew rapidly, with establishments eager to profit from the large numbers of workers and sailors seeking lodgings and places to eat and drink. The Reeperbahn was no longer famous for rope. It had become a nocturnal destination for those seeking drink, entertainment or women. As the 19th century drew to a close, the quarter was teeming with brothels, and prostitution had made the St. Pauli district in general, and the Reeperbahn in particular, famous throughout Europe. However, there was more to the expanding Reeperbahn than cheap drinking dens and prostitution. The opening of the Millerntor gate had also prompted a marked growth in theatres and coffee shops. People came to the Reeperbahn to be entertained, and this entertainment also included reputable theatre shows and music halls.

As the population grew at a dramatic rate the demographic was changing. The district was no longer just the preserve of sailors, dock-workers and rope-makers. Relocation from the Great Fire and the boom in industry had seen many factory workers, looking for cheaper accommodation, move into the newly built tenement buildings that were springing up around St. Pauli. These tightly packed terraces, developed at right-angles to the main road, were crowded and dimly lit – typical dismal dwellings for the workers at the sharp end of the Industrial Revolution.

These poor conditions bred discontent among the populace. As Matthew Jefferies notes in his book, *Hamburg – A Cultural & Literary History*: 'Hamburg's spectacular expansion in the Imperial era was inevitably accompanied by growing social tensions. Demands for social and political reform were principally articulated through the Social Democratic Party of Germany (SPD) and the free (socialist) trade union movement, both of which developed strongly in the late 19th century and would turn Hamburg into a red bastion for much of the 20th century.' And, of course, nowhere were these social tensions more tangible than in the working-class environs like those of St. Pauli. As noted by Chris Sanderson, over crowding was a major issue in the district. This led to the frequent practice of 'hot-bedding' – the sub-letting of beds, by the hour, to those tenants that could not afford their own dwelling. Squalid living arrangements, coupled with a poor diet, made conditions in the tenements and slums of St. Pauli and the nearby *Gängeviertel* in the Neustadt district ripe for disease and, in 1892, an outbreak of cholera claimed up to 10,000 lives in the city, with many victims drawn from the working-class housing by the docks.

As Jefferies mentioned, during the course of the late 19th century Hamburg became a stronghold of the German trade union movement. He states that by 1890 there were 84 active trade unions with close to 40,000 members in the city. These formal trade unions mainly represented skilled or semi-skilled workers, with most unskilled or casual labourers remaining unrepresented. However, the first large-scale industrial action in the city – an 11-week 'unofficial' strike by upwards of 16,000 workers – was organised by dock workers at the end of 1896. The industrial action was eventually suppressed with many dockers being sacked or imprisoned, but the strike did help trigger an upsurge in union membership in the years that followed. At the same time as the growth in trade union membership the broadly socialist Social Democratic Party also experienced an upsurge in support. However, it has been argued that the SPD never truly represented the views of many of St. Pauli's working-class population, as not only did the SPD fail to support the 1896–97 dock strike, but they frequently distanced themselves from the numerous wildcat strikes organised by groups of casual dock workers. It is worth noting that many of the following uprisings did not break out in St. Pauli but in districts such as Barmbek, Eimsbüttel and Hamm. In other words, during the German revolution that followed, St. Pauli appears to not have been one of the main centres of rebellion.

Although hundreds of miles from the frontline, Hamburg suffered greatly during the First World War, and none more than its poorest residents. A Royal Navy blockade all but closed the normally bustling port and, with food supplies dwindling, rationing had to be introduced. In 1917 food riots broke out among the city's malnourished population. As the war drew to a close, events at two large naval ports provided a spark for the 'German revolution' of 1918. A mutiny by sailors in Wilhelmshaven and Kiel, furious at their commanding officers' decision to launch into a final, pointless battle with the British Grand Fleet, that began on 29 October 1918 soon spread with soldiers and workers backing the rebellion. In Hamburg on 6 November 1918, more than 40,000 workers, sailors and soldiers assembled peacefully on the open expanse of St. Pauli's Heiligengeistfeld to declare a republic. The revolt spread quickly across the rest of the German Empire, and by the time of Germany's acceptance of armistice on 11 November, the Workers' and Soldiers' Councils had seized power in the majority of cities. As is well documented elsewhere (Chris Harman provides an overview of the German revolution and the Weimar Republic from the perspective of a socialist historian in his book, *The Lost Revolution: Germany 1918 to 1923* the path of the German revolution was to differ significantly from its Russian counterpart of 1917. It soon became apparent that divisions among those striving for a true workers' revolution were leading to political fragmentation and a dilution of ideals. The Weimar Republic was formally established in January 1919, but only after bitter infighting between the more moderate SPD and the Communists (KPD) – whose own formation had been a result of a merger only weeks previously between the Independent Social Democratic Party of Germany (USPD) and the more radical Spartacist League.

Despite the aftermath of the Great War and the social upheaval of the first years of the Weimar Republic, Hamburg was able to remain relatively autonomous. The SPD took control of the Senate in 1919, working in coalition with both the German Democratic Party (GDP) and, later, the German Peoples' Party (GPP). The SPD attracted criticism from more radical quarters by awarding important positions within government to members of the old Senate. Although the SPD argued that it was beneficial for positions of prominence (including the city mayor) to be held by people with a vested interest in the promotion of commerce and trade, it was viewed by many as further kow-towing to the needs of the old order.

In St. Pauli, the communist KPD, the main opponents of the SPD, maintained a healthy level of support throughout the 1920s and into the 1930s. By then a failed communist uprising led by Ernst Thälman had claimed more than 100 lives. At dawn on the morning of 23 October 1923 Thälman orchestrated a series of attacks on a number of police stations, hoping to gain control of Hamburg by force – he failed. Not only was the death toll from the revolt high, reprisals also saw thousands of communists arrested and the mistrust between the SPD and the KPD deepen.

In St. Pauli living and working conditions remained poor throughout the 1920s, with hyper-inflation dramatically escalating the problems faced by the area's working class. Strikes remained a constant feature in the docks throughout the 1920s, as workers continued to demand an improvement to their pay and appalling working conditions.

The fall-out from the Wall Street Crash in 1929 was felt acutely in Hamburg. Here was a port and a city that relied on global trade and the impact of the crash was disastrous. As historian Keith Lowe states, 'trade kept Hamburg working, and once starved of it the city fell apart: industries failed, food and fuel became desperately scarce, and the people increasingly angry.' Lowe was actually referring here to the effects of the British Naval blockade on the city at the end of the Great War, but his observation was just as relevant to the situation in Hamburg in the aftermath of the Wall Street Crash. Unemployment soared and this was amplified in a district like St. Pauli, where many of its residents relied on casual labour and were therefore the first victims of a downturn in trade. By 1932 a staggering 40 per cent of the population of Hamburg was unemployed. The city was broke, reliant on bailouts from the Finance Ministry in Berlin to survive.

The crisis played into the hands of a new form of radicalism: the Nazis of the NSDAP. In a city, and indeed a nation, on its knees, people were looking for someone to blame, and the National Socialists of the NSDAP had identified scapegoats in abundance. In a climate of desperation and with a populace feeling let down by the existing political alternatives, the Nazis took advantage. They preyed on fear and pointed the finger of blame at everyone from the Socialists, Communists and Jews to the international powers that had dealt Germany such a poor hand at the end of the Great War. In short, the prevailing economic conditions were perfect for a new kind of extremism to flourish. In Hamburg, the Nazi party had secured three seats on the Citizens' Assembly as early as 1928. By 1932 electoral support for the Nazis had increased dramatically and saw them gain 51 seats out of 160 in the Citizens' Assembly. This radicalism wasn't confined to the ballot box: running battles between the Nazis and the Communists (who still garnered a sizeable percentage of votes, especially in working class districts) took place regularly on the city's streets. On 17 July 1932, in a battle that became known as 'Altona Bloody Sunday', the two sides clashed when the communists tried to prevent almost 7,000 Nazis holding a rally in a working-class area of Altona. The battle left 18 dead and hundreds injured.

To this day there is considerable historical debate regarding Hamburg's acceptance of National Socialism. The Nazi vote in the city was always several points below the national average, yet party membership was higher. Within weeks of Hitler's rise to absolute power and the election of an NSDAP-dominated senate by Hamburg's Bürgerschaft on 8 March 1933, thousands of opponents of the regime in the Hamburg area had been rounded up. Political parties were banned and trade unions that had links to the outlawed SPD were dissolved. The city's thriving free press was closed down and important positions in every walk of life were filled by Nazi sympathisers.

Through Hitler's pursuit of rearmament, Hamburg's docks cranked back into life, dragging with them the rest of the city's ailing economy. Hitler's requirement for new battleships got the big shipyards back in business, with the famous *Bismarck*, at that time the world's largest battleship (sunk on 27 May 1941), launched by Hitler himself in February 1939. Historian Christoph Nagel notes that according to Herbert Müller, a late FC St. Pauli player who used to work in the Blohm & Voss shipyard, Hitler was greeted with palpable hostility in the docks.

Of course, the internment in concentration camps on the edge of the city of the majority of the Nazis' political opponents did not signal an end to the persecution of Hamburg's inhabitants. A relatively cosmopolitan port city, built on hundreds of years of global trade, provided rich pickings for the Nazis. The city's Jewish population, along with foreigners, gypsies, homosexuals and those with disabilities, were all easy targets. For some, Hamburg's position as 'The Gateway to the World' proved helpful as it provided an opportunity to escape persecution by fleeing overseas – it is estimated that by 1935 a quarter of Hamburg's Jewish population had emigrated – however, those that stayed had to get used to increasingly restrictive laws as well as random acts of violence.

Then, on the 8-9 November 1938, Goebbels launched his 'Kristallnacht' pogrom. In Hamburg, like the rest of Germany, Jewish homes and businesses were ransacked or set ablaze. The city's main synagogue was destroyed and Jewish cemeteries were desecrated. In Hamburg, during the 'night of the broken glass', nearly a hundred Jews lost their lives, and in the weeks, months and years that followed thousands of Jewish men, women and children were rounded up, put on trains and sent to the Jewish ghettos of Eastern Europe and then, ultimately, on to the concentration camps that were the horrific manifestation of Hitler's 'Final Solution'.

The outbreak of war in September 1939 came as no surprise to the citizens of Hamburg. The frantic assembly of Hitler's naval fleet in the city's dockyards was tangible proof of a regime preparing for conflict. In preparation the city had also embarked on a massive programme of air-raid shelter construction. When the war came, the authorities knew the city would be targeted from the air. Hamburg's strategic importance as a port and a centre for warship and U-boat construction, large-scale industry and oil refineries all but guaranteed that. By 1941, there were more than 1,700 shelters and bunkers across the city that could provide shelter for nearly a quarter of a million people. Nineteen forty-two saw the construction of two enormous flak towers on the periphery of the Heiligengeistfeld in St. Pauli. To the north, bordering Feldstraße, the enormous Hochbunker served both as a flak tower targeting enemy aircraft and as a huge air-raid shelter designed to hold up to 18,000 people (although not totally completed by the time of the 1943 'firestorm', the Hochbunker was thought to have provided refuge for many more than the 18,000 it was designed to hold). The concrete walls of the bunker are three and a half metres thick and its ceiling five metres thick. Unsurprisngly, the Hochbunker survived the war, and remains a domineering feature on the Heiligengeistfeld, its grey concrete bulk impossible to destroy without undermining the stability of the other buildings in the area. Its post-war usage ranged from a Cold War bomb shelter to a media centre, offices and nightclubs. Another large bunker was also built at the southern end of the Heiligengeistfeld and was used during the war as a telecommunications hub, but was destroyed in 1974. Although when FC St. Pauli redeveloped its Südtribüne in 2007 tunnels were discovered that were thought to link the former Südbunker with the Hochbunker to the north, and caused the redevelopment of the stadium to slow for a short while as they were filled in.

The spectre of the Great Fire of 1842 still hung heavily over the city and in addition to shelters the authorities bolstered fire defences and trained huge numbers of firemen and wardens in the hope that they could stop fire spreading through the tightly packed buildings. In the most fanciful attempt to avert destruction, the *Binnenalster* (inner Alster) lake became home to a fake, floating city in the hope that British bombers would mistake this reconstruction for the heavily camouflaged 'real' city centre (however, the British had received intelligence about this and on 18 July 1941 the story was all over the British press). As Keith Lowe states: 'Hamburg was probably better prepared for catastrophe than any other city in the world.' Of course, as Lowe understood, nobody could've quite predicted the intensity of the destruction that would be unleashed on Hamburg from above, quite simply because there was no historical precedent.

During the early years of the war, air-raids on the city were intermittent; damage and loss of life was still very real when the raids came but for many of the city's residents the disruption to sleeping patterns and the regular inconvenience of relocating to a shelter once the warning siren had sounded was a far greater nuisance. With decent air defences and an abundance of places to shelter, it seemed in the first years of the war as if the threat from the skies had been somewhat over-egged.

All this changed during the last week of July in 1943. Between 24 and 29 July around 1.7 million bombs fell on the city. In the first night alone more than 350,000 individual incendiary bombs were dropped by the RAF, predominantly on the north-west and western districts of the city which, of course, included St. Pauli. The raids weren't confined to the hours of darkness, American bombers capable of flying at much higher altitudes, and therefore less vulnerable to anti-aircraft fire, continued the assault during the day. However, Operation Gomorrah, as the raids were codenamed by the Allies, was only just getting under way. This was to be a sustained wave of bombing the like of which had never been seen before.

The raids continued on the morning of 26 July, although the British raid that night was significantly disrupted by thunderstorms. The most destructive phase of the bombing began on the night of 27 July. More than 700 RAF planes took part in a bombing raid that hit the city's east end. Unusually warm weather conditions combined with a carefully considered mix of high-explosive and incendiary bombs produced a 'firestorm'. This caused fierce winds to sweep through the streets, consuming everything in their path. Temperatures at the heart of the firestorm are thought to have exceeded 800°C. As a result, a large swathe of the city was burnt to cinders and people were literally swept off their feet and sucked into the huge fireball. Large numbers of the dead had sought protection in the city's air-raid shelters. Many were simply incinerated by the intense heat of the firestorm; others, particularly those who sought refuge in the city's numerous cellar shelters, died of asphyxiation as the fire sucked all the oxygen out of the air.

Even after the firestorm of 27–28 July the bombing continued. Hamburg was subjected to further raids on the night of 29/30 July, with more than 700 aircraft targeting the city's northern edges. The damage was substantial but didn't recreate the firestorm of two days before. The final raid under the banner of Operation Gomorrah on 3 August was disrupted by more bad weather, forcing most of the bombers to divert from Hamburg and drop their load on secondary targets elsewhere.

Operation Gomorrah killed more than 42,000, with an estimated 37,000 wounded. The destruction to buildings and infrastructure left more than 900,000 people homeless. The area at the heart of the firestorm, Hammerbrook, was reduced to rubble and ash. Photographs record an eerie, almost alien, landscape with just the foundations of buildings poking through mounds of ash. On the north banks of the Elbe, east of the Alster lake from Hammerbrook to Barmbek, there were scenes of incomprehensible devastation. The area became known as the 'dead city'. By contrast, the district of St. Pauli, though still heavily damaged by the raids, escaped the total destruction that had occurred to the east in Hammerbrook, Hamm and Rothenburgsort. Avoiding total annihilation was probably partly due to luck – the bombing raids, despite meticulous planning by the British and Americans, weren't always successful in hitting their exact targets – but may also have owed something to the presence of the massive flak towers on the Heiligengeistfeld, which undoubtedly gave some protection to the immediate vicinity.

St. Pauli may not have felt the full force of the Allied raids, but the district suffered as much as the rest of the city from the longer term fall-out from Operation Gomorrah. In the weeks that followed more than one million people left Hamburg in an organised programme of mass evacuations. Those that stayed were faced with a huge clean-up operation. The first priority was to recover the bodies of those who had perished. It is estimated that in the days that followed the raids more than 10,000 bodies were removed from the streets. However, this was only the start of a long and gruesome process of recovering the dead from the rubble of the city. Prisoners from the concentration camps were drafted in to carry out the jobs that those working voluntarily could not face: the mass removal of charred remains from bunkers and shelters where hundreds of civilians had met their death. The authorities were in a race against time; worried about the outbreak of disease, they were desperate to clear the dead from the streets. Eventually, the 'dead city' was cordoned off with access forbidden – a burned-out hole at the heart of Hamburg. When it was eventually rebuilt after the war it was not as a residential area but as a commercial sector.

If the primary aim of the 1943 raids had been to reduce one of Germany's most important cities to rubble, disrupt production and demoralise its civilian population, thus shortening the war, then this was only partially successful. Hamburg lay in ruins, but its destruction didn't bring about a quick resolution to the conflict. There remains a school of thought that argues that, of course, the raids disabled the city and dramatically slowed down the production of arms and goods needed by those fighting on the frontline, thereby significantly weakening the German war machine. But the war in Europe raged for another two years and slowly people returned to Hamburg. At first, only those forced by the regime returned to help clear the city, but soon civilians came back to live among the ruins and to slowly start to rebuild their lives. Electricity and gas supplies to many areas resumed much sooner than those responsible for carrying out the raids would've expected. Slowly but surely Hamburg went back to work.

When the city was finally liberated by British troops on 3 May 1945, many of the soldiers were shocked by the devastation that greeted them. Here were battle-hardened soldiers, who had witnessed their own unimaginable horrors, still stunned by what they saw as they entered Hamburg: mile upon mile of bombed-out streets, an almost apocalyptic vision that would stay with them for the rest of their lives. And, amid that destruction, a population eeking out an existence. The almighty raids of 1943, and those smaller bombing raids that continued for the duration of the war, had left a city in ruins, but they hadn't broken the spirit of its inhabitants.

It is interesting that the destruction of Hamburg was viewed for a long time as a historical footnote to the mass destruction that followed in Dresden and then further afield in Hiroshima and Nagasaki. However, in recent years historians have looked in great detail at Operation Gomorrah and its place in history. Historians WG Sebald and Jörg Friedrich were among the first to reassess the morality of the bombing, with Friedrich going so far as concluding that the British decision to use area-bombing tactics which they knew would inflict untold civilian casualties could be considered a war crime. Friedrich's work, while controversial, certainly prompted renewed debate among historians about the strategies used in the Hamburg raids of 1943. Keith Lowe's book, *Inferno – The Devastation of Hamburg, 1943,* first published in 2007, retraces the story of the 'firestorm' from the perspectives of those on the ground in Hamburg and those taking part in the raids in the sky. It is an informative and engaging book that outlines the events as they happened and leaves you feeling sympathy for those involved on both sides. It is essential reading for anyone looking for a balanced and comprehensive understanding of Operation Gomorrah and the devastation it unleashed.

The inscription on the simple brick and stone memorial on Hamburger Straße, just across the road from Mundsburg Bahnhof, encapsulates perfectly the sense of sadness and the futility of war, it reads, 'On the night of 30th July 1943, 370 persons perished in the air-raid shelter on the Hamburger Straße in a bombing raid. Remember these dead. Never again fascism. Never again war.'

As was to be expected, the post-war reconstruction of Hamburg was a drawn-out process. Temporary accommodation in the form of thousands of corrugated tin Nissen huts (the German prefab equivalent) was a stop-gap measure for those made homeless by the bombing. As Martin Jefferies points out, 'some 51 million square yards of rubble had to be removed before roads could reopen and new homes be built.' He continues: 'Much of modern Hamburg, from the foundations of the widened Ballindamm and the Kennedy-Brücke to the Volkspark, with its HSV football stadium, is built on rubble.' Yet, slowly but surely, buildings started to emerge from this debris.

FC St. Pauli also suffered directly from the bombing. The stadium on the Heiligengeistfeld, despite its location between the two enormous flak towers, had been completely destroyed during a bombing raid in the later stages of the war. In the middle of such devastation, members of the club worked tirelessly to build a new home on the Heiligengeistfeld, directly opposite the old fire station. From the rubble materialised a stadium built to hold 30,000 spectators. Astonishingly, the new ground was inaugurated on 17 November 1946 with a match against Schalke 04 just 18 months after the cessation of hostilities.

At the first elections after the war, the Social Democratic Party of Germany (SPD) returned to power, and remained in control of the city for much of the 20th century. Hamburg benefited from the German 'economic miracle' of the 1950s and '60s. A building boom helped regenerate the city and provided a kick-start to the post-war economy.

In the dockyards, ship building remained important and the port was quick to adapt to the changing markets of the post-war era. Trade with the newly created Eastern bloc diminished, but this was more than compensated for by demand from Western Europe and beyond. Today, the port welcomes huge container ships, bringing with them thousands of containers a week, containing goods, mostly from the Far East, bound for the rest of Europe. Even at the start of the 21st century the port of Hamburg remains a gateway to and from the rest of the world.

However, by fast forwarding to the 21st century, we have bypassed some of the important contributions Hamburg in general and the St. Pauli district in particular have made to modern culture. And, as we shall see in subsequent chapters, an understanding of the post-war history of the district of St. Pauli is vital to understanding the modern history of its football club.

The post-1945 history of St. Pauli is one of almost cyclical boom-and-bust – in fact this seems to be the pattern for the history of the district in general. It is the story of a district that has endured good times and bad in a rollercoaster ride that wouldn't be out of place at the funfair on the Heiligengeistfeld.

By the late 1950s, St. Pauli was back on its feet again. The docks were up and running and once again sailors and dockworkers as well as ordinary Hamburg citizens flocked to the area looking for a good time in more – or less – reputable establishments. The Reeperbahn was booming, but while prostitution, strip clubs and drinking dens remained as popular as ever, a new scene was emerging with music at its epicentre.

Hamburg is regarded by some as the birthplace of the 'Exis' (short for existentialist) youth movement, whose followers were hated by their mortal enemies, the Rockers. These young hipsters looked to the French writers Jean-Paul Sartre and Albert Camus for inspiration and dressed predominantly in black, often sporting roll-necked sweaters and smoking Gauloises. They were different, bohemian, and they were united by rock and roll music and, in time, some of those among their ranks would be credited with restyling the biggest rock and roll band in history.

In 1958 Bill Haley had played a concert at the Ernst-Merck-Halle that prompted a riot that had to be quelled by police – live music was becoming a real crowd-puller. As the new decade dawned, music venues were springing up on the Reeperbahn and on Große Freiheit – an infamous, neon-lit side street that housed a variety of insalubrious clubs, strip joints and porn cinemas. The demand for live music continued to grow and as it did attracted a number of hard-working rock and roll bands from the United Kingdom, among them The Jets, Derry and the Seniors and Rory Storm and the Hurricanes. These bands played punishing evening-long sets to diverse audiences of hardened sailors and the bohemian Exis drawn to St. Pauli by the prospect of live rock 'n' roll. Then, in the summer of 1960, a band arrived in Hamburg who would change popular music forever, The Beatles. Although, of course, nobody knew that yet; they were just another group of lads, hair thick with Brylcreem or liquid paraffin, prepared to belt out rock and roll standards for hours on end. The Beatles, including drummer Pete Best, recruited a few days before they left Liverpool, and bassist Stuart Sutcliffe, made their Hamburg debut on 17 August at the Indra Club (a venue that had only just started putting on live rock 'n' roll acts after noting the popularity of these acts elsewhere on Große Freiheit).

The Beatles played a total of 48 nights at the Idra, with each session lasting for between four and six hours. They slept in the storeroom of an adjacent cinema, the Bambi-Kino, roughing it on old camp beds. In October 1960, allegedly after complaints about the noise from an irate old lady who lived in an apartment above the Idra but also because the crowds did not meet the expectations of club owner Bruno Koschmider, they were switched to another venue also owned by Koschmider, the Kaiserkeller, a bit closer to the Reeperbahn, where apparently sustained by German slimming pills that provided an amphetamine-like kick, they alternated sets with Rory Storm and the Hurricanes (whose drummer happened to be a certain Ringo Starr).

Playing in front of rough, sometimes violent, audiences at the Kaiserkeller and mixing with prominent members of St. Pauli's underworld undoubtedly gave the band a resilient edge they had lacked before arriving in Hamburg. They learned to improvise, hone their skills as musicians and make the transition from youth to adulthood. Hamburg has also been widely credited with developing their image too. Sutcliffe started dating Astrid Kirchherr, a member of the Exis and a promising young photographer who had discovered the Beatles in the

Kaiserkeller (in whose rowdy surroundings she initially felt 'totally out of place'). Kirchherr is often credited with getting the band to ditch their old style and reliance on orthodox '50s rock and roll imagery – the teddy-boy quiffs and the drainpipe trousers – encouraging them to adopt the French influenced mop-top that would eventually be labelled 'The Beatles Cut.' Astrid Kirchherr's photographs from 1960 show the band, still sporting their rock 'n' roll quiffs, at the Dom funfair on the Heiligengeistfeld. The photos capture the band brooding against a backdrop of fairground machinery. Even given their location, it is fanciful to suggest that The Beatles had any awareness of FC St. Pauli or the construction of its new home stadium on the Heiligengeistfeld just yards behind the funfair where they were photographed. George Harrison's famously oblique quote about his football allegiance, 'There are three teams in Liverpool, and I prefer the other one,' make it rather improbable that FC St. Pauli, then playing its football in the Oberliga Nord, registered on the band's radar– and vice versa: In interviews for *FC St. Pauli. Das Buch,* members of the team at that time admitted freely that the emerging Hamburg Beat scene was not much to their taste and that they preferred to spend their nights elsewhere. It is interesting to note how close, and at the same time how far apart, the two different worlds of football and music were.

During their first stay in Hamburg, The Beatles not only polished their craft – they developed a style, something that would begin to set them apart from their contemporaries back home. And home was where The Beatles were heading, albeit unwittingly. In November 1960, it was discovered that George Harrison had been working as a minor and he was swiftly deported. The rest of the band stayed but Paul McCartney and Pete Best soon found themselves in a spot of bother after they were reported setting fire to a condom in their lodgings in the Bambi-Kino. Although an act of vandalism that did no lasting damage, the boys were arrested and spent the night in custody. The band's first spell in Hamburg was coming to an end, and after switching to a new venue on the Reeperbahn (the Top-Ten Club), they were soon found to be performing without work permits and were forced to return home.

In early 1961, with Harrison turned 18, the band returned to Hamburg and embarked on a 98-night residency at the Top-Ten Club. Stuart Sutcliffe left the band in July 1961, to enrol at the

Hamburg College of Art and work on his paintings. Sutcliffe, who had been suffering from increasingly severe headaches, died of a brain haemorrhage on 10 April 1962. The band were informed of his death on returning to Hamburg on 13th April for another residency slot, this time at the newly opened Star Club on Große Freiheit. McCartney took over Sutcliffe's position on bass and soon Pete Best was dispensed with by the band's manager Brian Epstein. Best's replacement was someone who certainly knew the ropes of the St. Pauli scene, Ringo Starr. With their most famous line-up complete, The Beatles' time in St. Pauli was reaching an end. Chart success in the United Kingdom was calling them home. The band played their last gig at the Star Club on New Year's Eve 1962, leaving Hamburg shortly afterwards. Lennon is famously quoted as saying 'Liverpool was where we grew up. Hamburg was where we came of age' and this is undoubtedly true. In the dark clubs of the Reeperbahn and Große Freiheit the band learnt their trade, while their beatnik friends among the Exis helped them grow beyond the confines of traditional rock and roll.

The Beatles played St. Pauli during the boom years of live music on the Reeperbahn. They helped define a period in the early 1960s when the district was at the cutting edge of pop culture. As the decade progressed other cities would take over the mantle, but the importance of the 'Hamburg Sound' in kick-starting a cultural revolution should not be underestimated.

Even during the boom years of Germany's economic miracle, St. Pauli remained a tough working-class district, substantially poorer than other areas of Hamburg. And by the mid-1980s the area was once again falling on hard times. The world had moved on and, with live music no longer the draw it had been in the '60s, the area around the Reeperbahn once again concentrated on serving up its diet of partially sanitised sleaze. However, the mechanisation of cargo fuelled by the container revolution was in full swing, and international shipping was beginning to deploy skeleton crews operating on fast turnarounds, so that they simply weren't in port long enough to sample the delights that the district of St. Pauli had to offer. The AIDS crisis of the 1980s hit the Reeperbahn hard.

In the early part of the decade there had been upwards of 1,000 prostitutes working the district, many plying their trade in large brothels, like the six-storey Eros Centre. By 1988, the Eros had closed its doors for the last time and the number of prostitutes in the district had more than halved. Nowadays, the most prominent of St. Pauli's brothels are confined to the Herbertstraße, a side-street walled off since the 1930s, where women sit behind glass waiting for custom. The Reeperbahn still has its fair share of women illegally working the streets, but trade is at much lower levels than in the hey-day of the 1960s and '70s.

In the 1980s, away from the neon glare of the Reeperbahn and Große Freiheit, the St. Pauli district continued to be an area that reflected the social deprivation of the era. As a result of recession, inner cities across Europe had experienced an exodus of jobs and people to the more palatable surroundings of the suburbs. As a result, buildings were left empty and fell into disrepair. In an era before urban regeneration became both fashionable and profitable, this meant that working-class districts, already suffering from years of neglect, were left to rot.

As we have seen, St. Pauli has long been a place where those living on – or forced to live on – the margins of society have sought refuge, with cheap rents and a tolerant outlook providing a welcome contrast to other parts of the city. The recession that gripped Germany in the 1980s was most keenly felt by its youth. School leavers struggled to find work. Unemployment meant young people couldn't afford to leave home and get a place of their own. The large number of empty buildings in areas of Hamburg and West Berlin provided an opportunity for communities of squatters, looking to forge new ways of communal living. One such community grew up around the Hafenstraße on the north bank of the Elbe in St. Pauli.

Here, in the autumn of 1981, several neglected, council-owned houses that were destined for replacement with modern office blocks were first squatted. Over the next decade, the squats on the Hafenstraße would become among the most famous in Germany, bringing together a diverse collective of punks, anarchists, and disenfranchised youth. The anarchist website *www.ainfos.ca* states that 'the cornerstone of these communities was communal living, and the creation of radical social centres: info-shops, bookstores, coffeehouses, meeting halls, bars, concert halls, art galleries, and other multi-use spaces where grassroots political, artistic and social culture were developed as an alternative to nuclear family life, TV dreams and mass-produced pop culture. These highly political, social communities took their lead from similar movements that had developed in Italy in the 1960's were referred to as "Autonome".'

In St. Pauli, once again, a community of society's 'outsiders' was trying to establish an alternative way of living. Viewed in a historical context, the squatters on the Hafenstraße were the latest in a long list of so-called 'undesirables' to make the district of St. Pauli their home. As we shall see, the occupants of the squatted houses of the Hafenstraße would play a defining role in transforming FC St. Pauli from an underachieving German football club into a cult phenomenon.

It is at this point, in the early 1980s, where the history of the district of St. Pauli and the history of its football club collide head-on. Those residents of the Hafenstraße who made the half-mile journey from their squats to the Millerntor stadium changed history. This is where the story of FC St. Pauli's transformation from a nondescript German football club to a 'Kult' phenomenon begins. It is here that the district's 'outsiders' embraced football.

MATCH

MINI

You'll Never Walk Alone!
Alemannia Aachen 1 FC St. Pauli 3
2. Bundesliga
Saturday 15 March 2009, 2.00pm, Tivoli

Alemannia Aachen 0 FC St. Pauli 5
2. Bundesliga
Monday 17 August 2009, 8.15pm, Neu Tivoli

BUOYED BY A couple of successful trips to the Millerntor, I decide it is time to branch out and experience an away game as a St. Pauli fan. I have a loose set of criteria for this: I want to visit other grounds renowned for both atmosphere and character (the presence of impressive old-school floodlight pylons was a consideration too) and I want to travel by train, preferably with under three changes from St. Pancras. With this in mind, all roads – or rails – lead to Aachen.

Aachen, pronounced *Ark-en* rather than *Atch-en* (my lack of even the most basic pronunciation of place names had embarrassed me when discussing possible away games with fellow UK-based fans on my previous trip to Hamburg) is situated in a little nook on the German–Belgian–Dutch border. It's Germany's most westerly city and, as such, sustained substantial damage during World War Two. It was also the first German city to be captured by the Allies on its surrender in October 1944. The cathedral, which survived the war time assault on the city, is the resting place of Charlemagne, the famous middle-ages empire builder and King of the Franks. The reason Aachen had registered on my radar was nothing to do with its place in history as a favoured retreat of a medieval powerbroker and everything to do with it being on the high-speed rail link to Köln. My dislike of flying means the route from London to Brussels to Hamburg via Köln was my preferred, if elongated, way of getting to the Millerntor. As the train begins its approach into Aachen you are alerted that you have entered Germany not by a passport inspection or a sudden change in the architecture or landscape whizzing by outside, but by the incessant beeping of a carriage full of mobile phones which alerts you that you've switched networks to a German mobile provider. In fact, as the train slows down, you notice that the houses still have a very Flemish feel to them.

When passing through, I'd often wondered whether modern-day Aachen has benefited to some extent from being a named stopping point on the reliable, high-speed, Thalys service that connects Paris to Amsterdam via Köln, Brussels and Liège, in much the same way as Lille has flourished since the Eurostar's arrival. On a purely football level, it's fair to say that Alemannia Aachen hasn't benefited in quite the same way as LOSC Lille in recent years.

The history of Alemannia Aachen, much like FC St. Pauli, is one of lower league mediocrity. Stalwarts of the second division, the club has also spent time in the regionalised third tier of German football. In 2005–06 the club clinched promotion to the Bundesliga for the first time in 36 years; unfortunately, the success was short-lived and the club were relegated back to 2. Bundesliga the following season. However, it wasn't the team's performance that persuaded me to make the short (ish) trip to Aachen, it is the stadium. The Tivoli is another of those atmospheric old-fashioned football stadiums, with terraces on three sides that mean that 17,600 of the 21,300 capacity are standing places. The Tivoli is probably best known for the 'Würselener Wall', a steep bank of open terracing at the north end of the ground that's home to Aachen's most fervent fans. The Tivoli is the sort of stadium the Taylor Report did away with in England long ago, but whose rugged, windswept terracing inspires more passion than a hundred identikit modern stadia. Sadly, despite its immense popularity with both Aachen fans and visiting supporters, it too was about to be replaced with a shiny new stadium for the start of the 2009–10 season. As such, this represented my last chance to visit the old Tivoli.

For this trip, I enlist two mates. We decide to make a weekend of it – St. Pauli's game in Aachen was on the Sunday afternoon, which meant we are also able to take in the Rhine derby between 1.FC Köln and Borussia Mönchengladbach in Köln. This split-city, dual game approach had worked well the previous season when we'd combined a visit to Hamburg to watch St. Pauli defeat FSV Frankfurt with a trip down to Bremen to watch Werder against FC Energie Cottbus.

Like all of my great European rail–football adventures thus far, the whole trip is nearly scuppered before we make it to London. Two of us are travelling on the milk-train from Milton Keynes to Euston, while my other friend is trying to get to King's Cross. Both lines are hit by delays and cancellations that necessitate three unfit middle-aged men running to the Eurostar terminal at St. Pancras from our respective stations, while updating each other of our progress via mobile phone. We get there, which is fortunate, because it would require making every connection *and* every connection running to time if we were to leave London at 7.00am and be in our seats in the RheinEnergie Stadium in time for the 3.30pm kick-off.

Once again, we speed through Aachen heading for Köln accompanied by the trill of mobile phones switching their allegiance from Belgian to German network operators. At Köln station there is just enough time to dump our bags in the slightly scary, automated, bag-storage device and get on the tram to the stadium. The heavy police presence at the ground is our first indication that this is a fiercely contested local derby with no love lost between the two sets of rival supporters. My St. Pauli fixtures thus far, had all been rather low key-affairs, against relatively 'friendly' opposition.

This is different. There is historical bad blood between these two, compounded by some Ultra' flag-stealing shenanigans prior to the previous encounter between the sides. The entire 'Gladbach block just to our right are dressed in black and intent on letting off an impressive selection of flares, that make their section of terrace look like a particularly sinister, well attended bonfire party. The game, despite an impressive 2-4 away win for 'Gladbach, never really grabs the attention like the crowd, and before long we are back on the tram heading for our hostel and a couple of beers in its cosy bar.

Of course, Köln v 'Gladbach is nothing more than a diversion, and after a leisurely start to Sunday we are back at the Hauptbahnhof getting the train to Aachen for the weekend's main event.

On arrival in Aachen, a modest station with an appealing stone frontage, we ask a couple of fans in St. Pauli scarves for directions to the stadium. They reply in perfect English. Nothing unusual there, except by chance we'd randomly stumbled across the two other fans from the St. Pauli UK Messageboard attending the game. They decide they are going to walk, but suggest the station-to-stadium bus as a less arduous alternative, and within minutes we cross the station forecourt, board the free courtesy bus and are on our way to the ground.

We actually see the new stadium first, its hulking yellow frame visible as we make our surprisingly hilly journey to the Tivoli. Once there, we wander round until we find the away section. Despite being a good 90 minutes until kick-off, a fair number of St. Pauli fans are milling around. We have to wait until the Fanladen buses roll into town so we can meet Stefan and collect our tickets. Waiting around outside, we watch the USP get their collection of flags through the security check and also have time to browse the mobile club shop, that I later find out accompanies the team and fans to all away games (well, we can't afford to miss a merchandising opportunity can we, now?)

Once we get our tickets – an incredible €8,50 – we haul our way up the steep concrete steps, utilising the wonderfully yellow-painted handrails, to the away section of the terrace tucked into one corner at the opposite end of the ground from the Würselener Wall. In one sense, it is like stepping back in time to one of the lost terraces of our youth. There's more than a whiff of old grounds like Brighton's Goldstone or Millwall's Old Den about the Tivoli. We take our place under the huge floodlight pylon and contemplate a beer from the distinctly old-school beer hut.

As kick-off approaches, the stadium fills up steadily, with the Würselener Wall looking packed out with a good 30-minutes to go. The St. Pauli fans are in good voice as usual; you can only presume it is the same down the other end, but of course, one of the drawbacks of a huge open terrace (aside from getting a soaking when it rains) is that most of the noise disappears into the ether.

It is an open game, that sees St. Pauli grab a relatively rare 3-1 away victory. Again, it isn't the match that keeps us captivated but the non-stop singing and exuberant atmosphere in the away section. Again, the air is heavily scented with tobacco and marijuana smoke, but as non-smokers we choose to supplement the on-the-pitch entertainment with regular trips to the beer hut. As someone who never drank when watching football in the UK, I now make sure I always have a beer when watching football in Germany. Partly because there are no ridiculous laws preventing me from doing so, and partly because it adds to the atmosphere. However, on this occasion I get it all wrong and end up missing the second of David Hoilett's two goals; although not actually seeing the goal doesn't prevent everyone in the beer queue celebrating as if they've scored it themselves.

This is a good team display capped with a fine individual performance from a hitherto inconsistent Hoilett – if you'd said at that point he'd go on to make an impact in the Premier League, I'd have questioned your judgement. However, somewhere between that performance for St. Pauli, a name change to 'Junior' and a return to Blackburn Rovers (where we'd loaned him from) he transformed into a decent player.

The highlight for me comes halfway through the second half when someone in the bowels of the Tivoli flicks a switch and the huge floodlights flicker into life, illuminating a dank spring afternoon. It makes the trip to this beautiful old stadium complete, yet knowing this ground is nearing the end of it's lifespan tinges the occasion with sadness. I know it seems strange to feel nostalgic for a ground you've only just visited, but having lost so many great old stadiums in Britain, the loss resonates all the more. Soon I know the club will move lock, stock and barrel a few hundred metres down the road. The new stadium will be pristine, modern and hi-tech, but I doubt it will ever be thought of with the same fondness as the old Tivoli. Ho hum, I guess that's the price of progress.

After the game, and another beer (I cling onto my plastic cup printed with a nice floodlit panorama of the Tivoli) we are bussed back to the station and have an uneventful journey back home via Brussels.

It has been another successful trip and more importantly, a ground soon to be lost forever, ticked off my list – just in time.

As it happens I will see the old Tivoli again sooner than I imagine. Call it fate, or the fixture computer, but St. Pauli are paired with Aachen in the second game of the 2009–10 season. It is also the first competitive game to be played at the New Tivoli. The fact that it is also picked for the dreaded Monday night TV slot also works in my favour as it means I can take the train to Aachen and be checked into my hotel with a few hours to spare before kick-off.

I am travelling on my own this time, which is okay as I have plenty of work with which to occupy myself on the train, and the journey flies by with me working away feverishly on my laptop. There've been a few warnings about a planned neo-Nazi march on the German St. Pauli forum in the lead-up to the game, but when I arrive in the early afternoon, the town's residents are enjoying a peaceful afternoon in the warm summer sunshine. As far as I know, there is no reported trouble on this occasion, although the problem of the far right raises its head again when FC St. Pauli visit Aachen in February 2012, including a threat to plant a bomb in the away section.

My hotel, though close to the Tivolis (note the plural) is right on the edge of town and turns out to be one of these new, largely unstaffed hotels, where you need to enter a complicated series of letter and numbers into a key-pad just to get into the reception. But it is okay, and has free wi-fi, which is handy for work.

Once again, I find myself waiting for the Fanladen bus, although this time the scene is very different – lots of freshly laid concrete approach roads and concourses, along with the obligatory glass and steel of a new stadium. The giant letters on the side spelling out 'Tivoli' is a nice touch, but otherwise from the outside there isn't a lot to distinguish it from countless other new stadia or indeed a jumbo-sized DIY superstore. Still, the Aachen fans both inside and outside the ground seem in good spirits, and try as I might, there is no way of having a look inside the club shop that doesn't involve at least a 45-minute wait, as the place is totally rammed.

I get my ticket – still a very reasonable €12,50, although an increase of nearly 35 per cent in the five months since March – and make my way to the away fans section, a steep segment of terrace wedged into the corner of the new stand. Being a Monday night fixture, the St. Pauli fans continue their protest against the broadcaster DSF with plenty of banners and a boycott of chanting for the first ten minutes. However, the rest of the 32,000 crowd make a fair amount of noise as they look to christen their new stadium with a win. FC St. Pauli, who'd opened the season with an unconvincing, last-gasp, home win over Rot Weiss Ahlen have other ideas. Marius Ebbers opens the scoring on 24 minutes, and in one of those surreal moments you occasionally get as a football fan we find ourselves 4-0 up at the break, each goal being celebrated with an increased sense of incredulity. St. Pauli have simply swept Aachen aside with a fast-paced display of counter-attacking football, a style that would reap dividends throughout the 2009–10 campaign. The poor Alemannia Aachen fans, dressed in their striking combination of yellow and black, have the shell-shocked appearance of a hive of bees that have collectively used their stings and are waiting patiently for the inevitable. This certainly isn't the house-warming they'd expected.

Rouwen Hennings adds a fifth goal four minutes from time, sending the away fans into further raptures and the home support heading for the exits. The players, who look almost as shocked as us fans, then make their way over to the away section to rousing applause.

The celebrations are extensive, but after a few minutes I notice the mood has changed. Not speaking much German, it is hard to pick up on what exactly has happened, but it seems one of our fans has been injured celebrating the victory. The atmosphere in our section of terrace changes from one of unbridled celebration to one of confused uncertainty. I decide to make a move and am probably one of the first 100 or so fans to leave the away section. As I make my way down the terrace, the looks on the faces of those that have been near the front speak volumes. As I continue down the stairs, I spot a distressed-looking Stefan from the Fanladen standing at the mouth of the section of concourse that provides access to the pitch. I ask him what has happened and he says that a fan has fallen from the terraced section onto the concrete below. He adds that it doesn't look good. Looking out towards the pitch I can make out a team of paramedics treating the injured fan. It is a good 15 foot drop from the bottom of the terraced section to the concrete floor below, and from what I can make out the fan had fallen face down onto the concrete. Although no one could be sure the extent of the injuries, I am left with that sickening feeling that this is really serious. Feeling upset and useless, and with more fans starting to make their exit seeing for themselves what happened, I decide to make my way back to the hotel.

I step out into the throng of Aachen fans leaving the stadium. They seem unaware of the incident, their slumped posture and stilted conversations being the product of an embarrassing home defeat in their new stadium. On the 10-minute walk to my hotel I see the flashing lights of a couple of ambulances parting the crowds walking in the road. Their destination might be the New Tivoli, but equally they could've been heading somewhere else entirely. I make it back to my room and switch on my laptop and head for the FC St. Pauli German fan forum. News starts to trickle through about a fan being injured after falling from the away block. However, it is difficult to separate truth from conjecture on internet forums at the best of times, let alone when what you are reading has been mechanically translated from the original German by an online search engine. Shortly before I log off, the fan forum is closed. I was later to find out that this was a precaution to both slow down misinformation and out of respect to the injured fan's family. At the time I could only assume it meant the worst.

I lie awake for ages, thoughts racing, hoping that I've misread the reasoning behind the forum being closed-down and reflecting on how the incident could've happened in a brand new, safety-checked stadium. I have to be up early to get the train back to Brussels, so I log on again about 6.00am. By now, most of the German news sites are carrying the story. Fortunately, everyone's worst fears hadn't been confirmed; the fan made it through the night, although he was still in a critical condition. He had broken both arms and suffered serious head injuries after falling five or six metres from the away section, through a canvas awning and onto the concrete below. Several players who had witnessed the scene, including the young striker Deniz Naki had been led away in tears. Doctors in the hospital in Aachen had placed the fan in an artificial coma in the hope that the swelling to his head injuries would subside.

As I am up early I decide to walk to the station. It is a bit of a trek, but it allows me time to clear my head. It is going to be another warm summer's day, but at 7.30am there is a pleasing crispness to the air that hints at Autumn being not many weeks away. I walk past lots of out-of-town retail units, not really noticing the New Tivoli, until I spot the giant letters that spell out its name. There is no one about, and certainly no trace of last night's events. I reflect again on how a brand new stadium could be christened in such a horrific fashion. I walk on, to the old Tivoli, still perfectly intact and playing host to Aachen's second team for one final season before demolition. Again, I feel the pull of the old stadium, and a thought crosses my mind briefly: 'What if last night's game had been played here?' But it is stupid to think like that; accidents can happen anywhere. I take a couple of pictures of the obsolete stadium signage and the floodlights against the pale blue morning sky. Again, there is nobody around, apart from the odd jogger. The only thing that reminds me it is a weekday morning is the steady build-up of cars at the traffic lights.

There aren't that many of us waiting on the platform for the early Thalys service bound for Köln, Brussels and Paris, but standing a few feet from me, looking weary, is FC St. Pauli chairman Corny Littmann. Perhaps, any other day I would've plucked up the courage to talk to him, but he seems lost in his own thoughts, and has probably been up all night trying to support those involved in the incident. The rest of my journey home is uneventful. I still have work to do, so put my headphones on and switch on the laptop. It has been a strange trip, an astonishing away win and what should've been one of the highlights of the season, rendered totally irrelevant by a horrible, horrible accident.

As the days go by, it emerges that the injured fan was called Mini, a member of the Mexikaner fan group, who'd fallen from his position at the front of the terrace as the players had come over to the crowd to celebrate. As well as the broken arms, he had also broken his cheekbone and upper and lower jaw. Questions were asked about the stadium design, but on the whole people seemed to conclude that it was a terrible accident. This strikes me as an incredibly balanced reflection on events. In fact, the only real – and totally justifiable – anger is reserved for a tabloid newspaper that published pictures of Mini as he lay injured on the floor inside the stadium. Get well messages flooded in from fans all over Germany and beyond, and support from club officials and supporters' groups was overwhelming. At the next home game against MSV Duisburg, on the request of Mini's family and fan club, an emotional rendition of 'You'll Never Walk Alone' was sung prior to kick-off.

Although Mini's condition stabilised, much uncertainty over his recovery remained. It was an incredibly stressful time for his family, especially his sister, who took on the role of spokesperson for them. Mini stayed in hospital in Aachen until mid-September, when doctors were sufficiently happy with his progress that he could be moved to a hospital in Hamburg to continue his rehabilitation, closer to family and friends.

Mini spent the autumn undergoing extensive rehabilitation and was finally declared well enough to return to the Millerntor to watch St. Pauli's 3-1 win over 1860 Munich in October when he sat alongside Corny Littmann in a box in the south stand. Reflecting on his accident, he stated just how lucky he'd been to survive and thanked everybody, from the hospital staff who'd treated him to the fans and officials of both FC St. Pauli and Alemannia Aaachen. He had no memory of the incident itself or the match that preceded it. For the return match against Aachen in January, Mini was able to take to the pitch to relay his thanks to both sets of supporters – it was another incredibly emotional moment for Mini and for those supporters who had prayed hard for his recovery.

The St. Pauli website caught up with Mini again in February 2012, just before St. Pauli travelled to face Aachen at the Tivoli for the first time since his accident. Despite losing sight in one eye and suffering from back pain, Mini remains as committed to FC St. Pauli as ever.

For me, it had been two very different trips to Aachen. The first had been an enjoyable step back in time to an atmospheric, if slightly down-at-heel, stadium. The second had been a surreal experience, part dream, part – *very real* – nightmare. I'm glad I took the time to visit the old Tivoli (which has since been reduced to rubble to make way for housing) but for various reasons, I'm not in a hurry to return to the New Tivoli. I'll know, for sure, the next time I visit Aachen, but after the trills of network-searching mobile phones have subsided, I'll stay on the train and head for Hamburg or, perhaps, another as yet unvisited away ground.

Mini

By way of a postscript, and proof that sometimes lightning can strike twice: just four months later, in December 2009, another St. Pauli fan was seriously injured after falling from a fence between the standing and seated area of the away section prior to FC St. Pauli's 5-1 win in Koblenz. Kick-off was delayed for ten minutes, and the fan was taken to hospital and also placed in an artificial coma. Once again, fans rallied round with collections being made to help pay for medical bills. Fortunately, he also made a good recovery. However, this accident, coming so soon after Aachen, continued to keep fan safety in the stadium in the spotlight.

Chapter 3
JUST ANOTHER FOOTBALL CLUB

THE FACT THAT Germany had no national, professional football league until the early 1960s season tells us that the development of football in the country was very different to the UK's. Up until the inaugural Bundesliga campaign in 1963–64, German football had been played on a regional level, with five Oberligen, dividing teams along geographical lines.

However, the late arrival of a national league isn't the only difference between football's development in Germany and the UK. The way in which football clubs came into being is markedly different from the British model. Football began to gain popularity in Germany in the last decade of the 19th century, but it was treated with suspicion bordering on contempt by the country's establishment and was even dubbed 'the English disease'. The roots of this disdain for football came from the long-established 'gymnastic movement' or *Turnen*. As Ulrich Hesse-Lichtenberger stated in *Tor! The Story of German Football*: 'Long before football arrived, physical training in Germany was dominated to an astonishing degree by the gymnastics movement. The German obsession with the teachings of these stern contortionists goes a long way to explaining why sport (as opposed to *Turnen*), and especially professional sport, had such problems taking root in Germany.' As Hesse-Lichtenberger observed, this obsession with gymnastic activity had its origins in military failings and Napoleon. More specifically the Prussian army's crushing defeat by the French at Jena and Auerstedt in 1806. The defeats cost Prussia dearly in terms of land and influence and as a direct result of these military embarrassments came a massive reform of the Prussian army and German society as a whole. Conscription was introduced and in order to get recruits fit for purpose, schools were encouraged to develop a programme of physical education.

In the half a century that followed Prussia's humiliation at the hands of Napoleon's army gymnastics took hold in the country. Clubs began to spring up, giving members the opportunity to participate not only in traditional gymnastic exercises but also other pursuits that included swimming and hiking. Devotees of gymnastics, such as Friedrich Ludwig Jahn, believed that gymnastics were quite different from typically English sports like cricket, golf, horse racing and billiards (and later football, of course). These 'English' sports were the complete opposite to gymnastics; as Hesse-Lichtenberger states, 'gymnastics was for the people. It created unity, not separation. It existed for the good of the whole, not for the self-esteem of a select few.'

Yet, these 'English' sports did slowly take root in Germany. In fact, football was brought to the country in the 1860s, before the foundation of the Football Association in England formalised the splitting of the codes between (Association) football and rugby. Football was especially popular among students attending the numerous English schools that were well established in most major German cities at the time; the only uncertainty is the particular code that these students (and English workers) were following. Indeed, the club credited with being the first 'football' club in Germany, Football Club of Hannover, actually began playing rugby.

The situation in Hamburg echoed that found elsewhere. René Martens states that the first clubs to play football in Hamburg were Cito and Excelsior, both formed in 1887 and, interestingly, both playing on the Heiligengeistfeld, not a million miles from the future site of FC St. Pauli's homeground(s). Of course, St. Pauli's cross town rivals Hamburger Sport-Verein (HSV) also claim 1887 as the year of their birth. Once again, there is a great deal of ambiguity in this claim. Working backwards, HSV in its current recognisable form came into being in 1919 with the merger of three Hamburg clubs that had all been significantly weakened after the Great War. The new club then took its foundation date from the oldest of the three clubs, Sports-Club Germania, founded in 1887. Adopting this lineage, HSV could claim to be one of the oldest football clubs in Germany only Sports-Club

Germania started life as an athletics club. They only began playing football in 1891, when six Englishmen joined, bringing with them their enthusiasm for all things Association football.

It is partly due to this confusion that modern-day FC St. Pauli used to run with the tag line, 'Non-established 1910', until very recently. It's a good gimmick, part appealing to the club's outsider/rebel status, but also poking fun at their more illustrious rival's birth claims.

Modern-day FC St. Pauli can also trace its roots back to the gymnastic movement of the mid-to-late 19th century. The Hamburg-St. Pauli Turnverein von 1862 (the Hamburg-St. Pauli Gymnastics club) was founded, as the name suggests, in 1862, although you could shave ten years off that foundation date if you consider that Hamburg-St. Pauli Turnverein was pre-dated by the MTV – Männerturnverein in Hamburg (Mens' Gymnastic Club) which was founded in 1852, but that is taking things to extremes! It wasn't until the last years of the 19th century that Hamburg-St. Pauli Turnverein began to experiment with other games, including football, on the wide expanses of the Heiligengeistfeld. Research for *FC St. Pauli. Das Buch* found the first recorded instances of football in the Hamburg-St. Pauli Turnverein in 1899, although still in a non-competitive, purely recreational manner. The games were played within the Spielabteilung (Games section), which had been established in April 1896.

The future FC St. Pauli's first competitive match was played against a team from the Aegir Swimming Club, registering a 1-1 draw (the re-match, which immediately followed the first one, saw St. Pauli's side record an impressive 7-1 win). Two years later, an equally momentous decision was taken, when St. Pauli's familiar brown and white kit was adopted.

In January 1910, St. Pauli TV joined the 3a class in District III (Hamburg/Altona) of the NFV's (North German Football Association's) football league for the second half of the season. In the spring of that year the club was formally recognised as a full member of the Norddeutscher Fußballverband (NFV), paving the way for its full participation in the 1910–11 league competition. Unfortunately, no evidence for the exact joining date (*Beitritt*) to the NFV has survived. It is almost certain, though, that it was *not* 15 May 1910, the date that has been used by the modern-day club as the date on which it was (non) established, as there are earlier mentions of the membership in club protocols of that year.

In 1919, St. Pauli TV achieved promotion to the top Hamburg league for the first time. However, this success was short lived and the club spent much of the next decade bouncing around between the divisions. The next significant date in its history came on 5 May 1924, when the ever expanding Sporting and Games section of Hamburg-St. Pauli Turnverein von 1862 voted to break away from the original organisation to create an entirely separate football club. Thus the 1924–25 season was the first in which the club competed under the name FC St. Pauli, finishing in sixth place out of eight teams, with HSV snatching top spot.

The club of the 1920s and 30s was a very different proposition to the club today. It was largely the club of the local bourgeoisie. The district's workers were much more likely to play for, or be supporters of, the Arbeiter-Turn-und-Sportbund (Workers' Gymnastics and Sports Association) clubs. As Chris Sanderson notes in his dissertation, 'in 1935, FC St. Pauli claimed in its 25th anniversary book that players from workers' clubs such as Komet Blankenese and Billstedt Horn would deliberately foul and kick FC St. Pauli players they saw as being right-wing.' Perhaps, this perception of FC St. Pauli as a bourgeois club with right-wing tendencies goes some way to explaining the club's actions during the Third Reich, or perhaps, if they wanted to continue to exist as a sporting entity, they were simply left with very little choice.

The ramifications of the Wall Street Crash of October 1929 were felt, not just in the United States but also throughout the industrial powerhouses of Europe. Germany's Weimar Republic was particularly vulnerable as American loans designed to hasten recovery from the Great War ceased. The country fell victim to mass unemployment and hyper-inflation. In desperation, the people turned not to the moderate conservative parties, but to the extremes of the political left and right. Both the Communist party (KPD) and the Nazi party (NSDAP) significantly increased their electoral share in the late 1920s and early 1930s. However, political in-fighting on the left of the political spectrum weakened its position and allowed a party of the extreme right, the National Socialist Workers Party of Germany (NSDAP) to rise to prominence. In the elections of September 1930, the NSDAP claimed more than 18 per cent of the vote, becoming the country's second largest party. Just two years later, against a backdrop of increasing violence on the country's streets, in the second round of Germany's Presidential elections Hitler's polled more than 38 per cent of the votes. Hitler's success at the ballot box was enough to force President Von Hindenburg's hand and on 30 January 1933 he appointed Adolf Hitler as Chancellor.

The arson attack on the Reichstag, the German Parliament building, on 27 February 1933 provided Hitler with the perfect excuse to annul the constitution and suspend civil liberties, leading to the arrest and detainment of many communists and social democrats. Another election followed in March 1933 despite rising tensions on the streets and although the Nazis mobilised Storm Troopers to violently intimidate voters the party didn't gain the overall majority it expected and was forced to seek a coalition partner. However, although the ballot box had propelled Hitler as far as Chancellor he was prepared to compromise no longer. The continued suppression of the communists and intimidation and imprisonment of members of the Social Democrat Party enabled Hitler to pass his pivotal Enabling Act which gave him the absolute power he craved and allowed him to rule by decree. The Nazis had successfully suppressed their opponents and seized power, an act that had immense ramifications in all aspects of life, including football.

In June 1933, Jewish people were expelled from sports clubs. It was part of the Gleichschaltung – the bringing into line – which tightened the Nazi grip over all aspects of German life. Far from resisting these changes, the Deutscher Fussball-Bund (DFB, the German Football Association) had jumped the gun somewhat, placing an article in *Kicker* magazine (which, as Ulrich Hesse-Lichtenberger points out, was founded by a Jew) stating that 'members of the Jewish race, and persons who have turned out to be followers of the Marxist movement, are deemed unacceptable.' Clubs quickly followed the DFB's advice, expelling Jewish members. FC St. Pauli, at this point in its history still very much a club of the bourgeoisie, acted no differently to other German clubs. There was one exception, though. In 1933, the brothers Otto and Paul Lang founded FC St. Pauli's rugby department after having been expelled from another Hamburg club, SV St. Georg, on the grounds of their Jewish faith. The brothers left FC St. Pauli early, probably in 1934 or 1935 – there is no recorded evidence if they were forced or quit by their own choice. However, it is difficult, even unlikely, to conclude that the club, as an entity, enthusiastically embraced Nazi policies and ideologies. Like all German institutions, they didn't really have a choice but to adopt these new laws and rule changes. Within the club there were certainly those who went along with Nazi policies, perhaps, just to keep the club functioning. There were probably also those who sympathised with the Nazi viewpoint. The fact that the club survived the 1930s as an independent entity goes some way to supporting this view. Chris Sanderson highlights that, according to respected St. Pauli historian, René Martens, 'such attitudes helped the club retain its independence during the 1930s despite Nazi plans to amalgamate a number of local clubs into a new club, SV Hamburg-Mitte.'

Even the level of involvement of prominent individuals with the NSDAP in the 1930s through to the end of the war is difficult to completely establish. The name that resonates down through history most when thinking about individuals with links to the Nazis is the long-serving former club President, Wilhelm Koch. Koch, a former goalkeeper for St. Pauli TV, was elected President in 1931, a position he held for 14 years, until the end of the war. Wilhelm Koch's membership of the NSDAP has never been in dispute. He joined the party in 1937. However, his commitment to the Nazi cause has been widely questioned. It has been suggested that Koch's hand was somewhat forced, and that he joined the Nazi party in order to remain in his position of President. The fact that he didn't join the NSDAP until as late as 1937 supports the idea that he wasn't an ideological supporter, but someone who felt he had no choice but to join the party. It would also appear that Koch was reticent about the use of the club's stadium and training facilities for Nazi sporting events, with Koch wanting the ground used exclusively for football. The fact that no other records of his active involvement with the NSDAP exist aside from his membership form further support this viewpoint. The extent of Koch's links to the Nazis was investigated by Frank Bajohr, Senior Researcher and Lecturer at the University of Hamburg and author of many books on Nazi Germany. He concluded that Koch had no ideological links to the regime, nor did he play an active role in Nazi party politics.

Wilhelm Koch did benefit from the Nazi regime, specifically the Aryanisation of the economy. In 1933, he took over the running of the export company where he was employed when the company's two Jewish owners fled to Sweden soon after Hitler's ascent to power. However, correspondence exchanged between Koch and the company's owners while in exile shows a friendly relationship, with Koch looking to keep the company running rather than having taken an active role in seizing assets from its founders.

Koch was removed from his position as President of St. Pauli at the end of the war, as a part of the process that saw former members of the NSDAP removed from positions of power by the Allies. However, just two years later Wilhelm Koch was re-elected as President, a position he held until his death in 1969. A year later the Millerntor was renamed the Wilhelm Koch Stadion in his honour. As the nature of FC St. Pauli's fan base changed during the late 1980s and '90s supporters began to question the stadium being named after a former member of the NSDAP. In 1997 a motion was put forward at the club's annual meeting proposing a change of name. A year later, in October 1998, a resolution was passed with a narrow majority, to change the stadium name, and since the start of the 1999–2000 campaign the stadium was switched back to the Millerntor.

While Koch's links to the NSDAP appear to be circumspect, motivated by necessity, there were other figures connected with the club who were decidedly active in the Nazi party and who appeared to share its ideology. Otto Wolff was born in 1907 in Kiel and came from a middle-class background. He played for FC St. Pauli for ten years from 1925. A forward, more specifically a right-winger, he also helped them out during the 1939–40 season. Unlike, Koch, Wolff had been quick to join the NSDAP, doing so in 1930, and over the course of the Third Reich he assumed positions of political importance in Hamburg.

Wolff was actively involved in the Aryanisation of Jewish property, from which he benefited personally, acquiring two houses formerly belonging to Jewish families between 1939 and 1942. In 1940, he was appointed 'Commissioner General of the Economy' for Hamburg and it was in this role that he was central in the organisation of forced labour at the Neuengamme concentration camp. The camp, about 15km south-east of Hamburg, housed around 100,000 prisoners over the course of the war. The camp memorial at Neuengamme lists the names of 20,400 victims (although the actual death toll is thought to be nearer 26,800). Another 17,000 prisoners died during the evacuation and closure of the camp by SS officers at the end of the war. Many of these prisoners died after being crammed onto four ships at the end of April 1945. They were kept on board for several days with no access to food or water. Hamburg Governor, Karl Kaufmann later claimed that these ships had been destined for Sweden, although reports suggested that there had been plans in place to scuttle them with the prisoners still on board. Neither of these scenarios came to pass. Instead, on 3 May 1945 the ships were attacked in a raid by the RAF. They'd mistakenly believed they were being used to evacuate SS personnel to Norway. The loss of life was staggering. By this stage in the war Wolff had reached the high rank of SS-Standartenführer. Unlike Koch, his role during the Nazi rule of Germany seems beyond doubt.

As a member of the SS, Wolff was imprisoned at the end of the war by the Allies. However, he was released in April 1948. After release, Wolff set up an insurance company with former Governor Karl Kaufmann. He also returned to FC St. Pauli, playing for their 'old boys' team during the 1950s. In 1960, Wolff was awarded the 'Golden Badge of Honour' in recognition of his work for the club. His obituary in the club programme in 1992 even praised him for his role supporting the club during the war years. It is only relatively recently that Otto Wolff's role during Nazi rule has been brought fully to the fore (it is thought previously that not many club members were aware of his role) and in 2010 a motion was passed at the club's AGM posthumously stripping him of his 'Golden Badge of Honour' because of his activities during the Third Reich.

René Martens, Frank Bajohr and other historians have worked hard researching the extent of the club's cooperation with the NSDAP. This work has recently being augmented by the work of historian Gregor Backes, whose paper regarding FC St. Pauli's role during the Third Reich was published to coincide with the club's centenary celebrations in 2010. It is a detailed account of the club and its relationship with the Nazis, made all the more impressive by the same constraints that have hampered others researching the period: the fact that most of the club's archive, including lists of members, was destroyed during the Allied bombing of Hamburg. This lack of documentation has made it particularly difficult in tracing the fate of the club's Jewish members, although it is known that the club had two Jewish members, Otto and Paul Lang, as late as 1934. This perhaps lends credence to the theory that the club as a whole was not ideologically motivated to comply with the Nazi regime. Backes believes that the club did not actively seek ideological or political closeness to the Nazis, yet neither did club officials make a stand against the regime (although this was something that would've been incredibly difficult to maintain). Jewish members were still excluded. The club's youth departments were still reorganised in accordance with the guidelines of Hilter Youth, promoting the ideals of physical well-being (in readiness for conflict) and the 'Leadership' principle. Backes states: 'In summary, we can say that the FC St. Pauli adapted to the regime after some hesitation, but more for club than ideological reasons.' In short, during the period of Nazi rule, the club predominantly acted in self-preservation, adopting NSDAP policies but seemingly to preserve its own status. Of course, the lack of detailed records from the period hinders further research and while the club as a whole may have acted in accordance with self-interest, as we have seen, there were certain individuals with closer ideological ties to the Nazis.

It is reasonable to conclude that FC St. Pauli between 1933 and 1945 remained a conservative institution, happy to toe the line for a quiet life. There are no recorded examples of heroic resistance to Nazi rule, individual or otherwise. Obviously, historical context makes comparisons to the club's modern day anti-fascist stance futile. There is, however, one nice cameo. Club members and supporters of FC St. Pauli during the Third Reich may have found open resistance to the Nazis impossible, but pockets of resistance did exist in certain parts of Germany. Prior to the club's away game in Köln in September 2012, members of the St. Pauli fan scene laid a wreath at the Köln–Ehrenfeld cenotaph in honour of a group of youngsters called the Edelweiss Pirates who openly opposed the Nazis. This group rebelled against the forced regimentation of the Hitler Youth, often ambushing their patrols and beating them up. They were particularly active in and around Köln, Oberhausen and Düsseldorf, and many paid a high price for their defiance. When caught, some members were released with shaven heads while others were shipped to concentration camps. In November 1944, several members were publically hanged in Köln. Members of the contemporary St. Pauli fan scene were keen to honour the bravery of the Edelweiss Pirates, particularly as in recent years there has been increasing concern over the rise of far-right fan groups at clubs like Aachen, Dortmund and Duisburg. The rhetoric is simple: lessons must be learned from the past, the far right must never again be allowed to rise to prominence. Recent work by the club and local historians to understand the role FC St. Pauli and its members played during the Third Reich is part of the ongoing process to stop the horrors of fascism happening again.

There is one more ever present reminder of St. Pauli and the Third Reich. As Uli Hesse points out in his article for *The Blizzard*: the enormous bunker on Feldstraße continues to loom large over the Millerntor, yet people rarely talk about it. The huge concrete structure was both an air-raid shelter and a site for a battery of anti-aircraft guns during the war. It is an omnipresent reminder of Hamburg's past – one that hasn't been destroyed because the explosive force needed to raze it to the ground would cause irreversible structural damage to nearby buildings as well as the U-Bahn system. It is now home to offices, studios and a nightclub, but it is rarely out of shot when the television cameras covering St. Pauli games pan to the north end of the Millerntor. Occasionally, a few hardy St. Pauli fans will congregate on its roof waving huge flags, providing a juxtaposition of past and present: reclaiming St. Pauli's most prominent structure from its Nazi past.

In a city that suffered extensive damage due to the Allied bombing raids, the presence of the two huge flak towers on the Heiligengeistfeld meant that the district of St. Pauli escaped relatively lightly in terms of bomb damage, although there is photographic evidence of the destruction and devastation to the district and eye-witness accounts of the Reeperbahn in flames. Unfortunately, the club's pre-war home was totally destroyed. Determined to get the club playing competitive football again, a huge volunteer effort was mobilised to build a new stadium on the Heiligengeistfeld in the corner of Glacischaussee and Budapester Straße, under the watchful eye of both the now demolished Südbunker and the Nordbunker. Thanks to the hard work of hundreds of volunteers, the new ground was completed in record time, all the more remarkable considering the level of destruction Hamburg suffered and the effects this had on infrastructure in the immediate aftermath of the war. The stadium itself was a tidy affair, with three sides of open terrace complemented by a covered stand on the west side. On 17 November 1946, the stadium was inaugurated with a friendly match against Schalke 04. The game ended in a 1-0 win for FC St. Pauli in front of a crowd of 30,000.

The members and supporters of St. Pauli, who had worked so hard on the reconstruction of the stadium, were to be rewarded in spectacular fashion. The team had won the 1946–47 district league, piping Hamburger SV to the title, but quite unexpectedly, they would go on to experience one of the most successful seasons in the club's history. Just a few months on from the friendly win over Schalke 04, FC St. Pauli resumed action in the newly created Oberliga Nord. The 1947–48 season would prove to be historic, giving rise to a team that would be referred to simply as 'Die Wunder-Elf' or 'The Miracle Eleven'. The genesis of 'Die Wunder-Elf' is a story set against the tribulations of the times. The 1947–48 season saw FC St. Pauli amass an impressive 22 wins, two draws and just three defeats. Incredibly, Hamburger SV's record was exactly the same. Both teams were tied at the top of the Oberliga with identical records. FC St. Pauli's goal difference was superior, with 73 goals scored and 20 conceded compared to HAV's record of 66:17. However, top spot in the league was awarded not by goal difference or goals scored but by an aggregate of the scores in the two league games between FC St. Pauli and HSV. St. Pauli had won 1-0 in the away game but had fallen 2-0 in their new stadium on the Heiligengeistfeld. As a result the league title went to Hamburger SV.

However, second place in the Oberliga Nord was still good enough to qualify for the first National Championship since the war. On 17 July 1948, FC St. Pauli took on Union Oberschöneweide in the quarter-finals in Berlin's Olympiastadion. More than 80,000 people watched 'Die Wunder-Elf' destroy their opponents 7-0 including a hat-trick from Heiner Schaffer and two goals from Fritz Machate. The victory set up a semi-final against 1. FC Nürnberg at the Rhein-Neckar-Stadion in Mannheim on 25 July 1948. FC St. Pauli found themselves 0-2 down at half-time, but heroically pulled back to 2-2, with goals from Heinz 'Tute' Lehmann and Machate forcing the game into extra-time. But the club's dream of reaching a Championship final was shattered in the 94th minute when a Hans Pöschl volley was enough to send Nürnberg through to the final where they defeated 1. FC Kaiserslautern 2-1.

The run to the semi-finals was a remarkable achievement for FC St. Pauli and the story behind 'Die Wunder-Elf' was equally fascinating. Much of the team's success can be attributed to Karl Miller. Miller, the son of a butcher, born in Hamburg's Neustadt district, immediately adjacent to St. Pauli, had made his debut for FC St. Pauli in 1932–33. He achieved considerable success playing for Dresdner SC during the war, helping them win two Tschammerpokal's (predecessor to the DFB Pokal) in 1940 and 1941, before returning to Hamburg at the end of hostilities.

Back in Neustadt, Miller returned to his father's butcher's shop, a move that proved crucial for the formation of 'Die Wunder-Elf.' In post-war Germany, food was scarce and Miller was able to lure many of the stars of Dresdner SC and other players from the east by offering to supplement meagre rations with meat from his father's shop. Among those inticed in this way were former international Alfred 'Coppi' Beck and future national coach Helmut Schön (who only played very occasionally, by his own accounts, as he preferred to stay with his wife and son in Dresden). It wasn't just the sausages that induced so many distinguished players to FC St. Pauli. Unlike Dresden, Hamburg was located in the British zone of occupation, and offered many the safety and security they didn't feel they would get in the Russian sector. As Hans Apel (former finance minister and St. Pauli fan) commented in an interview for the *Mythos of St. Pauli* documentary in 2010: 'There came this guy (Karl Miller) and he told the players three things. First of all, the Russians can't catch you, the club will have a fantastic stadium in the near future and they can give you food. That was worth more than a giant transfer fee, or anything else back then.' Sausages and security turned out to be the cornerstones on which one of the greatest sides in the club's history was built.

After 1947–48, 'Die Wunder-Elf' went on qualify for the national championships in the next four seasons, making another two quarter-final appearances: drawing 1-1 with 1. FC Kaiserslautern in Bremen in 1949, before losing the replay 4-1 and falling at the same stage to SpVgg

Fürth a year later in Gelsenkirchen. By the 1950–51 season the national championship had moved to a two group format with the winners of each group contesting the final. Unfortunately, despite wins against FC Schalke 04 and SpVgg Fürth, FC St. Pauli bowed out, finishing bottom of their group. The following season the club finished third in the Oberliga Nord and missed out on the national championships. Five years after Karl Miller had lured the players to Hamburg with the prospect of supplemented rations, many of the players began to move on or, like Miller, who'd quit football at the end of the 1948–50 season aged 37, retire from professional football. As a result, the glory days of 'Die Wunder-Elf' were at an end.

League form tailed off for the rest of the 1950s but on 7 June 1959, the Millerntor did play host to some famous overseas visitors in the shape of Santos from Brazil, who played against a side selected from several Hamburg clubs. The Santos side included an 18-year-old Pelé, who helped his side to a 6-0 victory before being mobbed by autograph hunters, keen to get the signature of one of the stars of the previous year's World Cup in Sweden.

The early part of the 1960s was an important time for German football in general and FC St. Pauli in particular. The 1963–64 season heralded the start of the Bundesliga, a new national first division bringing together the top sides from the five Oberligen. Calls for the formation of a new national league had grown louder as the 1950s progressed. West Germany's relatively poor showing at the 1962 World Cup in Chile (a 1-0 quarter-final defeat at the hands of Yugoslavia) is often viewed as the decisive factor behind the formation of a national league. But in truth, German club sides had often struggled against their fully professional counterparts from elsewhere in Europe throughout the 1950s and, increasingly, the country's best players were being lured away to other clubs on the continent.

Places in the new Bundesliga were awarded to clubs through a complicated and quite opaque qualification process that looked at Oberliga results over the previous ten years alongside each club's financial viability, as well as other factors that appear to have been chosen somewhat deliberately to achieve the desired league profile. Hamburger SV were among the first tranche of clubs chosen by the DFB in January 1963 when the final 14 places were awarded in the May of that year. FC St. Pauli weren't included. As a result of the creation of the Bundesliga, the tiers below the top division were re-arranged and St. Pauli found themselves playing in the Regionalliga Nord, the second tier of German football. They finished that first Regionalliga Nord season of 1963–64 as champions, which put them into the promotion play-offs against teams from the three other Regionalligas. Unfortunately FC St. Pauli finished bottom of their group.

The club itself was on the move again at the start of the 1960s. The land on which the stadium had been lovingly constructed by fans after the war was requisitioned for the 1963 Internationale Gartenbau-Ausstellung (International Horticultural Exhibition). The city of Hamburg (after some deliberations which included relocating the stadium near the municipal park in a different part of town) decided to build a new ground just a few hundred yards away on the Heiligengeistfeld. Construction of the Millerntor began in 1960. The stadium was initially built to hold around 32,000, with terracing making up three-quarters of the ground, and the covered benches of the Haupttribüne completing the stadium. The shallow terracing and the low roof of the Haupttribüne served the club well for more than 40 years, until the gradual renovation of the Millerntor began in 2007. Unfortunately, the builders had neglected to install drainage for the pitch. The stadium was opened as planned (with a 4-7 defeat in a friendly against Bulgarian champions CDNA Sofia on 29 July 1961), and subsequent league matches were played at the Millerntor, which by that time had the reputation of being Hamburg's most modern football stadium. However, the notorious Hamburg rain that autumn and the subsequent winter left the playing surface an unplayable quagmire – which did not stop FC St. Pauli from playing there, often enough scoring impressive victories like a 7-4 win against Oldenburg in April 1962.

Several attempts to remedy the sorry state of the pitch failed miserably (*FC St. Pauli. Das Buch* has the whole account – for example, 500 large holes had been drilled and filled with sand just before a league match against VfV Hildesheim in January 1962, a measure which bizarrely was repeated in May 1962 with equally dismal results, attracting puns like 'Sand Pauli' in the press). After St. Pauli defender Heinz Deininger broke his ankle in a friendly match, FC St. Pauli went on 'football strike', with the club's board refusing to compete at the Millerntor until the missing drainage was built and the pitch repaired.

In June 1962, the city of Hamburg finally agreed, and the KiezKickers temporarily left their new home again, to play in SV Victoria's Hoheluftstadion, the stadium with the oldest seated stand in Hamburg. On 10 November 1963, FC St. Pauli finally returned onto the pitch at the Millerntor to play the first game in their revamped new home against VfL Wolfsburg. As debuts go, it was pretty perfect: 2-0 up at half-time, St. Pauli racked up another four goals without reply in the second half.

In 1965–66 they again won the Regionalliga Nord, but this time tantalisingly missed out on promotion to the Bundesliga by two goals, finishing behind Rot-Weiss Essen on goal difference. The club qualified for the play-offs four seasons in a row between 1970–71 and 1973–74 but couldn't make the final push required to top their play-off group and win promotion to the Bundesliga.

FC St. Pauli finally reached the promised land in 1977. The team topped the Bundesliga Nord at the end of the season, finishing four points clear of Arminia Bielefeld to win automatic promotion to the German top flight.

The club's first season in the Bundesliga got off to a solid start, with a 3-1 win over Werder Bremen in front of 20,000 fans at the Millerntor. Unfortunately, board members of FC St. Pauli took the disastrous decision to move 12 of the club's 17 Bundesliga home games to Hamburger SV's Volksparkstadion. It was a decision motivated by financial rather than footballing reasons. It was hoped that the move to the Volksparkstadion would prompt higher attendances and thus higher revenues. Unfortunately, the impact on the team would be more costly, yielding just seven points (two wins and three draws) in the 12 'home' games played in the suburbs.

Ironically, the most memorable moment of that season also took place at the Volksparkstadion. It was the moment that came to define the club's first foray into the German top flight. The 6th Spieltag, on 3 September 1977, saw FC St. Pauli back at the Volksparkstadion for their away fixture against city rivals Hamburger SV. HSV were enjoying a period of considerable success, having won the DFB Pokal in 1976 and going on to win the European Cup Winners' Cup in May

1977, defeating Anderlecht 2-0 in Amsterdam. The 1977–78 season had also seen the arrival of Kevin Keegan from Liverpool for a fee of £500,000. There was a sense of great expectation surrounding Keegan, with HSV fans hoping his arrival would spur them on to the club s first title since the inception of the Bundesliga. St. Pauli took the lead on 30 minutes with Franz Gerber slotting the ball home. Gerber, in the second of three spells at the club, was a prolific goal-scorer and would later return to manage the club between December 2002 and March 2004. The derby remained finely balanced until the closing moments when Wolfgang Kulka assured himself of his place in St. Pauli folklore by firing home from eight yards, sending the St. Pauli fans in a crowd of 48,000 into a state of hysteria. Not only were they in the Bundesliga for the first time, they had beaten their city rivals on their home turf. It was a historic result and a legendary performance that would have to wait 32 years to be equalled, when on a cold February night in 2011, Gerald Asamoah bundled in the only goal of the game to again secure victory at the Volksparkstadion.

Unfortunately, the derby victory did not provide a springboard for further success, and it soon became evident that FC St. Pauli's first experience of life in the Bundesliga would be brief. A week after the derby victory, they were back at the Volksparkstadion for a 'home' game against Borussia Dortmund. They found themselves 5-0 down after just 49 minutes. Some respectability was added to the scoreline with St. Pauli pulling back three goals, but Dortmund still ran out 6-3 winners.

The reverse fixture against HSV, St. Pauli's 'home' game was also played at the Volksparkstadion, but there was to be no repeat of the famous 2-0 victory. Another Gerber goal put St. Pauli 1-0 up, but in the end, a topsy-turvy game was settled by a late Felix Magath goal that saw Hamburger SV secure a 3-2 victory.

The decision to stage home matches in the Volksparkstadion backfired both on and off the pitch. The anticipated hike in attendances never materialised. The Dortmund goal-fest, in early September, had been watched by just 9,000 fans, while the game against VfL Bochum in November attracted just 5,000. The final match of the season, a 'home' fixture against 1. FC Köln, was watched by 25,000 fans. However, this influx of fans was partly due to Köln needing a win to secure the title. On an improbable afternoon of Bundesliga football, second-placed Borussia Mönchengladbach beat Borussia Dortmund 12-0, while 1. FC Köln put five past St. Pauli in Hamburg. The title went to Köln, though 'Gladbach ran them impossibly close, narrowing a ten-goal deficit in goal difference to just three goals by the end of the afternoon. It made for an exciting climax to the season, at the top end of the table at least. At the other end FC St. Pauli finished last with just 18 points, 12 points adrift of safety. They'd occupied last place from January and had dropped into the relegation zone, never to escape, as early as the 13th Spieltag in October.

The highpoint of the season was undoubtedly the derby win over Hamburger SV. As is humorously highlighted in *FC St. Pauli. Das Buch*, the win would have landed the club with the somewhat unwieldy moniker, 'Europapokal-der-Pokalsieger-Sieger Besieger' which translates as the equally difficult to say, 'European-Cup-Winners'-Cup-Beaters', a reference to the fact that lowly St. Pauli had managed to defeat the reigning European Cup Winners' Cup winner. However, marketing in those days was not what it was by the 2001–02 season, when FC St. Pauli presented themselves with an even more impressive accolade. After beating reigning World Club Champions, Bayern Munich, they emblasoned the legend, 'Weltpokalsiegerbesieger' on a T-shirt produced to celebrate the 2-1 victory over the mighty Bavarians.

The 1978–79 season was fairly unremarkable, with the club finishing sixth on their return to the Bundesliga Nord. However, by this time FC St. Pauli was on the verge of bankruptcy. Their poor financial health and dwindling support made what happened next even more remarkable. A club that for the first 70 or so years of its history had led a largely unremarkable, conservative existence was about to undergo a metamorphosis into something unique in German football. The 1980s would see FC St. Pauli gradually transform from a club to a 'Kult.'

Chapter 4
FREIBEUTER DER LIGA

The metamorphosis from club to 'Kult'

EVEN DOC MABUSE, the man who first flew the Totenkopf on the Gegengerade, can't be sure of the exact date when he picked up the iconic skull and crossbones flag at a stall at the Dom and took it to the Millerntor stadium, but it must have been around the mid-1980s. In fact, it didn't go directly from the Dom to the stadium. Mabuse's flag had been used as a decoration in the Volxküche on the Hafenstraße until he stapled it to a broomstick and took it with him to the Millerntor (at this time still, officially at least, named the Wilhelm Koch Stadium). However, by such random acts of chance legends are made and myths are created. In the 30 years since, Mabuse has seen his Totenkopf adopted, appropriated and subverted by everyone, from his radical comrades to corporate marketing consultancies. Yet still the Totenkopf remains the defining symbol of FC St. Pauli, whether stencilled on a fading sticker stuck to a lamp post on Budapester Straße, worn on a hoodie by youths in cities from London to New York or emblazoned on the roof of a Mini Cooper, suspended from the scoreboard inside the stadium. Despite the rampant commercialisation, the St. Pauli Totenkopf is *still* a symbol of something radical, something different.

In the early 1980s, Mabuse was squatting in the occupied tenements on the Hafenstraße, part of the punk scene that developed around them. For Doc Mabuse, the punk lifestyle is no passing fad or affliction of youth. He lived on the Hafenstraße for 14 years, and today lives with a collective of punks at a trailer park on Gaußstraße. Although he burnt the original flag some years ago, a Totenkopf still hangs from the wall of his trailer. However, today Mabuse, like several other pioneers of the alternative scene at the Millerntor, now watches his football at nearby – and considerably less commercial – Altona 93.

As a member of Hamburg's punk scene Doc Mabuse understood the significance of the Totenkopf. For squatters in the early 1980s on the Hafenstraße in St. Pauli, in the tenements of West Berlin and elsewhere in Europe the Totenkopf was a symbol of both rebellion and defiance. The Totenkopf would occasionally be seen hanging from the windows of occupied houses and flats. Throughout history the white skull and crossbones on a black background or the 'Jolly Roger' (itself a corruption of the French 'Jolie Rouge' or pretty red, more of which in later chapters) has been directly linked to pirates, poison and death. In more recent times it has been appropriated for military use, a visual device to inspire those fighting under it and at the same time strike fear into the enemy. During the Second World War the Jolly Roger was used by military units on both sides of the conflict: British submarines flew the flag on surfacing after returning from successful missions. Meanwhile the 3rd SS Panzer Division Totenkopf were named after the symbol, which translates literally as 'death's head'.

However, the punks, anarchists and Autonomen of the 1980s undoubtedly took their inspiration from the Totenkopf's pirate heritage, perhaps even making the link between themselves as the modern-day descendents of those seafaring renegades who lived outside the boundaries of the law, daring to defy authority. It is perhaps over emphasising the link, but there is nevertheless a connection between the 'alternative living project' of squats like the Hafenstraße, with its mistrust of the state, refusal to recognise borders and commitment to collective living and the pirate 'utopias' that many believed existed on the Barbary Coast of Africa in the 16th, 17th and 18th centuries. Indeed, anarchist author Peter Lamborn Wilson goes so far as to say that that these 'utopias' were early forms of autonomous proto-anarchist societies in that they operated beyond the reach of interfering governments and embraced unrestricted freedom.

Of course, being a port city, Hamburg has its own pirate heritage, and no pirate is more famous than Klaus Störtebeker. Almost as many myths surround his life as that of FC St. Pauli itself. First, 'Störtebeker' is only a nickname that in old German means (he who can) 'empty the mug with one gulp,' appertaining to Störtebeker's ability to drain a four-litre mug of beer in one attempt. Then, according to legend, the mast of Störtebeker's ship had a core of pure gold that was melted down to cast the apex of St. Catherine's church in Hamburg. Even his death is shrouded in legend; after his capture in 1400 or 1401, the senate of Hamburg sentenced Störtebeker and his crew of 73 men to death. It is then said that the pirate struck a deal with the Mayor of Hamburg; it was that every man that his own headless body could walk past on the quayside after his execution would be spared their own life. Legend has it that his headless corpse walked past 12 men before being tripped up by the exectutioner with a wayward foot.

In the centuries that followed his death, many of these myths have been embellished to the point of fantasy, and Klaus Störtebeker remains a popular figure especially among the more romantic members of the left in Hamburg. For them he was the embodiment of a medieval class war waged against the wealthy Hanseatic League. Indeed in 1985, amid the tensions surrounding the squatted buildings on the Hafenstraße, the Störtebeker centre (an anti-fascist meeting point) was set up in one of the houses with financial help from the Green Party. Later, German punk band (and staunch St. Pauli fans) Slime even recorded a song in his honour. There is one more curio that links Hamburg's most famous pirate to its football club. In January 2010, a 600-year-old skull, complete with spike protruding from the top, and believed by many to be Störtebeker's was stolen from Hamburg's History Museum. At the time of the disappearance it was reported that members of a St. Pauli fan club were questioned in regard to the theft – whether this is true or simply wishful thinking on the part of journalists looking for an angle is not known. The truth was not so fanciful: the eventual recovery of the skull led to two homeless men, who had stolen it hoping to sell it on, being charged with the robbery.

It is interesting to reflect on the historical significance of Doc Mabuse's decision to purchase a Totenkopf and take it with him to the football. This simple act has had an enormous impact in terms of symbolism, politics and profit, on both the fans of FC St. Pauli and the club itself. Within a decade of that first makeshift flag fluttering from a broom handle on the Gegengerade terrace, FC St. Pauli were firmly established as the 'Freibeuter der Liga' or 'the pirates of the league'. As for Mabuse, in a recent interview he reflected with a wry grin and more than a hint of sarcasm that if he'd only thought to trademark 'his' symbol, 'then I would probably be a millionaire now.'

While the origins and symbolism of the Totenkopf are an important part of the modern-day history of the club, the growth and radicalisation of FC St. Pauli's fan base was about more than just a flag, however potent the symbol. It was about a demographic of people who had traditionally shunned watching professional football, taking to the terraces in increasing numbers, changing and developing the nature of the German fan scene for ever.

The empty houses of the Hafenstraße were first squatted in the autumn of 1981. As mentioned in the previous chapter, West Germany, like much of western Europe, had been gripped by recession since the late 1970s, and the district of St. Pauli had been hit particularly hard. However, in Germany the strength of the unions had minimised the effect of the economic downturn on the country's blue-collar workers; instead it was those leaving school and university who were particularly badly affected. Young people were finding it impossible to find work and to afford their own place to live. This stagnation and lack of opportunities for the young, coupled with the previously documented urban decline, provided fertile conditions for those looking for an alternative way of life. Empty buildings in run-down areas like St. Pauli provided somewhere for this mixture of disaffected youth – the unemployed, punks and anarchists – to create viable social spaces in which to live, socialise and establish community projects like soup kitchens, meeting rooms and bookshops. Perhaps the most formally organised groups in this loose collective were the Autonomen, often referred to as the 'Black-Bloc'. The Autonomen movement had begun in Italy in the 1970s where they achieved notoriety through their successful use of direct action, including industrial action, rent strikes, squatting, street-fighting and university occupations. Economic conditions in West Germany (and neighbouring Holland and Denmark) during the 1980s led to similar Autonomen groups being established, all looking to reject what little the mainstream had to offer them and to develop their own alternative ways of living with minimal interference from the state.

The Hafenstraße, unlike other squats in the area, managed to avoid the police's usual strategy of evicting squatters within 24 hours, remaining largely unnoticed for the first few months and not making themselves known until the summer of 1982, shortly before the *Bürgerschaftswahlen* (local elections for the city state of Hamburg). To avoid controversy and public unrest, the senate decided to negotiate. Over the next few months the squatters and the council exchanged dialogue over the threat of eviction and the cost of repairing the buildings (which was considerably cheaper than the proposed plans to build a new development of offices). This dialogue would rumble on for years. Sometimes the relationship between the squatters and the council would be reasonably cordial (often around the time of local elections) and at other times it would be extremely strained or virtually non-existent, especially when aggravated by police raids on the buildings and the subsequent arrests. In the summer of 1983, the police encircled a demonstration trapping people in the buildings in a dispute that became known as the first Hamburg lock-in. By the end of 1983 another compromise was reached with the authorities, securing the future of the Hafenstraße for the short term.

The apartment blocks of the Hafenstraße were fast becoming a significant centrepoint for the Autonomen movement in Germany and beyond. The make-up of the Hamburg squats differed from their counterparts in West Berlin, where they were often dominated by students and middle-class drop-outs. The Hafenstraße squats were more diverse, drawing heavily from what American-born author George Katsiaficas, in *The Subversion of Politics*, refers to as the 'lumpenproletariat'. Perhaps it was this higher percentage of working-class squatters on the Hafenstraße that helped forge the links with FC St. Pauli? Although, as we have seen, the club had no particular affiliation to the working class, and indeed for the majority of its existence had been more of a bourgeois institution, football *per se*, in Germany, as in Britain, had remained the sport of the working class.

Despite this the game had long been treated with a suspicion bordering on contempt by many members of the left-wing intelligentsia (again, in Germany as in England). Indeed, the politicisation of fans on the terraces had a distinctly right-wing flavour to it during the 1980s. The far right had started to infiltrate stadiums and took hold in the politics of many fan groups. Mirroring the problems British fans experienced with the National Front in the late 1970s and early 1980s, German football was developing a particular problem with neo-Nazi groups. In December 1984, fans of Hamburg SV and Borussia Dortmund were actively involved in far-right Molotov cocktail attacks on the squats of the Hafenstraße. In fact, as the 1980s progressed, violence became a regular occurrence on the Hafenstraße, fuelled partly by a media frenzy that claimed that members of the German terrorist group the Red Army Faction (RAF) were being hidden in the buildings.

Tensions continued to escalate and in October 1986, the police laid siege to the houses, destroying goods and furniture and evicting squatters from six of the flats. This heavy-handed action sparked a spontaneous demonstration in which 2,000 people marched on the Hafenstraße, only to find the area cordoned off by police and declared a prohibited zone by the council. Demonstrations continued and spread to other parts of Germany and even into Holland and Denmark. November saw ugly scenes between protestors and the police and on 20 December a crowd of 12,000 marched through the streets of Hamburg in solidarity with the Hafenstraße, demanding an end to police victimisation. Public pressure on the council continued into 1987, and by the autumn the Hafenstraße occupants and the council finally reached an agreement, drawing up a contract that granted the residents some security against eviction and police persecution. In response, the Hafenstraße occupants released a defiant statement: 'The Hafenstraße is officially secured. We recognise that the struggle continues and that it is only one part. Our real aims are not fulfilled through the contract. We continue working towards self-determined, autonomous lives and continue building resistance against repression.'

The clash of ideologies between this collective of punks and anarchists and the council and police was far from over, and would again flare into violence, but it was around this time that the passion and politics of those radicals on the Hafenstraße would become entwined with the history of FC St. Pauli.

The decline of the district of St. Pauli, in the late 1970s and early 80s, had been mirrored by its football club. After that single season in the Bundesliga in 1977–78 the club was in seemingly terminal decline. Despite finishing the 1978–79 season in a credible sixth place in the 2. Bundesliga Nord, the club had its playing licence withdrawn by the DFB due to financial problems. Relegated to the Amateur-Oberliga Nord, the club was flat broke with players occasionally having to use their own transport to get to away games. Despite finishing top of the Oberliga Nord in 1980–81 the club missed out on a return to the second tier of German football due to 2. Bundesliga's reorganisation into a single national league. The club missed out on promotion again in 1982–83. Despite finishing top of the Oberliga Nord, they then finished bottom of a four-team, round-robin promotion play-off group, losing all three matches. FC St. Pauli had better luck in 1983–84, despite finishing second behind Werder Bremen II in the regular league season, as the team, referred to as 'The Young Savages' due to their youth and raw enthusiasm, won promotion to 2. Bundesliga along with Blau Weiss Berlin in the play-offs. Once again a disappointing 17th-place finish saw the club's stay in the second division limited to just one season.

St. Pauli looked destined to spend the 1980s yo-yoing between the second and third tiers of German football as they bounced back from the disappointment of relegation to again top the Oberliga Nord in 1985–86. A decisive 3-0 victory over Rot-Weiß Essen in the penultimate play-off game secured FC St. Pauli promotion back to 2.Bundesliga.

It is worth considering the attendances for games played at the Millerntor stadium over this period. Gates had dropped dramatically from the club's solitary season in the Bundesliga in 1977–78 when crowds had averaged 13,776. A season later the club was averaging just 2,396. They recovered slightly, ebbing and flowing as the club bounced between the regional Oberliga Nord and the 2. Bundesliga. Although capable of much higher attendances for big matches in the league or cup, the club had finished the 1985–86 Oberliga Nord campaign averaging around 4,000 spectators in a stadium that had a potential capacity of over 20,000.

Low attendances in German football in the early 1980s weren't unique to FC St. Pauli. In that same 1985–86 campaign the average attendance in the Bundesliga was just 17,600 (compared to 26,100 in 1977–78 and the astonishing 42,101 in 2010–11). At the start of the new decade the domestic game in Germany was going through a similar slump to that of its English counterpart. Despite Hamburger SV being crowned European Cup winners in 1983, the dominance of Bayern Munich and the flair of Borussia Mönchengladbach in

European competition during the mid-1970s seemed like a distant memory. It was clear that Italian club football was in the ascendancy, if not in terms of European trophies, then at least in the salaries clubs could afford to pay Europe's top players. Off the pitch there were serious concerns over spectator safety and the spread of hooliganism. German football had been rocked by a near tragedy that occurred at Hamburger SV's Volksparkstadion at the end of the 1978–79 season. The ground was packed with fans celebrating the club's title win. Fans inside the renowned 'Block E' section of terracing were packed tight against the fence that separated the terrace from the pitch. In the crush a small section of the fence gave way, and fans started to pour through the tiny opening with many being badly crushed and injured along the way. Four were placed in intensive care. Although a variety of different factors made direct comparisons between this incident and the tragedy of Hillsborough in 1989 circumspect, it was a chilling portent of what could happen when fans were packed into overcrowded enclosures with no viable means of escape.

Hooliganism was a major factor in the change in mood in German football in the period. A number of clubs had problems with hooligan gangs, often with direct links to neo-Nazi organisations. A Hertha Berlin fan group named Zyklon B, after the gas used in Nazi death camps, set fire to a train. Out in the suburbs Hamburger SV had its own hooligan problem. Gangs of skinheads with Nazi sympathies began to assemble on the West Terrace of the Volksparkstadion. Many young, unemployed working-class lads were coveted by neo-Nazi groups, preying on the economic uncertainties of the time and homing in on the issues of unemployment and immigration to peddle their fascist views. The leader of the neo-Nazi Aktionsfront Nationaler Sozialisten (ANS), Michael Kühnen, ordered his followers to recruit new members direct from the terraces. In a tragic incident, another Hamburger SV fanclub *Die Löwen* (the Lions) kicked to death a 16-year-old Werder Bremen fan in a clash with a Bremen fan group.

Plenty of Hamburger SV supporters were dismayed at the change in atmosphere inside the Volksparkstadion. And despite HSV going through something of a golden age at the end of the 1970s and start of the 80s some of these fans started to attend games at the Millerntor. The contrast was striking. The Volksparkstadion was a vast bowl with a cinder track putting distance between players and fans. The Millerntor, on the other hand, was tight and compact, designed for football. And, unlike HSV, there was no hooligan element shouting fascist slogans or intimidating fellow fans. For English fans, steeped in decades of city rivalry, crossing the line and changing from one team to another is unthinkable, yet in Hamburg at that time the intense rivalry that exists today simply wasn't there. Unsurprising really, as for the vast majority of the two clubs' history they had operated at different levels. Indeed, although St. Pauli had traditionally drawn large parts of its support from workers and residents around the port, many football fans had watched both sides.

As we have noted, these were dark times for German football. It was hardly surprising crowds were on the wane: star players tended to be hoovered up by Bayern or sold abroad, the recession meant that money was tight among football's traditional working-class fan base, hooliganism was rife in and around stadiums and far-right groups were starting to organise and target football matches as a vehicle to spread their violence and hatred. Ulrich Hesse-Lichtenberger, author of the excellent *Tor! The Story of German Football*, summarised perfectly the state of the game when reflecting on his own experiences following Borussia Dortmund during the period: 'The thing I remember most vividly about the early to mid 1980s is feeling completely lost, standing on a half-empty terrace, a group of around 50 neo-Nazi thugs goose-stepping around waiting for the police to arrive to get the action going... at least that was better than the away games, which could be quite risky affairs. Especially if you had a punk hairdo and torn jeans.' Against this depressing backdrop the changes that were starting to occur at FC St. Pauli were all the more remarkable. At the Millerntor, punk hairdos and torn jeans were about to become a regular sight on the steps of the backstraight of the Gegengerade.

There was no orchestrated plan for the residents of the Hafenstraße, the punks or the Autonomen to take over the terraces at the Millerntor. In hindsight, you could argue that had it been a deliberate, pre-meditated decision to attend, infiltrate and radicalise a football club. It would have been a thing of genius; after all, the terraces of a football club provide a highly visible platform to express your viewpoint in great numbers and had increasingly been used as a strategy by various elements of the far right. The reality at the Millerntor was different. Here the change was gradual and organic. Many followed the lead of Doc Mabuse and his friends, but the process took time, and although these new fans carried their politics with them to the stadium, this wasn't their raison-d'être. In the first instance, the fans from the Hafenstraße started visiting FC St. Pauli because it was fun and, crucially, it was local. As mentioned previously, football, although a working-class pursuit, had always been treated with disdain by left-wing intellectuals, viewed in many ways like the passive dope of religion – a diversion from true revolutionary activity. However, the young punks and anarchists of the Hafenstraße paid little truck to the values of the old left. They were young and they wanted fun and excitement to go along with their political idealism. Many also still loved the football they had played in their youth. With a football club on their doorstep, spending a Saturday afternoon at the stadium seemed like a fun thing to do.

One such young punk was Sven Brux, a prominent figure in what was about to unfold at the Millerntor. He had moved to the city to be involved in the punk scene but still loved his football. In an interview with Chris Sanderson, conducted in 2009, he said, 'There was never any plan to take over the Millerntor. The people from the Hafenstraße and around them just started going to the Millerntor stadium for the same reason as every single football fan everywhere: either to have a nice afternoon with friends and beer or to see a good footie match. Or both!'

At the start of the 1986–87 season, fresh from promotion from the Oberliga-Nord, St. Pauli fond themselves back in the 2. Bundesliga. Those first few home games saw the trickle of punks and anarchists from the Hafenstraße turn into a regular group of around 60 to 70. They congregated on the shallow terrace of the Gegengerade, standing directly behind the dugouts on the halfway line in what, in time, would become known variously as the 'Black-Bloc' or the 'Hafenstraße-Bloc'. Of course, this faction did not all herald from the squats down by the harbour – in the months and years that followed they were joined by others, who, while not directly involved in the Hafenstraße community, sympathised with its sentiments and supported the politics and ideology that this new fan scene brought to the Millerntor.

Bringing the politics of the left into the stadium wasn't the act of dry sloganeering that might've been expected. These new fans had come to football for enjoyment and the chants emerging from the Gegengerade were full of irony and sarcasm. Using humour, they provided a new twist on popular political chants of the day: 'Never again fascism! Never again war! Never again the Third Division,' and 'Who are the betraying rats? Social Democrats! Whose betrayal will we never see? Surely it is St. Pauli.' As René Martens explained, previously at political gatherings the question of who would never betray the masses was always answered by a cry of 'Anarchy!' Now, with a partly ironic twist, FC St. Pauli was being proclaimed as the saviour of the people. These new fans wanted something different, something fun but with meaning; they created 'happenings' on their section of the Gegengerade. It was certainly different, unlike any other terrace culture at the time. At other grounds neo-Nazi fans chanted their hateful, racist slogans; at the Millerntor fans used sarcasm and irony to spread their messages of anti-fascism and working-class solidarity, cleverly subverting regular football chants in the process.

But what of the 'old-school' fans of FC St. Pauli? How did they take to the new arrivals? Like other German clubs FC St. Pauli had its own, traditional, denim-clad 'Kutten' fan groups, and while most of St. Pauli's existing fan base were apolitical, this didn't mean that the terraces of the Millerntor were entirely free of supporters with right-wing sympathies – even if these views were not usually overtly expressed. How did this mix of existing football fans take to the new arrivals? It is probably true to say that the impact wasn't immediately obvious; initially these 'new' fans weren't big enough in number to change the atmosphere in the stadium overnight. It is also interesting to note that the fans from the Hafenstraße decided to base themselves on the back straight of the Gegengerade and not on the Nordkurve, the most popular terrace at the time. Perhaps this was a conscious decision not to impose on the traditional fan base, or perhaps it was because the punks and squatters wanted their own free space, an area of the stadium they could call their own, in which to enjoy each other's company and begin to generate an atmosphere that reflected their image. Or maybe they just wanted to enjoy a decent view of the game.

Certainly, the fluctuating attendances at the Millerntor during the period contributed to the acceptance of these new fans. There simply wasn't the volume of existing fans to oppose them. Attendances ebbed and flowed during the 1986–87 season, often dependent on the status of the opposition. The 60 or so punks from the Hafenstraße inside the stadium for an opening day 4-2 victory over 1. FC Saarbrücken were part of an impressive 9,000 crowd. However, a victory over KSV Hessen Kassel by the same scoreline in October 1986 was watched by just 4,600. Interest in FC St. Pauli in the 2. Bundesliga was always a little higher than when they were playing in the regional third tier, but there was clearly enough capacity for this new 'alternative' fan scene to grow – and that's exactly what happened over the following couple of seasons.

With the benefit of hindsight it is easy to reflect that the 1986–87 season was a pivotal moment in the history of FC St. Pauli. After an inconsistent start to life back in the 2. Bundesliga – and an embarrassing 6-0 reverse against Hamburger SV in front of 58,000 fans at the Volksparkstadion in the DFB Pokal – the team gained momentum and in the Rückrunde (the second round) found themselves in the running for promotion. They even climbed as high as second (an automatic promotion slot) after a 1-0 win in Oberhausen in May 1987. But, even as the season built towards a dramatic climax, with St. Pauli still very much in the hunt for promotion back to the top division, attendances still fluctuated wildly. Against league leaders Hannover 96, more than 17,000 packed into the Millerntor to watch a match often credited as bringing the 'Mythos of St. Pauli' into the public eye – St. Pauli staged a heroic, yet ultimately unsuccessful, comeback from 1-4, to 3-4 (with late goals from Dirk Zander and Dietmar Demuth) in a dramatic game that endeared this spirited young team to all those watching. Yet the club's penultimate home game of the regular season saw just 5,000 fans watch a 1-1 draw with SG Wattenscheid despite automatic promotion still being a possibility.

FC St. Pauli finished that season in third place, resulting in a two-legged 'relegation' play-off against FC Homburg, who had finished third from bottom in the Bundesliga. The game really caught the imagination of both the Hamburg public and the wider German sports media, with fans queuing for hours for tickets for the game at the Millerntor. FC St. Pauli found themselves 3-1 down from the first leg, and facing a mammoth task to turn things around at home. By now it was late June, and the Millerntor stadium was completely sold out.

Photographs show the terraces packed with fans, hoping against hope for a miracle, while on the Gegengerade the punks and anarchists of the 'Black-Bloc' added a splash of colour to the cacophony of noise. Crucially, the game was broadcast live by RTL, thus the German public had their first opportunity to view the vibrant, enthusiastic atmosphere of the Millerntor, an atmosphere at odds with what was going on elsewhere in German football at the time. This was the point – that the myth of the 'alternative scene' at Millerntor started to take root in the minds of the German public and the media. The myth was helped by events on the pitch. Despite a tense, goalless first half (which meant St. Pauli still had the proverbial mountain of a 3-1 deficit to climb) this young, enthusiastic, raw team of 'Young Savages' simply refused to give in. A 71st-minute strike by Jürgen Gronau gave the Millerntor hope, although these hopes were dashed when Homburg were awarded a dubious penalty four minutes from time and made it 1-1. Yet, still this young side refused to give in, with Stefan Studer putting St. Pauli 2-1 ahead two minutes later. With the clock running down, these brave young players pushed for another goal to square the game on aggregate. Unfortunately, they couldn't find a way through. Yet, perhaps, something greater than promotion was confirmed that afternoon – FC St. Pauli had won the hearts, not only of the 18,500 capacity crowd inside the stadium, but also those of many fans watching at home on television. Not only that, but the refusal to give up, whatever the odds and however much time was left on the clock, cemented the view of FC St. Pauli as the determined underdog, the heroic loser – a viewpoint that not only fitted the history of the district, but also reflected many of the core values of the emergent alternative fan scene developing at the Millerntor. The football club, like the district had been at so many points throughout its history, were 'the outsiders', the rebels, the antidote to the malaise that so much of German football and fan culture was immersed in.

Thus far, it would seem that the transformation of FC St. Pauli from run-of-the-mill, lower division side to cult phenomenon was down to the actions of a handful of activists from the Hafenstraße and circumstance, but of course that is too much of a simplification. The district of St. Pauli was changing, undergoing another of its periodic reinventions. The lack of jobs due to the mechanisation of the docks, and the collapse of the sex trade due to AIDS, at the start of the 1980s, had left the district in what seemed like terminal decline. Businesses folded and people moved out. The population fell by 9,000 between 1970 and 1985. But slowly things started to change. The empty properties on the Hafenstraße had attracted the punks and Autonomen, but rents elsewhere in the district were cheap and this drew in increasing numbers of students, radicals, artists and those looking for something a bit different. In turn, clubs, bars and restaurants sprang up, catering for this new, alternative crowd who were more into music than strip-joints. The population was on the rise again, and with so many of these new residents moving to St. Pauli eager to engage and identify with the district, the 'happenings' at the Millerntor became an important, acceptable and enjoyable way to spend their leisure time. As we shall see in the following chapters, the district's transformation was not without its problems: the arrival of new residents, lured by cheaper rents and a buzzing social scene, served to raise rents and begin the inevitable process of gentrification.

However, as the 1987–88 season kicked off things were looking bright for the club. The heroic failure of the previous season had made the bond between club and district stronger. Attendances continued to fluctuate between a low of 5,100 against Rot-Weiss Essen on a Wednesday night in early September and a close to capacity 18,300 against Stuttgarter Kickers in a top-of-the-table clash in May, but slowly and surely the fan scene was changing and the Millerntor was becoming the place to enjoy a completely different football experience.

However, the impact of the 'Black-Bloc' and the alternative fan scene was not yet strong enough to influence club policy, and an interesting cameo occurred when, in September 1987, the club lobbied the DFB to change its name to 'FC Deutscher Ring St. Pauli' in a sponsorship deal with a local bank, who already had their name on the club's shirts. Fortunately, the DFB rejected the proposal out of hand, which is just as well as being named after a bank would have been at complete odds with the ideals and aspirations of the alternative fan scene.

On the pitch, in early November, after an inconsistent start, Willi Reimann moved across town to take the reins at Hamburger SV. His assistant Helmut Schulte replaced him and after demolishing Rot-Weiss Oberhausen 6-1 away from home in his first game in charge, the side never really looked back. The last home game of the season, a 2-0 victory over Oberhausen, watched by 14,200, all but sealed an amazing return to the Bundesliga. A substantial goal difference over the teams in third and fourth place meant that St. Pauli needed only a draw from their match with lowly SSV Ulm 1846 to seal promotion. The 800 fans that travelled to Ulm saw promotion achieved via Dirk Zander's unstoppable rising 25-yard drive and a 1-0 victory. About 5,000 headed to the airport to greet the team on their return to Hamburg and there were scenes of total chaos with Helmut Schulte and the players carried from the airport on the shoulders of the fans. A convoy of coaches, cars and buses snaked their way back into the city and headed to the Reeperbahn. Fans even got access to the police station and hung flags from the windows, drank champagne and danced with the police. FC St. Pauli, heroic losers only 12 months previously, were back in the Bundesliga.

MATCH

VOLCANIC ASH

1 FC Union Berlin 2 FC St. Pauli 1
2. Bundesliga
Saturday 17 April 2010, 1.00pm,
Stadion An der Alten Försterei

FC St. Pauli 1 SC Paderborn 07 2
2. Bundesliga
Sunday 19 May 2010, 1.30pm, Millerntor Stadion

I'VE LOST COUNT of the number of bemused looks I've had. Or exclamations of 'it takes how long? All that way for a game of football?' or the most common, 'wouldn't it be easier to fly?'

On a number of levels they are right. It is easier, quicker and usually cheaper to fly, but I have an irrational fear of flying, especially without my kids, and besides I really like trains. In another life, I could easily have become a trainspotter. Indeed, when they banned football at break times during secondary school, and after they cottoned on to our cunning plan of replacing the ball with a stone, I spent a large proportion of my breaks standing on steps that overlooked the railway track below watching trains. It was quite good fun and surprisingly social too. There must of been five or six of us who would regularly hang out there, mucking around, taking the piss out of each other and waiting for something vaguely exotic like a Class 37 to trundle by. One of our number was the real deal, a bona fide trainspotter, complete with the books and the stubby pencil to underline any engines he spotted. It's easy to take the rise (and, being teenage boys, we did) but in hindsight, I really quite enjoyed it. There's something strangely comforting about the whole routine of spotting a train and underlining it in a book. It's ground hopping or programme collecting by another name.

My mild obsession with trains was further indulged during classic 'Football Special' away trips with my father during the 1980s. We enjoyed some incredible away days, not really minding the fact we were crammed like sardines onto dilapidated rolling stock. One opening day of the season trip to Old Trafford on a boiling hot afternoon saw us parked just outside Crewe on the way home for what seemed like eternity, sweltering in the heat and with no refreshments on board. We watched as a dozen or so Watford fans decided to make a dash for the station and the cafe, only to witness the train start off in the opposite direction moments after they'd got off. We sat tight, without refreshment for the remainder of the journey, but the pint of Coke I sank, and no doubt the beer my Dad had, at the pub near Watford Junction was one of the best I've ever tasted.

Of course, it is easy to fondly reminisce about those days and all too easy to forget that we were often herded around like animals, frog-marched across the tracks from obscure platforms, kept waiting in the rain and cold to be escorted from station to stadium. But still, it is hard to shake the romanticism of it, football fans together, all travelling with a common purpose: I certainly treasure those memories, traversing the country with my Dad. And it gave you a good working knowledge of the UK rail network too.

All of this is mixed up in my preference for travelling to St. Pauli games on the train. People think I'm mental anyway just for following a football team in Germany, so I might as well throw an unorthodox mode of transport into the mix; it's horses-for-courses, or trains-for-tracks.

And for once, I hold the upper hand. As I wait on the platform at Bletchley station on the morning of 16 April 2010, I stand a reasonable chance of making it to my destination, Berlin. The same can't be said for the not inconsiderable number of UK-based St. Pauli fans who have planned to fly. Not that I take any comfort from this, quite the opposite.

I've been looking forward to putting names to faces for fans from the UK messageboard, but unfortunately an event of seismic proportions has other ideas.

On 14 April 2010, the Eyjafjallajökull volcano in Iceland erupted and spewed vast quantities of volcanic ash into the atmosphere. Over the next five or six days the ash cloud spread across Europe forcing a closure of airspace and a grounding of aircraft across the continent. Travel chaos reigned supreme. All across Europe people were stranded, and, of course, this meant those planning to travel to Germany for St. Pauli's fixture at Union Berlin by air were well and truly scuppered. I was lucky, my trains weren't affected and I was able to email Stefan from the Fanladen to assure him I'd make it through the ash cloud to meet him at the Stadion An der Alten Försterei.

As I often do, when making a journey deep into Germany, I plan to stop over in Köln for the night, and then get the milk-train to Berlin the following morning. On this trip there is the added bonus of taking in a Friday night game at Köln's RheinEnergieStadion. I've used this tactic before, when watching St. Pauli in Aachen, taking advantage of the fact that Bundesliga and 2. Bundesliga fixtures are spread out over the weekend. Last time, it had been the slightly intimidating local derby against 'Gladbach; this time I am content with a low-key game against VfL Bochum.

It results in a 2-0 win for the home side, but all I really remember about it was how off the pace German international striker Lucas Podolski looked. The following morning, I get up, shower and stumble from my hotel (conveniently located within the station itself) to my platform for the last leg of my journey to Berlin. With the newspapers still full of a Europe gripped by travel paralysis, I make my way smoothly to Berlin. I've expected the trains to be more crowded, as people sought alternative ways of getting about, but there are still plenty of spaces.

When I arrive at Berlin's impressive multi-layered Central Station, I am amazed at how quiet it is. The station itself is slick and modern with a glass-fronted exterior. Despite a history that dates back to 1871, the station, which had been badly damaged in the bombing during the war, fell victim to the post-war division of Germany with both mainline and S-Bahn services between East and West Germany eventually suspended. In 1989, not long after the fall of the Berlin

Wall, plans were afoot for updating the city's rail network, and central to this were plans for Berlin Hauptbahnhof, a transport hub that would be the meeting point for both North–South and East–West rail travel in Berlin. The station, built on five levels, finally opened in 2006.

Arriving in Berlin before 9am, I have time to kill before the game that afternoon. I step out of the station to be treated by a pleasant pale blue April sky, a sky devoid not only of clouds but also of the tell-tale vapour trails of aircraft that would normally criss-cross it. I walk across the river, taking in the Reichstag and the Brandenburg Gate. Despite the early hour, it still feels eerily quite for a capital city. There seems to be a distinct lack of tourists, perhaps they are still in bed, or perhaps like so many people over that weekend, they have fallen victim to the biggest disruption of European transportation since the Second World War. I am not complaining; it gives me plenty of time to take in the sights of such a historic city. I've always wanted to visit it, having vivid memories of the Wall coming down, as it did, the day after my 18th birthday. Indeed, I've always been incredibly envious of my mate, who the following summer, after completing his A-levels, went inter-railing around Europe, taking in post-unification Berlin first hand, and bringing me back what he swears was a genuine chunk of Berlin Wall. Unfortunately, over the intervening years, I'd mislaid what may or may not have been a bona fide piece of history. But having regaled my daughters with this story, I am keen to purchase them a chunk of 'Wall' as a keepsake of a divided Europe, that they'd barely comprehend. And how lucky am I? Just yards from the Brandenburg Gate, and for just a couple of Euros, I am able to purchase two lumps of concrete complete with 'authentic' spray-painted graffiti. I leave the shop with a smile on my face, thinking just how long the Wall would've been, had every bit of souvenir tat sold since 1989 been as authentic as it was claimed to be.

I wander around a little more, soaking in the history and at the same time learning a valuable lesson for the contemporary European traveller – using the mapping service on your smartphone to try and locate Checkpoint Charlie is not only incredibly frustrating but will also prove to be damned expensive.

Now, I have some interesting travel options for the next leg of my journey. It has become something of a tradition for St. Pauli fans when playing against Union Berlin to hire a boat and travel by river to the Stadion An der Alten Försterei, having a few drinks along the way. It would have been a pleasant way to see the city, but in the end I decide to stick with the train, taking the S-Bahn east to Köpenick. It is a fascinating trip: the route heading out from the centre of the city was like the concentric rings of a slice of tree trunk. At its core is modern, contemporary Berlin, a stylish confident modern metropolis; then the next major stop is Alexanderplpatz, with its ageing television tower, that once stood just over the border in Eastern Berlin, as a symbol of communism, watching and listening over the western enclave. Having recently read Anne Funder's *Stasiland: Stories from Behind the Berlin Wall*, it is hard not to cast my mind back to what life was like living under the constant surveillance of an increasingly paranoid regime. It is strange to think that anyone my age or older would have very real memories of life in the GDR. As you move further out (and East) the shiny, new regenerated Berlin slowly gives way to the tired-looking architecture of the Eastern Bloc, albeit now populated with a mix of discount off-licences and nail parlours. Eventually after about 40 minutes, the train arrives in Köpenick.

Aside from finally doing my bit of inter-railing and visiting Berlin, there's been a particular reason that I've opted for Union Berlin versus St.Pauli. If I'd waited a season, until St. Pauli's return to the Bundesliga, I could have chosen Hertha Berlin at the Olympiastadion, a ground that resonates with both history and controversy, from hosting Hitler's Olympics in 1936 right up to the Zidane headbutt in the final of the 2006 World Cup final. During that 2010–11 season Hertha were even sponsored by Deutsche Bahn, the German rail operator, a curio that would have dovetailed nicely with my train obsession. However, my attraction to the Union Berlin fixture was down almost entirely to their stadium.

Over the previous 18 months or so, I'd developed a fascination with the place. The Stadion An der Alten Försterei, which translates as 'the stadium near the old Forester's house', is another old-school football stadium, not too dissimilar from the Millerntor. It exudes charm, from the quaint, gated clubhouse on one corner of the ground (à la Craven Cottage) and its location in the woods, to the three sides of atmospheric, steep-sided terracing. It looked like a lovely stadium, and had always been high on my list to visit. However, one thing really made it stand out. Throughout the 1980s and '90s the stadium had fallen into a state of disrepair (nothing too unusual there, the same could be said for many English grounds, prior to the widespread rebuilding that took place following the Taylor report) but what made the Alten Försterei different was that the fans themselves rebuilt it. Not raised the money to have it rebuilt, actually rebuilt it, brick by brick. For much of the 1990s, the club had been living on borrowed time, the Deutsche Fussball Liga (DFL) insisting on a reduced capacity and only granting them season-long temporary licences to play at the stadium. In 2006, they didn't renew the licence, finally forcing the club's hand. There was talk of a new stadium, but this was given short shrift by the club's supporters – the message was clear: they wouldn't contemplate moving from their home. Work finally began on upgrading the stadium at the start of the 2007–08 season, and most of it was carried out by the club's fans. More than 2,300 of them contributed thousands of man-hours replacing the crumbling banks of cinder terracing with concrete and erecting the required perimeter fencing. Seats were upgraded, and undersoil heating (another league requirement) was also installed. Most impressively, roofing was added to the previously open-to-the-elements terracing. As much as possible was completed by this volunteer fan force, with specialist workers only called in when absolutely necessary. As a result, the club was able to keep costs to a minimum. Union had to play their home games at the Friedrich Ludwig Jahn Sportpark during the 2008–09 season, but returned home in July 2009 to inaugurate the renovated stadium with a friendly against city rivals, Hertha. What the collective effort of these fans achieved was truly remarkable. Not only had they updated their beloved stadium to modern standards, but they had retained, perhaps even enhanced its character – the roof capturing and amplifying the noise made by the fans on those three sides of terracing.

I am not disappointed, as I make my way from the station (part of the walk is indeed through woodland along a cinder path). Union fans outnumber their St. Pauli counterparts by about four-to-one, yet the atmosphere is jovial. Union Berlin, like St. Pauli are something of a 'Kult-club', something that stems from the Cold War days, when rivals, Dynamo Berlin's links with the Stasi brought them countless league titles while Union laboured away in the lower divisions with a solitary East German Cup win in 1968 to their name. During the GDR days, Union had the patronage of the FDGB trade union, and they gained the reputation of being a team of the people, rather than an instrument of the state. As such, the Stadion An der Alten Försterei became somewhere where those who opposed the regime could occasionally vent their political frustration obliquely through football chants. Even after reunification, Union's fortunes continued to wane: they were twice denied the licence to participate in 2. Bundesliga in the 1990s before finally winning promotion to the second tier of German football at the start of the new millennium. However, by the 2005–06 season they were back in the regional fourth division. Perhaps this yo-yoing of fortunes added to their 'Kult-status' as like St. Pauli in Hamburg, they seemed destined to be the underdog, forever in the shadow of Hertha Berlin. There was oft-voiced assumption that Union fans are also predominantly left-wing, sharing a 'fan-friendship' with St. Pauli ('blood-brother' badges showing both clubs are available on the internet); however, this is something of a grey area. The majority of Union fans are okay although attacks on St. Pauli fans aren't uncommon. One St. Pauli fan summarised the situation by saying, 'when you run into a Union fan, you never know whether he wants to buy you a beer or smash your face!'

Once through security, I am able to locate and share a beer with 'astro', a regular on the UK messageboard. We then take our places on the steep terracing in the guest block. Both sets of fans produce impressive choreos just before kick-off: the Union fans hoist an impressive mural across their entire end, while Ultrà Sankt Pauli distribute an array of brown and white flags. The teams enter the pitch down a set of steps from an impressively retro (yet at the same time futuristic) covered walkway – the sort of thing you'd expect to be linking a car park to a shopping centre in early '80s Britain.

The match itself is strangely muted. Perhaps, the unusual April sunshine drains both sets of players, but a St. Pauli side chasing promotion look strangely off the pace, falling behind to a soft free-kick on ten minutes. Charles Takyi restors parity nine minutes later, but St. Pauli, who never really look like winning, fall to an enviable goal from Benyamina with just three minutes left on the clock. The promotion push, while not derailed, is parked in a siding for another week.

Despite astro's offer I opt out of the boat trip back to central Berlin, as it would've been touch-and-go making my connection back to Köln. And so, with the skies still strangely silent I go about the journey in reverse. I am glad to have made it through the ash cloud (I didn't know it at the time, but one other UK fan had made it too, getting out of Britain prior to all flights being grounded). I am also glad to have ticked the Stadion An der Alten Försterei off my list – as I've spent a worryingly large amount of time perusing it on Google Earth and flicking through the daily photographic updates as the stadium renovation neared its conclusion. It makes me wonder what I'd give for something similar in the UK – a stadium, brought up to modern standards, but rather than a soulless identikit bowl of concrete and plastic, a stadium that provided three sides of safe standing. It was yet another reminder that in Germany football supporters' wishes are much higher up the pecking order than in Britain.

Just under a month later, I am in Hamburg for the final game of the season 2009–10. Following the defeat at Union Berlin, St. Pauli thrashed TuS Koblenz 6-1 at the Millerntor, before securing a historic promotion back to the Bundesliga (meaning the club would celebrate its centenary in the top flight) with a 4-1 away win at Greuther Fürth. The winning had prompted ecstatic scenes as St. Pauli fans invaded the pitch and celebrated with the squad, a celebration that included cult striker Deniz Naki standing on the roof of the dugout waving a club flag surrounded by a sea of supporters. I'd watched it on my laptop at home, but even with promotion secured I was relishing the opportunity of being at the Millerntor for the promotion party.

The final game of the season, against SC Paderborn 07 at the Millerntor, presented St. Pauli with the opportunity of winning the second division title. A win for St. Pauli and a draw or defeat for Kaiserslautern at home to Augsburg would give FC St. Pauli their first trophy in, well, forever. Rather than travelling alone for this one, Kathryn and the girls come with me. It was the weekend of the Harbour Party, so we thought it was an ideal opportunity for the girls to sample some of the city's attractions. We have an action-packed agenda that includes the not-to-be-missed *Miniatur Wunderland* model railway exhibition (this is truly spectacular; you don't even have to like trains to be in awe of its sheer size and attention to detail). We also take in the Harbour Party, although sadly the glorious sunshine that had brightened my trip to Berlin is replaced by more typical Hamburg weather, dull skies and rain showers. And while I am at the game, the girls have a day out at the zoo. But before that, on the morning of the game, we are booked in for a tour of the Millerntor. I'm not sure my excitement was matched by that of Kathryn, Bess or Charlotte, but they kindly go along with it. The tour is an interesting peek behind the scenes, and we are fortunate that one of our party translated the important bits (note to self, it would be really handy to learn at least some German!). I just wish I'd got to see the ground before the redevelopment of the South Stand, as the old, underground dressing room looked incredibly atmospheric, unlike the slightly anodyne corridors that lurk under the new stand. Bess had spent a couple of evenings the week before the trip making a card for the players congratulating them on promotion, and is hoping to leave it for them in the changing room, but unfortunately as it is a match day this is off limits, and Bess is set to go home disappointed. As the tour winds up, we ask our guide (in English, obviously) if there is anywhere we could leave the card she'd made. We are greeted with a beaming smile and a beckoning gesture as she unlocks the door back into the stadium and walks us down the corridor that leads to the changing rooms. The door is locked, but she dives into an adjacent room and borrows some tape from one of the physios and carefully attaches Bess's card to the dressing room door. Bess is as pleased as punch. It is another big thumbs-up for FC St. Pauli.

With the girls dispatched in the direction of the Tierpark, I take my place on the Südkurve, strangely nervous about the afternoon ahead. I really want to be here when the club wins its first 'national' trophy. Things start well with Marius Ebbers firing us ahead after 19 minutes. It is still early, but I seem to be the only one in my part of the Südkurve nervously checking my phone for news from Kaiserslautern – it is all good there, still 0-0. On the stroke of half-time 'El Capitano' Fabio Morena dwells on the ball, allowing Daniel Brückner to steal in for an equaliser. Still, there is plenty of time left.

The way the second half pans out teaches me something more of St. Pauli fans and German football in general. With Kaiserslautern still drawing, St. Pauli just need a goal to secure the title. There is me getting more and more uptight, while neither the players nor the fans seem that bothered. I later find out that in German football, promotion is the important thing, there is no particular emphasis on winning the title. Indeed, it is only in recent times that the second division even had a winner's trophy. I also subsequently find out that, with the blessing of boss Holger Stanislawski, the team had spent most of the week since promotion was secured in Fürth partying and very little time training. Fair enough. Matters are taken out of my hands (and the team's) when Paderborn bag an 81st-minute winner. I try to forget that Kaiserslautern had drawn 0-0 and that a St. Pauli win would secure the title and just join in the bonkers celebrations that are going on around me. As you can imagine, beer is thrown, the team are heralded by all four sides of the ground (the victorious Paderborn players even go into the away end to celebrate with their fans) and perhaps most tellingly, the St. Pauli players take it in turns to hold aloft a hub cap, a celebration that lovingly takes the piss out of the trophy awarded to the league winners, and that puts my obsession with silverware firmly in its place! This is St. Pauli; trophies really aren't that important.

Obviously, no one wants to leave the stadium, but I have to rendezvous with the girls at the hotel and get our early evening flight back to Birmingham. Strangely enough, for a run-in that ended in promotion, my brace of games had netted two defeats. Even stranger, both trips were book-ended by the volcanic ash cloud. The ash particles are still causing problems in early May, swirling around Italy and then curving back across the Alps closing airspace in their wake. We sit in the departure lounge watching airports close in Southern Germany, but fortunately we are sufficiently far north to avoid it all, and make it home without any bother. Now, if only I can persuade Kathryn and the girls that 16 hours on a train is a much more rewarding way of travelling to Hamburg. As they are among those who think I'm nuts spending that much time on a train, it will take an equally spectacular seismic shift to change their minds.

Chapter 5
MILLERNTOR ROAR!

THE BUNDESLIGA BROUGHT the crowds back to the Millerntor. During the 1988–89 season attendances hovered around the 17,000 mark, rising to more than 20,000 when clubs like Bayern Munich and 1 FC Köln came to town. The atmosphere at the Millerntor was loud and vibrant. The big clubs didn't enjoy playing in such an intense environment, especially Bayern, who were held to 0-0 in early November 1988, and whose coach Jupp Heynckes, along with several of his players, had to endure being showered with beer bottles and plastic glasses from the packed terraces in scenes that perhaps highlighted the fact that St. Pauli fans hadn't totally rejected the behavioural model of 'regular' football fans at the time.

Unlike their disastrous 1977–78 Bundesliga appearance, FC St. Pauli weren't drawn into a season-long relegation battle. Instead they spent the majority of the campaign in mid-table. In fact, FC St. Pauli would go on to experience three consecutive seasons in the Bundesliga, before in 1991 succumbing to relegation once more in the most heartbreaking fashion. However, not all supporters were happy. Helmut Schulte, manager at the time and subsequently sports director at the club, recalled that there were many fans who grumbled about the club's transformation – fans who looked back with fondness to the time before a sold-out Millerntor and the arrival of the 'Black-Bloc' on the Gegengerade.

There were other tribulations too. Hooliganism continued to plague German football, and hooligans with far-right sympathies continued to attack both the district of St. Pauli and fans of the club itself. On 21 June 1988, West Germany lost to Holland courtesy of a late goal by

Marco van Basten. The game was played at the Volksparkstadion and later that evening a large mob of HSV hooligans and neo-Nazi fans led an attack on the squatted buildings of the Hafenstraße. Far from being an isolated event, this first disturbance signalled the start of attacks on the Hafenstraße that carried on every weekend for months. Two years later, on 8 July 1990, violence flared again as thousands of people flocked to the Reeperbahn to celebrate West Germany's World Cup win over Argentina. This time the authorities had blocked the rioters' access to the Hafenstraße, so instead the hooligans fought with police and smashed up local pubs and shops.

Wary that shops and bars would be attacked once more when HSV hosted Hertha Berlin in October 1990, a group of around 2,000 fans and local residents held a counter demonstration in Hans Albers Platz. Despite a heavy police presence, there was a typical St. Pauli party atmosphere about the protest – yet another example of the people of St. Pauli using guerilla tactics of having 'fun' to get their message across. Yet, to conclude that both the club and the district of St. Pauli were free of far-right sympathisers would be a mistake. Even at the Millerntor there remained very small pockets of fans that held distinctly right-wing views.

Attacks on the Hafenstraße and nearby shops and bars by hooligans and neo-Nazis helped bring residents and fans even closer together. Damaging houses or intimidating, abusing and attacking fans at games was seen as an attack on the St. Pauli way of life. However, it was the actions of the club itself that did the most to unite residents and fans in solidarity.

Despite rising attendances and promotion to the Bundesliga, the club itself wasn't in good financial shape and had gone into the 1988–89 campaign DM 3.8 million in debt. But club officials had a radical plan to get the club out of its financial malaise. In January 1989, Vice President Heinz Weisener announced, without any consultation with members or fans, that the club had ambitious plans to build a 50,000 capacity 'Sport-Dome' on the site of the Millerntor stadium. Backed by a consortium of Canadian investors, the rebuilt 'all-seater' stadium was to be modelled on Toronto's Sky Dome. It would cost an astonishing DM 500 million and would transform not just the Heiligengeistfeld but the whole St. Pauli district. This wasn't to be just a football stadium, this was to be a multi-purpose venue based on the emerging North American model. The 'Sport-Dome' would also contain a swimming pool and ice-rink and would be able to host international tennis matches as well as numerous pop concerts. The plans also included an indoor shopping complex and a vast underground car park. The club would need to relocate to the Volksparkstadion while the stadium was built but the club would receive DM 10 million in compensation from the contractors. The idea was to transform the homely Millerntor into a modern multi-sport arena capable of hosting top international events. This new stadium would surpass the ageing Volksparkstadion and would form part of the city's ambitious bid to host the 2004 Olympic Games. From the outset, there seemed one obvious snag with the plans: in order for the Sport-Dome to break even it would have to host a staggering 200 events each year.

Local opposition was immediate and once again residents and fans were brought together by a common cause. Opponents of the scheme were quick to coalesce behind the slogan, 'St. Pauli Yes, Sport-Dome No'. Again the tactics honed by the squatters on the Hafenstraße in their dealings with the city council were applied to the Sport-Dome. Leaflets, petitions and demonstrations were used effectively to show the strength of the opposition to the proposals. This wasn't just about the transformation of the Millerntor; the district's way of life was again under threat. Yes, the atmospheric terraces of the Millerntor would be replaced by the bland conformity of an all-seater stadium, but the impact would be more widely felt by the district's residents and its plethora of small shops and businesses. Rents would rise, the district would grind to a halt on matchdays due to the increase in traffic and its whole character would gradually be eroded. As spring arrived, the campaign continued to gather momentum. In March 1989, more than 19,000 fans were inside the Millerntor to see a Dirk Zander goal give St. Pauli a 1-0 victory over Karlsruher SC and it would have been a fairly unremarkable game were it not for the events of the first five minutes. More than 6,000 leaflets had been distributed in and around the stadium prior to kick-off calling on St. Pauli fans to do the unthinkable: remain completely silent for the first five minutes of the match.

It is thought the silence lasted for between three-and-a-half and four-and-a-half minutes, but the Millerntor did indeed fall silent in a remarkable show of solidarity. Nothing of the sort had been attempted inside a German football ground before. Again, the strategies of the 'Black-Bloc' had been applied and adapted to the football context. Outside the stadium, fans and residents organised demonstrations against the development and gradually managed to influence the board of FC St. Pauli. Another demonstration was organised prior to the home game against Bayer Leverkusen on Friday 7 April – the first game to be played under the club's newly installed floodlights – but this time it truly was a 'celebration in the streets' as fans met at Sternschanze station to march to the stadium. FC St. Pauli president, Otto Paulick, had just announced that plans to build the Sport-Dome had been scrapped. Although Paulick stated that the scale of the opposition to the plans had 'opened the board's eyes', there was also a school of thought that there were genuine concerns about the investor's ability to finance the construction. Vice-President Hans Apel stated that the club did not want the Millerntor turned into 'a concrete north face of the Eiger.' However, Apel, a lifelong St. Pauli fan, as well as the former finance Minister for the Social Democratic Party (SPD), would have been only too aware of the huge financial risk a project like this represented. Yet, regardless of the reasoning behind the decision to abandon the Sport-Dome, this was a victory for the people of St. Pauli. The varied actions of the protestors, including silencing the vibrant atmosphere inside the stadium, had maximised exposure to the cause. Since the club's return to the Bundesliga, the media had been keen to buy into and enhance the 'mythos of St. Pauli'. The protesters had used and subverted this media stereotype for maximum impact – the most boisterous, fervent fans in the league falling silent (even if it was only for a few minutes) not only made good copy but brought the issue of the Sport-Dome to a wider audience.

The same solidarity shown by fans and residents in standing up to right-wing hooligans intent on smashing up the district had also helped them defeat a plan that would have altered St. Pauli forever. Also, the club itself was now aware of the growing influence that the fans were beginning to exert on important issues.

Free of the spectre of the Sport-Dome, St. Pauli fans breathed a sigh of relief. However, they still had plenty of other genuine concerns, not least their treatment at away games. Increasingly travelling supporters became targets for right-wing hooligan groups, but more worrying was the response of the authorities that frequently treated St. Pauli's large away following like criminals. While widespread racist chanting went unchecked inside the stadium, stewards and police gave St. Pauli fans a hard time. This culminated in FC St. Pauli's trip to the Olympiastadion for the game against Bayern Münich in May 1989. Fans were subject to strict searches and anyone wearing boots was asked to remove them, as they were deemed to be weapons. A group of fans, disgusted at the treatment of supporters in the Olympiastadion, wrote to the club asking them for space in the St. Pauli matchday programme to run an article rebuking the behaviour of the authorities in Munich, but the article was never published. As a result this group of fans decided to take matters into their own hands.

They launched *Millerntor Roar!* Buoyed by the success of the campaign against the Sport-Dome and inspired by the emergent fanzine scene in the United Kingdom, fans of FC St. Pauli established their own independent mouthpiece.

There had been German football fanzines before *Millerntor Roar!* but these tended to be small-scale publications linked to the hooligan elements of individual clubs. Unlike in the United Kingdom, by 1989 there was no established club fanzine network, nor an over-arching national fanzine like the UK's *When Saturday Comes*. It was from *When Saturday Comes* in particular that the newly-formed editorial group of *Millerntor Roar!* took their inspiration. *When Saturday Comes* had launched in 1986, the title borrowed from a song by The Undertones, and its first issue had a modest print run of 100. Although a number of club-specific fanzines pre-dated it – including Bradford City's *City Gent* and York City's *Terrace Talk* – *WSC* was the first fanzine of the era to widen its focus beyond the confines of an individual club. It is worth noting, however, that *Foul*, an independent, satirical supporters paper (the term 'fanzine' hadn't yet been invented) had been published between 1972 and 1976. The first issue of *When Saturday Comes* quickly sold out and sales snowballed. With the popularity of the English game at an all-time low, real football fans identified with the issues raised in *WSC* and enjoyed the mix of humour and discussion. The editors of *WSC* freely admit that they got their timing spot-on. Supporters were tired of being portrayed as hooligans in the press, being harassed by police, demonised by the Conservative government and ignored by their clubs and *WSC* provided a vehicle to express these concerns. The fanzine scene in the UK exploded, and by 1989 *When Saturday Comes* had made the transition from low-budget fanzine to an established and respected national magazine, clearly differentiated from the other football media of the time.

There were obvious parallels to be drawn between the events in the UK and the mood among supporters at the Millerntor stadium. St. Pauli fans needed a voice and *Millerntor Roar!* provided it. The first issue went on sale on 29 July 1989, prior to the first home game of the new season against Werder Bremen. Priced at 50 Pfennig its 16 pages mixed humour and politics along with practical details of forthcoming trips to Borussia Dortmund and Borussia Mönchengladbach. The print run of 500 copies was doubled for issue two and before long *Millerntor Roar!* was selling 3,600 copies per issue. The idea was to appeal to a broad cross section of supporters and not exclusively those of FC St. Pauli. It worked. *Millerntor Roar!* became the biggest selling fanzine in Germany, spreading the ethos of the club's supporters far and wide. As Tom Mathar states in *Mythos 'Politischer' Fan, Millerntor Roar!* was 'both the megaphone and the engine of the new fan movement.'

Part of the success of *Millerntor Roar!* was down to the way it linked the specific concerns of FC St. Pauli fans with the changes occurring in the district, while also referencing national and international concerns. The residents of the Hafenstraße had their own column which was especially important as by 1990 the relationship between the squatters, police and the city council, strained at the best of times, was again nearing breaking point. The area around the Hafenstraße had been declared a prohibited zone with everyone in the area forced to show their identity cards. In May 1990, the contract between the council and the residents was cancelled due to alleged criminal activity by the residents, although because the cancellation was not yet legally binding, the uneasy stand-off continued. The column in *Millerntor Roar!* might be viewed as inconsequential, but any opportunity to redress the balance against a media that readily attacked the Hafenstraße was welcomed. In January 1991, a court ruling approved the cancellation of the contract and in response to this *Millerntor Roar!* launched a campaign in support of the residents using the slogan: 'Hamburg without the Hafenstraße is like the Bundesliga without FC St. Pauli.' The fanzine produced leaflets and mobilised support for a demonstration in support of the residents which assembled at Gerhart-Hauptman-Platz on Saturday 9 February 1991 under a *Millerntor Roar!* banner, as a 'St. Pauli-Bloc' of protestors. Another banner that day was a huge one bearing the legend 'Hafenstraße – You'll Never Walk Alone!' It was a clear message of solidarity between residents and supporters. Being a fan of FC St. Pauli was fast becoming more than just about football. In the end, a bailiff charged with evicting the Hafenstraße residents refused to acknowledge the court ruling and eventually the mass eviction was overturned and it was decided that each individual occupant the council wanted to evict had to be taken to court separately. It was a victory for the residents of the Hafenstraße and they appreciated the support shown not only by the fans but also the players and officials of FC St. Pauli.

Despite the media betraying the Millerntor as a tolerant utopia, the fan base was not entirely free of right-wing idiots. In August 1989, FC St. Pauli lost 0-1 at home to 1. FC Nürnberg, but it wasn't the defeat that raised concerns, it was the racist abuse directed towards Nürnberg striker Souleyman Sané. For the majority of fans it was incomprehensible that fellow St. Pauli supporters could hold and voice such abhorrent views, and they set about changing opinions. *Redaktion Millerntor Roar!* produced a leaflet entitled 'Players and Fans Against Racism', which was signed by the team and crucially had the support of the older St. Pauli fan clubs from the Nordkurve – including 'Heilige Geister', 'Fanclub Tornado' and 'Fanclub Millerntor' – where much of the chanting had occurred. The leaflet called on the DFB to ban racist chanting and banners from the stadium.

In another incident, in October 1991, fans on the Nordkurve directed chants of 'Foreigners Fuck Off!' towards supporters of Turkish origin. Hamburg, along with other German cities at the time, had a growing Turkish immigrant community that often became the target of racist abuse. When one fan replied 'Fascists Fuck Off' he was set upon and beaten up by eight fans. The police and stewards went straight to the Turkish fans, totally ignoring the fact that it had been them that were attacked. Unlike a previous incident when the club refused to play a friendly against a Turkish side, deeming it too political, FC St. Pauli reacted swiftly to pressure from fans. *Millerntor Roar!* in conjunction with members of the local Turkish community proposed a stadium ban for anyone using racist language. The club quickly agreed. For the next home game, on 3 November 1991 against FC Remscheid, the club gave away 150 free tickets to the Turkish community. Turkish and German fans paraded banners proclaiming 'Resistance against Racism' and 'Against Racist Hatred, Self-Defence Now!' around the edge of the pitch before the match. The banners were warmly received by fans on all sides of the ground, with the crowd breaking into a chant of 'Nazis Raus'. The tannoy broadcast warnings to fans not to use racist language inside the stadium – it was a major step forward and was followed by a friendly against Galatasaray on 26 November that year. As a result of the actions of concerned fans led by *Millerntor Roar!*, by the end of that autumn the club had formally banned racist chants and Nazi banners from the Millerntor. That may seem normal today, but FC St. Pauli were the first club in Germany (and possibly Europe?) to formally ban such behaviour inside their ground.

Other problems persisted during the period. On returning to the Bundesliga, the club continued to give up home advantage for games against Hamburger SV, switching to the Volksparkstadion, in the hope that profits could be maximised and trouble kept to a minimum. This was an incredibly unpopular strategy among St. Pauli fans. Those who remembered the 1977–78 Bundesliga campaign were especially despondent, recalling the 12 'home' games that were moved to the suburbs and which yielded two wins, three draws and seven defeats. Attendances for the derby were higher at the Volkspark, but with predictable results: FC St. Pauli losing 1-2 in March 1989, holding out for a 0-0 draw in September 1989, then losing 2-0 in November 1990.

St. Pauli fans took matters into their own hands in spectacular fashion after the club decided to move the home game against Hertha Berlin on 5 March 1991 to the Volksparkstadion, citing the potential for trouble with the hooligans from Hertha. The club believed it was easier to control and segregate fans at the Volksparkstadion, disregarding the fact that many St. Pauli fans had themselves felt threatened and intimidated when playing fixtures there. Fans decided to arrange a boycott of the game and instead opened the gates of the Millerntor, so that they could listen to the game on their terrace via a radio broadcast. On a damp and wet March evening, 1,500 fans stood on the terraces of the Millerntor singing and chanting at an empty pitch illuminated by the floodlights. The game at the Volksparkstadion finished 2-2, but video footage from the Millerntor shows fans greeting each St. Pauli goal with ecstatic cheers, and a party atmosphere on the Gegengerade with fans drinking beer and dancing to the strains of *No Sleep Till Brooklyn* by The Beastie Boys (around this time, fans with an ear for a tune and an eye for fashion produced excellent 'No Sleep Till Millerntor' hoodies).

Sven Brux was involved in the organisation of the 'Ghost Game' and he commented on the uniqueness of the event: 'That was also one of those campaigns that nobody had done before – boycotting a game and having a radio broadcast in an empty floodlit stadium instead. A friend who was a radio journalist helped us with the technology. Donations were collected in buckets at the entrances and we had 1,500 people in the stadium who shouted encouragement at an empty but illuminated pitch – brilliant! The press reaction was hugely positive and we knew – we are St. Pauli; we can do anything.' While 10,000 fans still ventured to the Volksparkstadion for the Hertha game, the fans who organised the radio broadcast made their point: the Millerntor was home, and as integral to the fan scene of the late 1980s as the team itself, perhaps even more so.

Through *Millerntor Roar!* St. Pauli's emergent 'alternative' fan scene had found its voice. The fanzine had inspired people and shown people what could be achieved when fans worked together. Over the next four years, until the final edition in April 1993, the fanzine remained at the forefront of the St. Pauli fan scene, mixing fun and ironic comment with organised protests and campaigns against the mistreatment of fans by the authorities. Like *When Saturday Comes* in Britain, *Millerntor Roar!* was able to provide fans with a platform, just when they needed it most. It provided a focus for fan activism and, vitally, it reached out to new fans, encouraging them to join the cultural revolution that was underway on the terraces of the Millerntor.

However, *Millerntor Roar!* wasn't the only focal point around which St. Pauli fans could coalesce – as well as their own publication, fans also acquired their own space. In October 1989, a portakabin was wheeled into place behind the Nordkurve and, thanks to the influence of Vice-President, Christian Hinzpeter, Sven Brux was tasked with establishing FC. St. Pauli's 'Fanladen' (which translates literally as 'fan-shop' but is better described as a 'fan-project'). The Fanladen's initial hook was to help fans with tickets and transport to away games. However, its influence would turn out to be far greater. As we shall see, both Sven Brux individually and the Fanladen as a collective would go on to shape and define the modern-day image of the club.

MATCH
PLANES, TRAINS & AUTOMOBILES

SC Freiburg 1 FC St. Pauli 3
Bundesliga
Saturday 21 August 2010, 3.30pm, badenova-Stadion

FC St. Pauli 0 TSG 1899 Hoffenheim 1
Bundesliga
Saturday 28 August 2010, 6.30pm, Millerntor Stadion

I SIMPLY HAD to be at St. Pauli's first game back in the Bundesliga. As it happened, and not for the last time this particular season, the fixture computer did me a massive favour. In early August, St. Pauli would begin their first top-flight campaign since 2001–02 away at SC Freiburg in the heart of the Black Forest. For fans going from Hamburg it was awkward – a gruelling 920-mile round trip from the north to the south of the country, made by road or rail. I was much luckier: a quick scan of the internet revealed a choice of airports all within a reasonable drive of Freiburg. A long weekend in the Black Forest was too good to turn down and, as it was slap-bang in the middle of the school holidays, the whole family were off on another adventure.

Over the summer, my eldest daughter, fuelled in part by the excitement of watching the World Cup on the telly and by (nearly) completing her first Panini sticker album, was desperate to come with me to her first 'proper' football match. Most of the kids in her class had been down the road to the loathsome MK Dons, but she has been well schooled in the wrongs of franchise football. So, who better to watch in your first match than the very antithesis of soulless soccer, FC St. Pauli (the moral high ground never felt so good!). Now, you might think that taking a seven-year-old across Europe to a ground you've never visited before and to a country where you only speak two or three words of the language was a bonkers idea, but I was confident it would be okay. Over the years, St. Pauli and Freiburg fans have established a mutual respect based in shared anti-fascist beliefs, so I was sure that it would be a positive, safe experience for her. Once again, the Fanladen were brilliant – I explained that, if possible, seat tickets would be preferable as I wasn't sure how my daughter would cope in the standing section, and they were quick to email back saying it wouldn't be a problem, although they did point out that the seats would be considerably more expensive (a very Premier League €32).

The four of us take the early morning flight from Stansted to Baden-Baden. Things are going well: our Ryanair flight arrives early, rousing its bleary-eyed passengers with a triumphant fanfare on landing; then our hire car is upgraded to a snazzy black Mercedes A-class (now, I'm not one to get excited by cars, but this represented a considerable step-up from the battered red Citroen Berlingo – that the girls have christened Postman Pat's van – that I drive at home). With the paperwork complete and car seats installed we drive south to Freiburg. I have done research and Freiburg, though seemingly a pleasant enough city, doesn't suggest it would have enough to keep two girls, aged seven and four, entertained for the weekend, so we continue through the city and head for the spa town of Titisee. The road winds through spectacular scenery, hills covered in spruce and pine trees that give the journey a distinctly Alpine feel. We even spot the single-track railway that will take us back to Freiburg the following day for the match, snaking its way in and out of tunnels blasted in the rock. The town of Titisee sits at one end of a large lake bearing the same name (and said to have been named after the Roman Emperor Titus) and our guesthouse is a mile or so out of town perched delicately on the hillside. Its location turns out to be the only delicate thing about it. Having only really travelled in the north of Germany, I am not quite prepared for how different things are in the south. It is horrible to deal in stereotypes, but this felt stereotypically German. *'70s German.* A big burly man in a grubby vest and sporting a moustache as broad as it is long gestures us to our rather antiquated room – where it looks as though the dust and the décor hasn't been touched since 1976. There do not appear to be other guests, just us and the scary-looking proprietor. I think at that point it is fair to say Kathryn and I think we won't last the night, convinced the entire family will be chopped up and converted into Bratwurst come nightfall. We don't communicate this to the girls and, as it is still only mid-morning, we decide to enjoy our last day on earth by walking into the centre of Titisee to take in the sights.

As we stroll through the centre of the town with the girls in tow, it feels like we have lowered the average age of the population considerably. Titisee seems to be the hang-out of whatever is the German equivalent of the blue-rinse brigade. A bit like Eastbourne, but with beer and sausages by the lake, instead of afternoon tea by the bandstand. After a lunch, consisting mostly of beer and sausages, spent watching the plethora of pleasure boats and pedalos narrowly avoiding each other as they manoeuvre around the lake, we decide to head towards what looks like a roped-off swimming area.

The Black Forest is experiencing something of a heatwave and the cool dark waters of the lake look inviting. This turns out to be one of the best things we do. This swimming area is wonderful, a beautiful grassy expanse on the banks of the lake, that is home to a wonderful outdoor swimming pool, play area and, of course, access to the 'official' swimming area in the lake itself. It is also where all the other families with kids have been hiding. Admission for the four of us is €10, and with the girls happily alternating between the pool, the playground and the lake we know we've found a base for the next few days. As the afternoon sun moves across the sky, the temperature on the poolside thermometer creeps into the eighties. The lake itself is a welcome contrast: the geological product of a retreating glacier, it feels like the water – in mid-August – is, well, glacial. Speeding down the slide moored on a pontoon into the freezing cold lake is one of the most refreshing things I've ever experienced, and looking back I'm not sure who enjoyed it more – me or the kids.

Of course, we are here for the football, so after eking out the last of the evening sun by the lake, and getting something to eat in town, we head back to our guesthouse, knowing that if we survive the night, Bess and I will be heading off to her first proper football match and St. Pauli's first Bundesliga game in eight years the following morning.

Not only do we make it through the night, by morning the breakfast room in the guesthouse is packed with people, although fellow football fans seem in short supply. Most of the other guests appear to be gearing up for a day's walking or cycling. This really isn't football country, but it is reassuring at least to know that we aren't alone. About 11am, we jump in the hire car to head for Titisee station on the other side of town. I turn the key in the ignition – *nothing*. At least at home when my Berlingo refuses to start it's preceded by that strained wincing sound that tells me something's not quite right. The lights and the electrics on my hired Merc are still working and a little LCD display is telling me something in German. Faced with such a dilemma, I do what any 21st-century man would do – I consult my iPhone, frantically typing the car's error message into my handy translation tool. Kathryn, meanwhile, back in the real world, goes to see if anyone can help, which is just as well because it seems that 'seek assistance' is the exact message being displayed on the Mercedes' console. The 'assistance' comes in the shape of our burly hotelier, who seems fascinated by the whole affair. He too turns the key and gets nothing in response. After a few minutes of key turning, sighing and tutting, he gets out of the car and, raising his thumb and little finger to the side of his head, makes the international symbol for 'you'd better phone someone'.

After some frantic searching through the paperwork, I ring the car hire helpline. They are very helpful and, despite us being in the middle of the Black Forest, assure us that they will have someone out to see us within two hours. Unfortunately, Bess and I don't have two hours. We need to be on the train to Freiburg before then. So, after a bit of flapping on my part, we decide to get a taxi to the station while Kathryn and youngest daughter, Charlotte, will wait at the hotel for the rescue party to arrive. Not an ideal start to the day, but to come all this way and then miss the match will have been a real shame.

So the two of us get our scheduled train back to Freiburg. The view is as spectacular as we'd imagined the day before when we'd seen glimpses of the track from the car. The train snakes slowly along the hillside, seemingly clinging to the narrowest of ledges like a hulking, metal mountain goat. We both hold our breath as we emerge from a tunnel to find the train running parallel to the road a good 30 metres below. As trips to your first ever football match go, it will be pretty hard to beat. Bess spots the Freiburg fans in their bright red shirts as we pull into one of the stations on the approach to the city, and before we know it the train is full of football fans – handy, as I know we'll be able to follow them from the station in the general direction of the badenova-Stadion (their lower-case 'b' not mine!) on our arrival. Of course, I've done my Google Maps research and worked out that getting off at Freiburg-Littenweiler on the outskirts of town will mean a five-minute walk to the ground, but it is always nice to have someone to follow, especially when you've got a seven-year-old with you and you want to minimise getting lost. Originally, all four of us had planned to make the trip and the other two were (weather permitting) going to spend the afternoon at a splendid-looking outdoor swimming complex adjacent to the stadium, and had the car not broken down it would have been perfect. It is about two o'clock (kick-off 3.30pm) by the time we approach the stadium and the temperature is in the eighties.

We peer longingly through the entrance archway at the swimming pool, waterslides and acres of grass packed with families soaking up the sun, as we make our way to the ground. We are due to rendezvous with Justus from the Fanladen outside the away fans' section. The Fanladen has never let me down, but it is always a stressful moment as you stand outside the away end trying to spot them through the throng of football fans. I needn't have worried; after a bit of hanging around eating ice creams purchased from a nearby petrol station, Justus is located and we get hold of our tickets, Bess drawing admiring glances for her homemade St. Pauli T-shirt with a big heart on the front (an idea shamelessly stolen from the guys and girls from 'Nord Support' who wave the big brown and white heart flags on the Nordkurve at the Millerntor) and 'Takyi 13' on the back. When we sat down to make the T-shirt we hadn't realised that Charles Takyi had relinquished the 'lucky' – and immensely popular among players in Germany – number 13 shirt to his friend, and marquee summer signing, Gerald Asamoah, and that Takyi would be wearing '10' this season.

So, at last, after a convoluted journey involving planes, trains and knackered automobiles, we have made it to St. Pauli's first Bundesliga game since the disastrous 2001–02 campaign when they'd finished bottom with a meagre 22 points. We wind our way up to the very top of the two-tier stand that houses the away fans – our seats are on the very back row, high above the terracing and just in front of the police control room. The atmosphere is already building inside the stadium as both sets of fans, eager to get the new season under way, trade chants. It is sweltering and we are glad to be out of the sun at the back of the stand that also affords us a great view of the swimming pool to our left.

It is an important day for the club for sure, but it is more personal than that – it is my daughter's first game, a generational rite of passage. Now, I'm not naïve enough to think that this game of football will have the same relevance or resonance in her life as my first game had in mine (where an 8-0 win for Watford over Sunderland on an equally warm afternoon in 1982 fuelled a life-long obsession with football) but I sincerely hope it will be an experience she'll remember.

Thinking back nearly 30 years to my first match it wasn't the football I recalled, it was the obscure things, like stopping at the shop to buy chewing gum, the strange holes in the shiny red bucket seats (apparently, to let the water drain away when it rained) or the slow shuffle out of the stadium at the end of the game. Also, being St. Pauli, I hope – in that deluded way parents do – that she might remember the experience and it might give her confidence in later life to look beyond the mainstream, and not just accept what was served up in front of her, be it the all-powerful Premier League or the dross on *The X-Factor*. Like I said, I'm just your average delusional parent trying to indoctrinate my kids with my own opinions. In reality, it is impossible to second guess how – or indeed if at all – a seven-year-old will recall her first football match in years to come, but there are a couple of things that catch our attention as kick-off approaches.

First there are the huge, arching rainbows created by the combination of brilliant sunlight and pitch sprinkler system. I'm sure the rest of the crowd are pretty oblivious, but we are mesmerised by the dancing spectrum of light and water for a good five minutes or at least until, playing surface suitably watered, the tap is switched off. Second is the friendliness of the fans. Up here, in the expensive seats, is a slightly different selection of St. Pauli fans to those that I have stood with on the Gegengerade or the Südkurve. Not exactly a family crowd

– we only spot a couple of other kids – but an older cross-section of fans, slightly more conservatively dressed although, that said, a bloke with a stunning Mohican is sat a few rows down from us and crops up regularly in the video footage I shoot on my phone. However, they are incredibly friendly, and the blokes in front are very concerned that they are blocking Bessy's view, so much so that the chap directly in front of us decides he is going to move to the spare seat next to us to give Bess an uninterrupted view of proceedings. And, of course, discovering we are English only extends the warmth of their friendship. We discuss the usual differences between English and German football and I discover that the four of them have made the trip from Hamburg to Freiburg by car and are stopping the night in Freiburg before getting up ridiculously early to do the trip in reverse.

With the seat in front kindly vacated, Bess has an uninterrupted view of proceedings as the teams take to the field. St. Pauli emerge wearing a distinctly metallic-looking copper-coloured shirt that dazzles in the afternoon sun. Freiburg are all in white, which confuses us somewhat as all their fans on the train and walking towards the ground had been dressed in red. I guess German clubs now change their kits with Premiership regularity and it's just not possible for the fans to keep pace. Either that or the fans just prefer red.

The Freiburg Ultras' choreo more than makes up for the kit confusion, with a huge central banner hoisted towards the roof proclaiming their love for SC Freiburg, as the rest of the terrace holds up red and white cards to create a stunning opening day frieze – wherever I go in Germany, I'm impressed by the time, effort and devotion that goes into the choreo, whether from Ultrà Sankt Pauli or rival fans, it remains one of the key differences between German supporters and their British counterparts. Fan led 'Ultra' style groups like the Green Brigade at Celtic, Jorvik Reds at York City or Aldershot's Red Blue Army are doing their best to generate an atmosphere, but they are often small islands of enthusiasm in a sea of apathy. Whether it is because standing is forbidden in the top divisions or because a generation of fans have grown used to being passive consumers, spoon-fed Sky Sports hyperbole, the atmosphere at games in Britain bears no comparison to Germany. Waving a blue flag that's been provided for you by the club on a 'big' European night in the Champions League in an attempt to generate faux atmosphere is not the same as these dedicated groups of men and women, who give up large amounts of their spare time, often meeting in grim warehouses, to create spectacular fan-driven displays of support for pretty much every game. For this alone, Ultra groups (the politically sound ones, at least) in German football should be cherished.

The first half consists of two teams sounding each other out with one eye on the energy-sapping heat. St. Pauli's copper shirts are gradually losing their metallic sheen, as they become soaked in sweat. Nil-nil at the break, and the fact that St. Pauli don't look out of place in the Bundesliga is a welcome relief, especially after I'd watched our limp exit from the DFB Pokal at the hands of Chemnitz on the internet the week before.

We spend the interval drinking cartons of warm orange juice and making an intricate paper fan from the programme in a vain attempt to combat the heat. The teams have obviously benefited from far more substantial refreshment as the game resumes at a much higher tempo, with both sides creating openings, but it isn't until the 78th minute that the deadlock is finally broken. Freiburg's Makiadi breaks down the left, draws the 'keeper before playing the ball to Papiss Cissé who slots home.

With 12 minutes left we are one-nil down and a long way from home. Poor Bess puts a brave face on things, helped, I think, by the fact I'd spent all week explaining that it would be very unlikely for a newly promoted team to win away from home in their first game, thus mentally preparing her for the inevitability of defeat. And, anyway, it is still a beautiful afternoon, the fans are in good voice and there is still the prospect of an ice-cold swim in the lake to round off our day.

And then it happens. Fabian Boll sweeps in an unexpected equaliser from the edge of the area. I feel that unmistakable adrenalin rush that has kept me addicted to football all these years. I'm not sure if Bess feels it too, but she is jumping up and down like a lunatic, being high-fived by everyone around us. It is one of those freeze-frame moments, that can't be altered no matter how many times you look at the highlights, from a different angle, on YouTube. If I close my eyes I can still see the net below us bulging, and everyone around us going mental. Even if what followed is more dramatic, that is my memory of the day. It has a certain symmetry about it too: Fabian Boll had been the goalscorer when my old man and I went to our first game at the Millerntor back in 2007 and he's now been seen scoring by three generations of Davidsons – I like that. Freiburg have only been ahead for five minutes and with seven minutes remaining you sense everyone around us will settle for a credible opening-day draw.

What happens next seems to occur at high speed, as if fast forwarding through the highlights on video. With a minute left, new signing Fin Bartels breaks at pace through the middle of the park, his shot is deflected into the path of Richard Sukuta-Pasu (another new arrival on loan from Leverkusen) and he side-foots the ball into an empty net. If it is clichéd to say the away end is delirious, it is also untrue becauase there simply isn't time to celebrate the goal. Seemingly straight after the restart, St. Pauli break away again – perhaps the heat has finally got to Freiburg – and as Sukuta-Pasu outstrips the Freiburg defence, he glances up, deciding now is a good time to return the favour and plays a simple ball to Bartels, who puts the game beyond doubt. There are 91 minutes on the clock, but the last five minutes have passed in a blur. Now, the delirium kicks in. The people around us are congratulating Bess like she's slotted home the winner herself. I even catch the officer in the police control room giving her a cheery thumbs up from behind the glass. I'm not sure she really knows what's going on, but then neither do any of us in the away end.

As first games go, it is pretty much perfect. A winning return to the Bundesliga for the team and an afternoon of chaotic drama and high-fives for Bess. As always, there is no rush to leave the ground, the celebrations last for a good 15 minutes before anyone even thinks about leaving the stadium, and when we eventually decide to head back to the station, our exit is delayed by a further round of high-fives and an open invitation for Bess to attend all future St. Pauli fixtures, due to her status as a lucky mascot.

We are both still running on adrenalin as we wait for our train. Word has reached us via a text from Kathryn that our car is fixed and so we can relax on the train knowing that we've got a fighting chance of getting back to the airport the following morning. About 40 minutes later, we are back in the genteel environs of Titisee and heading for a lakeside rendezvous with Kathryn and Charlotte. They've had a pretty good day wandering round the shops, including a wonderfully atmospheric Christmas 'emporium' that was doing a surprisingly good trade despite it pushing 80 degrees outside, before finishing off the afternoon back at the lakeside swimming pool. Kathryn is also able to give me the lowdown on the car. We'd both assumed after ringing the helpline she'd be hanging around for a few hours waiting for the German equivalent of an AA patrol van to locate our hotel on the fringes of the Black Forest. We couldn't have been more wrong. About 20 minutes after we'd gone for our train, a smart Mercedes turned up and out hopped a team of three mechanics – all dressed in incredibly tight-fitting dungarees (Kathryn's words not mine!). They started the car first time, then politely asked if they could take the car to their garage in town to run some diagnostic tests.

Within half an hour they were back clutching a print-out of a report assuring us everything was fine. Then in perfect English one of the mechanics suggested that on starting the car, 'the driver may wish to depress the clutch which will avoid any further problems.' Oops. I was quite glad I wasn't there for that one. Still, in my defence I've never driven anything as remotely glamorous as a Mercedes before. How was I to know I'd disable €15,000 of technology by forgetting to press the clutch?

Suitably embarrassed by my lack of motoring knowledge and still boiling from our train trip, Bess and I break ranks and go for a quick swim in the lake. The pool area is shut, but plenty of other people are still swimming in the non-roped-off part of the lake, so we enjoy a refreshing dip, marvelling at the big brown fish that are totally unfazed by our presence.

With the car sorted and three points in the bag, we spend our last day stocking up on Christmas trinkets (although we can't quite run to the cuckoo clocks the girls have their eye on) and more swimming in the lake. Although our day begins curiously; as we venture down to breakfast we notice a crowd of about six people standing around our car. Apparently they are eager to see first hand this Mercedes that had 'broken down' the day before. They give us a wry smile as we pass by – and to think they say the Germans don't have a sense of humour? We also bump into one of the mechanics and his family picnicking by the lake – this really is a small town. Fortunately, his swimming shorts aren't as tight-fitting as his overalls and he is kind enough not to mention my inability to start a car.

It has been a good trip – Bess has loved her first game, and St. Pauli are off to a promising start in the top flight. And even better, the following Saturday, I will be in Hamburg for the first home game of the season, against Hoffenheim.

If FC St. Pauli is a club that's been reborn in a very different image, then so is TSG 1899 Hoffenheim. The metamorphosis that began in Hoffenheim at the start of the 21st century was very different in nature to St. Pauli's rebirth but it was no less dramatic.

Hoffenheim takes its foundation date from the formation of gymnastics club Turnverein Hoffenheim in 1899. However, the modern club was officially founded in 1945 after a merge with Fussballverein Hoffenheim. For the latter half of the 20th century the club spent most of its time in the lower reaches of Germany's amateur leagues. This changed when Dietmar Hopp, co-founder of the SAP software behemoth and former Hoffenheim youth team player, returned to the club as a major financial backer. Within a year they were promoted to the Oberliga Baden-Württemberg, the then fourth tier of German football. Then they were quickly promoted to the Regionalliga Süd. Their rapid promotions stalled for a couple of seasons, which heralded a change in tactics. Hopp brought in experienced players on higher salaries and was rewarded with promotion to the 2. Bundesliga for the 2007–08 season. Then, in true fairytale fashion (if you like your fairytales heavily bankrolled) they won promotion to the Bundesliga at the first attempt. The success didn't stop there. A remarkable start to the 2008–09 season saw them go into the winter break as 'Herbstmeister' (autumn champions). The team had amassed an impressive 35 points and 42 goals in the first round of matches, providing the benevolent Hopp with the perfect Christmas present.

Despite this quickfire journey from the regional leagues to the summit of the Bundesliga, 1899 Hoffenheim are not widely liked among German football fans. In fact, they are probably only eclipsed in the unpopularity stakes by Bayern Munich (or FC Hollywood as they are referred to by many). This unpopularity stems from the nature of their speedy rise through the divisions. There is the feeling that Hopp's heavy investment in what was essentially an amateur side runs contrary to the spirit of German football. The 50+1 ownership criteria in Germany is designed to prevent potential investors taking control of clubs as 50 per cent plus 1 share have to remain in the hands of its members in a non-profit-based organisation. The benefits are obvious: clubs can't be bought as playthings for rich businessmen and the interests of the members or fans remain paramount. For some there are downsides too: in 2009 the ruling was challenged by Martin Kind, president of Hannover 96, who wanted to see the 50+1 rule scrapped completely or at the very least modified. He and others believe the rule prevents German clubs maximising income and thus from competing at the highest level in European competition. When it was put to a vote, 32 of the clubs from the top two divisions voted against the proposal with three abstaining. This left Hannover 96 as the only club supporting the motion and means for the time being at least that the 50+1 ruling remains.

Hopp has always acted within the boundaries set by the DFL, yet Hoffenheim are still viewed by many fans as having been bankrolled into the Bundesliga. Not that Hoffenheim are the only club to benefit from external investment; both Bayer Leverkusen and VfL Wolfsburg are backed by huge corporations. Leverkusen were founded by the Bayer chemical and pharmaceutical organisation while both the city of Wolfsburg and its football team owe their existence to Volkswagen, who chose the location to build their car manufacturing plant in 1938. However, when the 50+1 rule was introduced in 1999, both companies were granted special dispensation to keep their majority shareholding as they had demonstrated ample commitment to the running of their football clubs. Perhaps because of this long history as 'workers' clubs' set up to provide sport and entertainment for their workforce, Leverkusen and Wolfsburg aren't usually mentioned in the same breath as 1899 Hoffenheim. And it is easy to see why fans of other 'unfashionable' German clubs might feel this way about the club. Here is a settlement with a population of around 3,000 that boasts a football club in the top tier of German football. Although Hoffenheim is best described as a village, it is really a suburb of nearby Sinsheim, which itself only has 35,000 inhabitants. Hoffenheim's new stadium, the Rhein-Neckar-Arena has a capacity of just over 30,000 – nearly enough to provide a seat for every inhabitant of Sinsheim.

This swift rise through the divisions, coupled with a reliance on an expensively assembled playing staff and an impressive new stadium, stands in direct contrast to everything that St. Pauli's fan base believes in. And, leaving the fans aside for a moment, the fixture provided the perfect contrast between the two clubs: FC St. Pauli, who were going to attempt to take on the Bundesliga with a small squad on a limited budget, and Hoffenheim where the purse strings weren't quite so tight. Having had their fingers burnt during a previous tilt at top-flight survival in 2001–02, St. Pauli weren't about to take any financial risks this time round. This fixture would be a real test of character for the team and would provide the first real litmus test for St. Pauli's chances of survival.

I arrive in Hamburg on the morning of the game after braving an early morning flight out of Birmingham. I've left the family at home for this one and am planning to get the train back from Hamburg to London the same evening. After picking up my tickets from the Fanladen, I find myself with time to kill before the 3.30pm kick-off, so I buy myself a ticket to the *100 Years of FC St. Pauli* exhibition that is being temporarily housed in a towering series of 46 interconnecting shipping containers (as used in the docks of Hamburg) on the pedestrianised area at the front of the Südkurve. Despite my non-existent German, there is plenty to see, with the sections devoted to the club since its rebirth as a 'Kult' phenomenon being particularly impacting. My favourite artefacts are two banners, one supporting the Pro 15:30 campaign that seeks a return to traditional kick-off times, complete with what I can only assume is the German equivalent of the TV test card as a background and the one that simply reads 'SAVE FOOTBALL! SMASH BU$INE$$!' It's a proclamation that's at once extravagant, unrealistic and now, due to its location in a museum that costs €7 to enter, ever so slightly ironic. But it's also a proclamation that's very St. Pauli and very appropriate considering the recent history of the day's opponents.

By the time I've emerged back into the daylight, the area around the stadium is starting to fill up with fans. I decide to join the queue of people heading into the Südkurve. As I wait patiently in line to go through the security check and ticket inspection (there are still no turnstiles to speak of either on the Südkurve or the Gegengerade) I am tapped on the shoulder. I'm unaware of any other UK-based fans over for the trip, certainly none that would be able to recognise me from my grainy forum atavar, and I am amazed to turn round and see that it is the bloke who had moved seats to enable Bess to see the week before in

Freiburg. As we shuffle slowly forward, he kindly suggests I watch the game with him and his friends behind the goal. I decline partly because I don't want him to be saddled with making polite conversation with me for another 90 minutes, and partly because – in my head – I am set to watch this game on my own. Although it's nice having company – after all I grew up going to football with my Dad and it does sometimes get a bit lonely journeying to and from the match – there's something nice about just being part of the crowd, with no one knowing you've journeyed halfway across Europe to get there, and just soaking up the atmosphere. After all, that atmosphere is the main reason why I regularly make the trek.

Once inside, and having bid farewell to my friend from Freiburg, I take up a good position on the Südkurve, near to the players' tunnel and with a good view of the Gegengerade terrace that runs at a right angle to me, along the length of the pitch. I still consider the Gegengerade my spiritual home, as it's where I was standing for my first fixture at the Millerntor, but I'm so grateful to the Fanladen for a ticket that I'm happy to stand anywhere. And the Südkurve, now the permanent home to the USP, is a pretty lively place to be.

There has been some pretty dramatic chances since my last visit. Back in May the Haupttribüne, directly opposite the Gegengerade, was a building site – a tangle of pre-formed concrete and scaffolding, that was partly obscured by a giant canvas mural of St. Pauli's favourite players. Now in its place stood a brand new, all-seater stand, its new seats positively gleaming in the late summer sun. The structure dwarfs the old Haupttribüne stand and divided opinion among the fans as early as the planning stages. The completed Haupttribüne contained almost double the number of proposed executive boxes, while luxurious, padded business seats cut a brown swathe through the stand, occupying the prime position from penalty area to penalty area. There were those supporters against the balance of executive facilities and business seats on principle, but there were also fans who supported the nature of the Haupttribüne's redevelopment, citing the need to compete financially with other, wealthier, clubs in the Bundesliga by developing and expanding matchday revenue streams. There were also those who saw this phase of the Millerntor's redevelopment as necessary to help fund the improvement of the opposite side of the ground, the run-down

Gegengerade. The revenue from sales in the Haupttribüne helped make St. Pauli's business model for redeveloping the Gegengerade as a modern 10,000 capacity standing terrace financially viable. As an idealist, I fall into the former group of fans anxious about the changes to the Millerntor, but as an infrequent visitor it is easy for me to identify with the old-school charm of the stadium in its dilapidated state. I don't have to concern myself with financial sustainability or stadium safety licences.

One thing is clear from my vantage point in the corner of the Südkurve, the distinction between the old and new realities facing St. Pauli are as clear as day: to my left the rebuilt Südkurve and Haupttribüne loom large over the ancient terraces of the Gegengerade and Nordkurve. Although my feet stand on the robust pre-formed concrete slabs of the present, I still yearn for the crumbling steps of the Gegengerade. Yet, while I fret about the heart and soul of St. Pauli being lost in the redevelopment, the fans on the Südkurve have taken a far more practical approach to the changes – something that wouldn't be tolerated in the same way in the anodyne all-seater stadiums back in the UK – and completely covered the relatively new Südkurve in stickers and graffiti. Rather than accept the civilising process of a new stand or stadium, the fans have set about absorbing the new stand into their world. Indeed, that summer, the grey of the steps leading up to the Südkurve had been painted in vibrant red, white and brown. The message is clear: the heart and soul of St. Pauli isn't going to be replaced by a new south stand.

The build-up of atmosphere and expectation bring my thoughts back to the present and Hoffenheim. The Millerntor is in good voice and even those in the business seats seem willing to participate in the call and response chanting led by Ultrà Sankt Pauli on the Südkurve. One thing I can't help noticing as the players walk back towards the tunnel after a goalless first half is the sheer size and physicality of the Hoffenheim players. It reminds me of my 'old' club Watford's return to the top flight of English football in the August of 1999. The Hornets had begun the season with a surprise away win at Portsmouth before coming unstuck against a physically stronger and quicker Wimbledon side at Vicarage Road a week later. That the defeat, to an average Wimbledon side, had an element of misfortune to it (the winner being secured through an own goal) hadn't masked the fact that the Premiership was an entirely different beast to the First Division. In the Premiership, mistakes and lapses of concentration were punished with routine efficiency. It's easy to write now in hindsight, but that's the uneasy feeling I have as the second-half kicks off at the Millerntor: that the things we've got away with in 2. Bundesliga may come back to haunt us in the Bundesliga.

Sometimes my inbuilt pessimism serves me well, cushioning the blow of the inevitable, and on 87 minutes, a corner is swung in from the right and sent crashing into the net from close range by the boot of Hoffenheim defender Isaac Vorsah. There is just time for the Millerntor to hold its breath as Max Kruse sends a low shot just past the post, but moments later the full-time whistle blows with the game finishing 1-0 to Hoffenheim. It feels like a cruel way to welcome Bundesliga football back to the Millerntor, but the degree of inevitability about the result, and the late timing of the winning goal is something that as St. Pauli fans we will have to get used to as the season unfolds. If last week in Frieburg seemed like a fairytale, this is the harsh wake-up call. Life in the Bundesliga is going to be a battle for survival.

Still, it is a pleasant evening in Hamburg and I have time to kill before beginning the mammoth journey back to London, so I am in no rush to leave the stadium environs and decide to have a leisurely beer at the AFM container behind the Gegengerade before heading back to the station for the overnight train to Köln.

Unfortunately for me, my early season sojourn following St. Pauli in the Bundesliga has one final twist, a last minute kick in the teeth to rival Hoffenheim's late winner. I won't go into great detail about the cancellation of my sleeper train to Köln (caused by storms in Denmark) or the blind panic and desperation of trying to sort out somewhere to stay and an alternative way of getting home at gone midnight in Hamburg Hauptbahnhof. However, after very little sleep and with my wallet considerably lighter, I manage to get a flight back to Heathrow, even making it home a couple of hours ahead of my scheduled arrival by train.

Eventful trips to Freiburg and Hamburg on consecutive weekends had brought to a close my 'live' viewing of the boys in brown until after the winter break, but for FC St. Pauli, the rollercoaster ride of life back in the Bundesliga was only just beginning.

Chapter 6
FANLADEN & THE AFM

IF YOU ARE an international fan reading this book and have already made the pilgrimage to the Millerntor then chances are you will have had first hand experience of both the Fanladen and the Abteilung Fördernde Mitglieder (Department of Supporting Members) or AFM.

Most fans travelling from abroad pick up their tickets from the Fanladen's headquarters, which have been moved from Brigittenstraße to the *Fanräume* (supporters' rooms, financed by a fan-driven initiative) inside the Gegengerade stand in June 2013. Most also stop for at least one Astra at the AFM container that was located for many years at the north end of the Gegengerade, but during the back straight's renovation was relocated at the Südvorplatz, outside the main entrance to the ground, until it too was integrated into the *Fanräume*. As a result, the Fanladen and the AFM often play an important role for those of us wanting to experience the atmosphere of a game at the Millerntor, but in truth this is just the tip of the iceberg. This chapter will give an overview of both organisations, what they do, and their relationship to the club itself.

The Fanladen's roots stem from a project set up in 1983 across town at Hamburger SV. As we have seen, in the early 1980s hooliganism was a growing problem in German football. Certain HSV fan groups had a reputation for violence and links to far-right organisations. The death in October 1982 of a 17-year-old Werder Bremen fan, Adrian Maleika, after clashes between HSV and Bremen fans, led to the creation of the HSV Fan Project. Its central premise was to educate young fans about the dangers of violence, political extremism, racism and alcohol abuse, while also providing them with a support network to raise their self-esteem and to overcome problems with drink and drugs.

Sven Brux, now St. Pauli's head of organisation and security, was asked to establish something similar at the Millerntor. He took up the post on 13 October 1989, after lengthy discussions with club Vice President Christian Hinzpeter and business manager Peter Koch. Hinzpeter, in particular, had seen the potential benefits of working with fans, and as a result Brux was given the responsibility of developing St. Pauli's Fan Project. From humble beginnings in a container located behind the Millerntor's Nordkurve the Fanladen would grow into perhaps the most respected fan-led organisation in Germany, if not all of Europe.

Sven Brux hailed from the Rhineland, but moved to Hamburg to serve his *Zivildienst*, a type of community service that was a longer form of West German national service. Sven had been a 1.FC Köln fan as a youngster but having discovered punk, he found it increasingly difficult to attend games at the Müngersdorfer Stadion due to the increase in right-wing fans. As mentioned previously, the 1980s saw a rise in hooligan activity and being a punk marked you out and put you at risk of both verbal and physical abuse. Brux stopped attending football for a while but once in Hamburg engrossed himself in the city's vibrant punk scene and soon found himself gravitating to the Millerntor. He played an active role in the launch and development of the *Millerntor Roar!* fanzine before setting up the Fanladen. As Sven himself stated in an interview carried out for the December 2012 edition of the Yorkshire St. Pauli fanzine, *Weisse Rose*, 'I was already involved in a fan-initiative against the plans at the time to rebuild the stadium, and was also in the editing team of the first St. Pauli fanzine, *Millerntor Roar!*, but was otherwise jobless... then I got the job for the short term at first, whereby the whole shebang took off...'

The first thing for Sven to do was to find somewhere more permanent to base the Fanladen, which he found in the vicinity of the stadium in a street called Beim Grünen Jäger The renovation of the premises took several months, during which time Sven found himself doing much of his work from home or from the pub. (Sven also had access to the premises of the HSV fan project in Holstenstraße, which might explain why he opted for the pub instead!)

Initially, Sven's main task was to act as a central point for selling tickets to away games and to organise transport. Until this point, travelling to away games wasn't commonplace and was virtually impossible to organise unless you travelled by car. Even the first trip arranged by the Fanladen attracted only around 60 fans. But steadily the numbers began to grow. Brux cites the trips to games as vital in spreading the newer, alternative fans' ideology across the country as well as providing an opportunity to tackle those St. Pauli fans who still held right-wing views. In an interview conducted by Chris Sanderson in 2008, Brux stated: 'So we infiltrated normal football supporters with this service thing – come to us; you get the ticket for the train very cheap, and, look here, you can have stickers against the Nazis... Of course it was a small scene, so we had contacts with them (racist fans): then we said, no we don't accept these flags, this sticker, this Nazi shit, but we did it in a good way, because on these long train journeys to away matches we talked a lot and set out our agenda.'

Brux underlined the importance of these organised trips in the same *Weisse Rose* interview: 'Offering organised away trips was really important, but also not too difficult. I just searched for a local coach operator that appeared trustworthy and also a contact person at DB (Deutsche Bahn) for the rail journeys. When I look back on it today it seems to me that at least the rail journeys were easier to organise in those days. Back then DB was still a state-owned company and we mostly got all the seats we wanted. And neither the Police nor anyone else got themselves involved at that time. The trips themselves were really funny; big riots or problems with the Police were, with exceptions, never part of the equation. You could also still smoke, drink and sing, whatever and how much you wanted.'

They must've been interesting times, with old and new fans of St. Pauli discussing politics on those long cross-country train journeys – a clash of ideologies that ultimately saw St. Pauli's left-wing fan base recognised throughout the country. Sven Brux spoke fondly of those early days: 'It was great because everything we did back then, nobody else had done prior to us, either in German football or internationally. Everything was new and the will to change things and break things up was very big. The self-confidence to be able to change things also increased constantly and with every successful campaign. You also have to know though, that back then the number of activists was much different to today. The circle of activists was limited to a small clique of perhaps 20–30 people, no more than that.'

The Fanladen's official birthday is recorded as 15 February 1990 when they moved to new premises on Beim Grünen Jäger Straße, just a few blocks away from the Millerntor. This new location helped to underline the Fanladen's status as an organisation independent of club control. However, Sven Brux was keen to point out that this independence was vital from the outset, and remains just as important today. He stated: 'If a fan representative or a fan project is to take seriously the interests of fans and, as such, give the fans a voice, it must also be able to speak freely, without fear of consequences. However, if the links to the club are too large (for example, by means of an employee relationship or too great a financial dependence), then the danger exists that, in the case of a serious conflict, the club would say, "Hey, we pay you, so you'd better shut your gob!" '

The new Fanladen occupied an office of just 25 square metres which had been previously been a hairdressers'. It was well used; editions of *Millerntor Roar!* were produced there, football was watched on television, beer was drunk and ideas were discussed. It was here that the now legendary 'St. Pauli Fans Gegen Rechts' (St. Pauli Fans Against Nazis) stickers were laid out using a combination of Letraset (sheets of Letraset being a tool of the trade for any aspiring fanzine writer in the 1980s) and a hand-drawn image of a fist smashing a swastika. From their beginnings in the Fanladen offices, these stickers went on to appear all over Europe, with millions being produced and distributed for free, and millions more being adapted by fans of other clubs wanting to display the same anti-Nazi message. The stickers' popularity hasn't waned. Even 20 years later the iconic 'St. Pauli Fans Gegen Rechts' frequently appears stuck to the back of seats, in toilets or on signage in football grounds, bars and pubs all over Europe. After just two years, the Fanladen had outgrown the former hairdressers and moved a few blocks to larger premises on Thadenstraße.

Very quickly the Fanladen became the hub of the St. Pauli fan culture; a meeting point for like-minded individuals, a place to discuss politics, drink and organise protests whether that be against the Nazis or against threats to the local area from continuing gentrification.

The early 1990s also saw the start of an enduring friendship between the fans of FC St. Pauli and Celtic. As you'd expect, Sven Brux was an influential figure in developing this. Brux had contact with the editorial team at the Celtic fanzine, *Not The View*; he travelled to Celtic Park and stood on the terraces, experiencing the incredible atmosphere of the Jungle. Brux also travelled with other St. Pauli fans to watch Cetic competing in Europe, making friends along the way. In 1992, members of the *Not The View* fanzine travelled to Hamburg to visit the Millerntor, drink and play football against a team from the Fanladen. The trip cemented the friendship and paved the way for regular visits from both sets of supporters. Much has been made of the political aspect of the friendship, with both clubs being joined under the banner of 'The Rebel's Choice'. There were certainly close links with Celtic's left-leaning, republican *TAL* fanzine, with many fans sharing a political ideology. However, the link with Celtic wasn't entirely political; the *Not The View* fanzine wasn't overtly political. Many of the Celtic fans travelled to St. Pauli for the beer, to have a party with new-found friends and to absorb themselves in the atmosphere of the Millerntor. Perhaps the bond became so strong because both sets of fans share so much common ground in the *style* of their support. For both, supporting the team unconditionally and generating an atmosphere exist independently from results on the pitch. This, along with a strong sense of social justice, rallying against everything from racism and sexism in football to victimisation by the police and the authorities, helped bond the two groups. It is a relationship that has continued to grow down the years, with an annual Celtic–St. Pauli party, attracting hundreds of Celtic fans to Hamburg every spring. In May 2010, as part of FC St. Pauli's centenary celebrations, the two teams met for the first time. Celtic ran out 2-0 winners at the Millerntor, but the result was the last thing on anyone's mind as thousands of Celtic and St. Pauli fans partied long into the night. Not that the Celtic–St.Pauli friendship has been to everyone's tastes. In an interview with Celtic fanzine *The Thunder*, a member of Ultrà Sankt Pauli noted a degree of unease among some at the Millerntor with some Celtic fans, 'who had no real interest in Sankt Pauli or in the game, only in the beer they could drink on the terrace and singing Celtic songs.' He continued: 'This lack of respect disturbed not only USP but also a lot of ordinary

Sankt Pauli fans. Even during this time, though, some USP members followed Celtic in Europe so weren't "anti-Celtic".' He followed this up by explaining, 'The relationship between Celtic and Sankt Pauli fans, including USP, has improved over the past few years due to the Celtic fans' involvement in the annual Antira football tournament and the change in fan culture at Celtic Park.'

As the Fanladen's reputation grew, so did the variety of projects that fell under its remit. The Anti-Racist tournament first organised by the Fanladen in 2004 has gone on to become an important annual event. bringing together left-wing Antira supporters' groups from all over Europe. The event has gone from strength to strength and between 25and 27 May 2012, 39 different supporters groups from 15 different countries gathered together to play football at the home of the St. Pauli amateur team on Waidmannstrasse (the tournament, when played in Hamburg, is usually held at the FC St. Pauli training ground, but redevelopment of the site over the summer prompted the change of venue).

In light of the ongoing repression from the authorities and the worrying rise in the number of far-right supporters groups becoming active inside German stadiums, the slogan for the 2012 Antira tournament was 'Reclaim your Stadium'. However, the Antira tournaments are about more than just football. The tournament represents a coming together of fans' groups sharing a similar ideology. The weekend's activities also included talks and lectures, with survivors from the Neuengamme concentration camp on the outskirts of Hamburg or contemporary witnesses of the Nazi regime coming to speak to the teams. There are tours around the St. Pauli district that highlight the ongoing battle against the gentrification of the area. Of course, the tournament also offers plenty of opportunities to socialise and party, with the evening given over to DJs, live bands and, of course, drinking. With fan groups travelling from as far afield as Cadiz in the southern tip of Spain, Tel Aviv, and Eastern Europe, the event is a true pan-European rallying point for Antifa activities, and one the Fanladen should be rightly proud of organising.

In 2001–02 the Fanladen pioneered, along with FC St. Pauli itself, another exciting social initiative. The 'KiezKick' project gives local youths the opportunity to play football for free in their neighbourhood.

The project was initially funded by the proceeds raised by a friendly match between FC St. Pauli and a celebrity side. Every week up to 60 local children, aged between seven and 18, take part in training sessions. The project has also set up 'girls only' training sessions on Thursday nights designed to get more girls playing football. The central premise of the project is to give children from the 'Kiez' (or neighbourhood) something to do other than wander the streets. The project has brought together children from a variety of social and cultural backgrounds and it also gives them the chance to enjoy football away from the pressures of results and performance.

The idea is that the kids have fun. The project is visited regularly by players of FC St. Pauli, and many of the kids visit the Millerntor for home games. This two-way process helps the children feel part of the club but also builds the FC St. Pauli players' association with the neighbourhood. The KiezKick project has won a number of awards since its inception in 2002, including the 'City of Hamburg Integration Award' in 2006 in recognition of bringing so many different nationalities and cultures together under the banner of football. The KiezKick project has undoubtedly been a success, but it still relies on donations from individuals, groups and organisations to allow it to continue, and as such the Fanladen continues to welcome donations to the project. On Saturday 9 August 2012 KiezKick celebrated its 10-year anniversary with a football party on the astroturf pitches behind the Nordkurve. The event was attended by more than 50 children, along with FC St. Pauli president, Stefan Orth, and goalkeeper Benedikt Pliquett.

The Fanladen also organises the 'U-18 Ragazzi', which provides social activities for the district's youngsters. Every Friday night between 5.00 and 7.00pm, kids can get together in the Fanladen to socialise and play a game of table football. When the weather is decent, the Ragazzi play crazy golf or host barbecues. As Stefan Schatz from the Fanladen explained the range of activities is varied, 'During the meetings we often organise a football tournament or do some cooking together, meet players, go skating... whatever comes to our or their minds.' Travel is also organised to away games, although not to every away game as the Fanladen are not allowed to organise trips if they clash with school commitments!

Over the years, the Fanladen has done a great deal of work in the local community, working with local youths suffering from police oppression, or with drug problems.

On top of this commitment to social work, the Fanladen along with the Fanclubsprecherrat of St. Pauli organises the 450 plus fanclubs and groups that are officially linked to the club. The Fanclubsprecherrat of St. Pauli (FCSR) is a body elected by members of the St. Pauli fan clubs. Not only does it form an umbrella for the numerous fan clubs, it is also an important member of various committees, including the Ständiger Ausschuss, Fanräume and BAFF (the national organisation of 'active' fan groups in Germany).

It is clear that the Fanladen is vital to both the St. Pauli fan scene and the local community. It has a varied and far-reaching role, but as Stefan Schatz states: 'Our daily work is dominated by dealing with tickets though. We get an amount of tickets for the home matches from the club for supporters' clubs and supporters from abroad. And also for away matches, as we organise the trips for the supporters, let it be by bus or train.'

The trips by special trains are worth a particular mention, as they are something of which Sven Brux and Schatz speak fondly, even if they have become a bit of a logistical nightmare. Brux's comments about the special trains have been documented above; Schatz was able to bring the joys of the train trips up to date: 'The special trains are big fun! We sometimes have special trains to near-distance matches like Hannover, Rostock, Braunschweig – these are mainly regional trains and cheap enough for everybody. The "real" special trains – like Dresden last season – are the trips with a bigger distance. We try to get comfortable old-school carriages and a bar-and-dancing-carriage. Obviously these trains cause more costs and it's always a little risky to organise it – and we have had some small disasters in the last years!'

In the interviews conducted for the *Weisse Rose* fanzine, both Brux and Schatz were asked how the Fanladen had changed over the years. Brux believed that the Fanladen had become much more professional, joking that these days the staff weren't allowed to drink alcohol at work. He also stated: 'There are significantly more regulations to adhere to and the colleagues (as well as their work) are observed significantly more in the public domain. The work has also become more specialist, which is indicated in the establishing of special projects like KiezKick or U18, where the foundations of preventative work are being laid.' Schatz, who has ten years' experience working in various capacities at the Fanladen, has seen his workload increase dramatically: 'Not only did we start many good projects during the last years which became regular projects without quitting other projects, but also the demands by the supporters, the club, the police, politicians, etc., are growing.' He continued, 'And also our work has changed a lot. On the one hand you have the ultra-culture which changed the audience a lot, on the other hand we are facing a massive public discussion about security issues. This has a massive effect on our work.'

With the Fanladen having moved from their home on Brigittenstraße to a purpose-built space in the Fanräume in the newly rebuilt Gegengerade, further changes are afoot. It will be interesting to see how being a physical part of the club will differ from being in the district itself. Schatz sees both the potential benefits and possible pitfalls: 'I think that we have a big chance to get closer to a bigger range of supporters as soon as we move to the stadium. I'm hoping that we will thus arrange a better communication between us and the club/ club's officials. On the other hand it'll be difficult to reach the regular St. Pauli kids passing the Fanladen nowadays and just coming in by chance.'

The move will give the Fanladen more physical space, a library of articles linked to fan-culture and a space for concerts and gigs. It is also hoped that there will be room for an FC St. Pauli museum next to the Fanräume, rather than the controversial police station that was originally proposed. Stefan, like most St. Pauli fans, has strong views on the citing of a police station in the Gegengerade: 'When you consider the fact that FC St. Pauli today would be nothing without the history of its supporters and mostly everything the supporters stand for today originates from the Gegengerade stand, it would be another nail in the coffin of the "mythos St. Pauli". Concerning the Fanladen, we are doing social work with youth and young adult supporters who are very often facing problems with the police. To have them as direct neighbours would be offensive to those who are seeking help in the Fanladen.'

The active role of the Fanladen in the St. Pauli fan scene has often brought it into dispute with the club. The Fanladen's independence from the club has been central to its success. As Sven Brux stated, 'There are always conflicts between fans and the club. Sometimes more, sometimes less; it's totally natural. If a fan representative or a fan project is to take seriously the interests of fans and, as such, give the fans a voice, it must also be able to speak freely, without fear of consequences.'

It helps that those working in the Fanladen have always been passionate St. Pauli fans first and foremost, as Stefan Schatz commented: 'Of course most people working in the Fanladen are and have always been St. Pauli fans before starting to work here, so sometimes we will get very emotional on things not happening in a way that we want them to, but on the other hand we are working professionals. Our job is to try to arrange communication between the club, the supporters and all other "players" involved.'

It is a difficult role that the Fanladen plays incredibly well. They have the trust and respect of the active fan scene in St. Pauli and they are also widely admired across Germany and the rest of Europe, often cited as the example to follow. It is almost impossible to measure the amount of good the Fanladen has done for both FC St. Pauli fans and residents, since Sven Brux got the organisation off the ground back in 1989. As international fans, although we are incredibly grateful for the service they provide, it is perhaps worth considering quite how much other good work they do, especially when you are hanging on for that all-important ticket confirmation email!

The AFM was established ten years after the inception of the Fanladen. It was set up to give supporters the opportunity to be a member of the club and thus have a say in the running of FC St. Pauli through voting at the club's AGM. Once a membership fee has been paid, you need to have been registered as a member for just three months and you are eligible to vote at the AGM. There are other benefits to membership that include a range of discounts, and crucially for those fans that live 100km or more from the Millerntor, the allocation of 100 tickets per game to the AFM. These can be applied for in advance, and along with those tickets offered by Fanladen, are perhaps the most common way in which international fans secure tickets.

The growth in AFM membership since 1999 has been staggering. By 2008, there were around 4,500 members but at the club's AGM in November 2012 the AFM reported that membership had broken the 10,000 barrier. With total membership now standing at around 18,000, it is clear to see that the AFM has grown into the largest single section of membership in a relatively short time frame. This has the obvious positive of extending the democratic scope of the club as every member has equal voting rights.

The other extremely positive impact of this surge in AFM membership is the amount of money and resources it can direct towards the organisation's primary function: supporting and developing youth projects. More than 80 per cent of the revenue raised from membership is pumped back into a variety of these projects linked to the club.

In 2001, the AFM worked with the club to establish the 'Young Rebels'. This led to a series of initiatives designed to expand the club's youth policy and make the promotion of homegrown talent a priority. At a time when the club itself was suffering financially, the prospect of it being able to draw on a well of homegrown talent was particularly appealing. However, it wasn't just about developing young players and putting them on a conveyor belt of talent that led to the first team. The project was also about extending the social and cultural role of the club in the local community and looking after the welfare of young players both on and off the pitch. One of the first things established under the banner of the 'Young Rebels' was a mentoring scheme, offering help and support with any problems whether football, school or work related.

Two years later the AFM set up a place for young players to stay, located next to the club's training facilities. Housing up to five players at a time, it fast became the hub of the mentoring programme and a space in which the youngsters could relax and socialise. The residence cost €278,000 to get up and running and is overseen by Claus Teister and two housekeepers. The house itself is modern and well equipped, with places for the players to work and relax. During the day, the five residents are joined by other young players, providing them with somewhere to spend their free time between training and school.

The AFM was also instrumental in developing the Youth Training Centre, something that became a mandatory requirement for clubs wishing to retain their professional licence. The AFM also helped establish an apprenticeship scheme, costing around €10,000 per year, linking youngsters with local companies and giving them the opportunity to develop other career paths for that time when football is no longer an option. The scheme operates under the banner 'You'll Never Work Alone' and is an acknowledgement that only a small percentage of youth team players make it as a professional footballers, and that an alternative career path is a necessity.

Perhaps the AFM's biggest project to date is the redevelopment of the club's training facilities at Kollaustraße. Working alongside the club, the training facilities are being totally overhauled and expanded to enable the Under-17 and Under-19 squads to share the new facilities with the first team. At the November 2012 AGM, Alexander Gunkel, AFM chairman, also reiterated the AFM's support for a museum in the new Gegengerade stand.

For a long time, the most visible aspect of the AFM for fans visiting the Millerntor has been the legendary AFM container that has now been replaced by the Fanräume. Open from two hours before kick-off until long after the final whistle, it was a meeting point or social hub for hundreds of St. Pauli fans each matchday. For each home game a different fan group took over the container, serving drinks and playing music – a ritual that has now been moved to the Fansaal. The music is usually eclectic and always loud, and varies depending on which fanclub is in control of the sound system. Fan groups are free to decorate the Fansaal in their own memorabilia and are 'paid' with a crate of Astra that they can either drink themselves or sell to raise money for their own fan group. The rest of the money raised from the not inconsiderable amount of Astra consumed each matchday is further funding towards the myriad of youth projects run by the AFM. Spending some time in the Fanräume both before kick-off and at the end of the game is integral to the St. Pauli experience. The atmosphere is always relaxed and the beer flows regardless of the outcome of the game.

As stated at the start of this chapter, the Fanladen and the AFM are essential contact points for fans travelling from overseas. It is also apparent how vital both organisations are to the continued vibrancy of the St. Pauli fan scene. With this in mind, next time you visit the Millerntor, stop for a drink in the Fanladen or the AFM, buy a T-shirt, stickers or a fanzine; take time to chat with the staff (or the fanclub serving the beer). By doing so, you will be making a small contribution to the fan culture at the Millerntor. And if you really want to be a part of it, take out an AFM membership, or set up a fan club of your own.

MATCH
I'M STILL STANDING

Borussia Dortmund 2 FC St. Pauli 0
Bundesliga
Saturday 19 February 2011, 3.30pm, Westfalenstadion

I CAN'T QUITE remember when I became aware of Borusssia
Dortmund and the Westfalenstadion. The club probably first flickered
across my football radar with their 1997 Champions League victory
over Zidane and Juventus in Munich. The Westfalenstadion itself
hosted the incredible Liverpool–Alaves UEFA Cup final in 2001
and must've pricked my conscience as most of the drama in that
match – Liverpool's first-half goals, Jordi Cruyff's late equaliser and
Delfi Geli's unfortunate golden 'own' goal – occurred in front of the
Westfalenstadion's colossal Südtribüne terrace.

It was the Südtribüne that really caught my imagination. I remained
an advocate of safe standing at football. The conversion of English stadia
to all-seater always seemed to me to be an excuse to sanitise the game
and sell this 'refined' and repackaged version back to us at an inflated
price. I remain convinced that the safety argument was just a handy
excuse. After all, it wasn't the terraces per se that were dangerous – it
was the horrendous organisation, policing and stewarding that were
problematic. As someone who was politicised by the tragic events and
subsequent injustice of the Hillsborough disaster, I wouldn't support
the return to standing at football matches if I thought that terracing

itself was responsible for loss of life. To my mind, the publication of all the official documentation relating to Hillsbrorough brought to light the lies and subsequent cover-up operation relating to the events of 15 April 1989. It wasn't terracing, it was shameful neglect and mismanagement that led to the loss of 96 lives. I'm not a Liverpool fan but I have proudly worn my 'Justice for the 96' lapel badge for many years, and like every other true football fan felt an overwhelming sense of relief when the Hillsborough Independent Panel absolved the Liverpool fans of any blame for the disaster.

With the quashing of the original verdict it felt like justice had finally been served. The scale of the cover-up surprised even the most hardened cynic but finally the perseverance of the families, who had struggled all these years with the lies that had been heaped upon them, had been vindicated. The return of terracing to football remains an emotive issue and I have total respect for the opinion of those friends and relatives of the people who died at Hillsborough who don't want to see a return to standing at football. However, there is a part of me that has always believed it can be done safely.

As my disillusionment with English football became more pronounced, I'd read about stadiums in Germany that could alternate between terracing for domestic games and all-seating for European competition. Most famous among these grounds was Dortmund's Westfalenstadion. The stats were impressive: a capacity of 80,720 for domestic fixtures, reduced to 65,718 for international competition. If the capacity alone wasn't impressive enough, the fact that 25,000 fans could be accommodated on Europe's largest terrace, the Südtribüne, was simply jaw-dropping.

As a result, ever since I'd first started visiting Germany for football, I'd had half an eye on Dortmund's fixture list. I'd tried a couple of times to divert via Dortmund when en route to watch St Pauli in 2. Bundesliga (Bundesliga and 2. Bundesliga fixtures tend to be on different days at the weekend) but the fixtures had never fallen for me. I'd managed to take in games in Köln and Bremen, but a game at the Westfalenstadion had eluded me.

In hindsight, I'm extremely grateful. I don't doubt any fixture at the Westfalenstadion would be an incredible experience but to go there *with* St. Pauli would be something else.

Even with Borussia Dortmund and FC St. Pauli in the same league attending the fixture wasn't going to be that straightforward. The game, part of Spieltag 23, could've been played anytime from Friday night to Sunday tea-time and the kick-off wouldn't be confirmed by the Deutsche Fussball Liga until a month or so before. The Friday fixture would be impossible due to work, and Saturday would be pushing it. As a result, I'd taken a keen interest in Dortmund's Europa League campaign. If BVB could negotiate the group stages it would guarantee a Sunday slot for our game – and guarantee my attendance. Unfortunately a 2-2 draw for Dortmund away at Sevilla wasn't enough to get them into the Round of 16 and, as a consequence, my trip was resting on a whim of the DFL.

To add to the suspense (in my head at least, I appreciate no one else was particularly bothered) the DFL kept me hanging on until mid-January before confirming the kick-off times for Spieltag 23. Finally, Dortmund v St. Pauli was scheduled for 15.30 on the Saturday – it would take some planning, but it was just about possible.

Once again, I opted for the train, and as a result my trip began with a frantic dash to Milton Keynes Central Station (central to what, I'm not sure; it sure as hell is not anywhere near the centre of Milton Keynes). As I walk towards the station I spot a young lad in a brown St. Pauli hoodie leaning against the wall. I take it as a good omen that, in the land of the concrete cow, anodyne shopping centre and Franchise FC, someone is sporting a Totenkopf – genuine fan or fashionista? I don't have time to stop and chat, I have a train(s) to catch. At least my trip appears to be blessed with better karma than in August when, on a rare plane journey to Hamburg, some idiot in an English Defence League T-shirt was flitting around the platform of Birmingham International station looking for aggro as I was heading for the airport.

By now I know the Deutsche Bahn schedule inside-out, so after an overnight stop in Brussels I get up early for the German equivalent of the milk-train to Köln. In Köln I have another of those chance meetings with fellow St. Pauli fans that seem to bookmark most trips. As I make my way up to the platform for my connection to Dortmund I bump into fellow members of the St. Pauli UK Messageboard – all London-based Port Vale fans and a sound bunch. After the final connection through to Dortmund I miss my rendezvous with Justus from the

Fanladen on the incredibly busy station concourse but after a quick call rearrange to meet outside the away fans' entrance at the ground. Before that there is time to meet a few more messageboard members at the Hövels Hausbrauerei micro-brewery including a long awaited (and much postponed, last time due to the volcanic ash cloud) link up with a fellow Watford fan, before getting the U-Bahn to the stadium.

My first glimpse of Signal Iduna Park (I was going to have to refer to it by its official, sponsored name at some point) from the train is a little underwhelming to be honest. Only the huge, yellow steel exoskeleton marks it out as distinctive, and even then there is more than a hint of Middlesbrough's Riverside stadium, albeit with a day-glo paintjob, about it. After being quickly and efficiently deposited at the stadium's U-Bahn stop, we amble towards the ground and its sheer size starts to become apparent. However, although it dominates the skyline, it isn't the hulking presence of the Westfalenstadion that initially catches our attention. Instead we are drawn to the antiquated stadium next door, its main stand seeming to be slowly consumed by the overbearing Westfalenstadion behind it. This shallow oval bowl was Borusssia Dortmund's home before the Westfalenstadion was completed in 1974. Stadion Rote Erde (Red Earth Stadium) has (or perhaps had?) a capacity of 25,000 with 22,000 of those housed on the shallow curve of terracing that encircles the pitch. From our angle the diminutive seated 'grandstand' looks like it is grafted onto the side of the new stadium behind it. The expanse of green these days plays host to Dortmund's second team, but the Rote Erde Stadion itself is a beautiful example of football from another age. The wonderful, old-school crush-barriers are still painted a crisp white and give the impression of hundreds of five-a-side goals marooned in the crumbling concrete of the terrace. Perhaps I should've done my stadium homework, but I wasn't really expecting to come to one of the largest stadiums in Europe and be blown away by the faded grandeur of its 1920s predecessor.

Dortmund first made plans to replace the Rote Erde Stadion in 1965. The following year they won the Cup Winner's Cup, triggering further demand for tickets. Sadly, funding was impossible to secure and the project struggled to get off the ground. However, in 1971, Dortmund replaced Köln as a host city for the 1974 World Cup finals, and the money set aside for stadium development in Köln was transferred to Dortmund. Both the timeframe and the budget were tight, if the new stadium was to be ready for the competition. It was, perhaps, these constraints that became the new Westfalenstadion's greatest strengths. Instead of including a running track, the usual prerequisite of large stadium projects at the time, Dortmund's new ground was designed – in an effort to constrain the costs – exclusively for football. Four prefabricated concrete stands were quickly assembled in close proximity to the pitch, thereby giving the stadium its intense atmosphere. The whole project was completed for DM 32.7 million (of which nearly DM 2 million was spent refurbishing the Rote Erde Stadion next door).

When the stadium opened in April 1974, it was hosting 2. Bundesliga football as BVB had been relegated from the top flight two years before. However, even in the second division crowds were high, and the ground had been filled to its 54,000 capacity during the four games played there at the 1974 World Cup.

After admiring the Rote Erde Stadion, my fellow English fans head off to find a pub (they'd already got their tickets for the seated section via the club) while I go to meet Justus and collect my ticket. Of course, the stadium I was now standing in front of had changed beyond all recognition since its inauguration in 1974. It had undergone several expansions, the most recent coming in the mid-1990s, when a second tier was added first to the East and West stands and then to the North and South stands. In the process the club expanded the Südtribüne, making it the largest standing area in Europe, dubbed 'The Yellow Wall'. The fact that this terracing, along with the away fans' terracing behind the opposite goal, can be converted between standing and seating feels like a wonder of the modern footballing world.

Eventually, through a combination of talking frantically into my mobile and exaggerated arm-waving I am able to locate Justus and pick up my ticket. It is a crisp, clear February day, but the wind is starting to bite and so it is time to head inside. Once through the ticket and security check – at an entrance *shared* by home and away fans, imagine that at Old Trafford or Anfield! – I head down a short flight of steps and notice the piles of bright yellow seats stored neatly, ready for that conversion from terrace to seating for international fixtures or European games.

I am in Block 8 of the Nordtribüne terrace, so have to go down more steps to an entrance that brings me into the stadium, right at the base of the away fans' section almost level with the pitch – not that I am looking at that. My attention had been diverted to a first glimpse of 'The Yellow Wall' at the other end of the stadium. Much has been written about that vast expanse of terrace, so I won't bang on about it too much, but seeing it pretty much full 30 minutes before kick-off is a sight to behold. In fact, the whole stadium looks huge. Turning round to look at our section, the terracing is dwarfed by an upper tier of seated St. Pauli fans stretching up to the heavens (and containing somewhere therein, my fellow fans from the UK). Cathedral, temple or opera house of football – take your pick, it is truly breathtaking.

I stand drinking it all in when, about 20 minutes before kick-off, there is a bit of bother to the left of me. A few fists are flying and I assume that a home (or rival) fan had decided to get in among the St. Pauli hardcore. Apparently, the incident is prompted by stewards not letting fans hang their banners over the advertising hoardings at the front of the stadium. This 'over-enthusiastic' police and stewards' response isn't the authorities' best move after the problems St. Pauli fans had experienced in the derby game against HSV the previous Wednesday night in the Volksparkstadion. Although a solitary goal from Gerald Asamoah had secured FC St. Pauli an historic away win against their local rivals, echoing the victory in 1977, much of the talk following the game was of police storming the packed away section after flares and smoke bombs were let off by the away fans at exactly 19.10 (the year the club was founded). The use of pyrotechnics at football games is an issue that has caused a lot of debate (I'm cautiously supportive of their use, although I can see the problems and danger that they cause) but the heavy-handed action of the police, charging fans in full riot gear and using pepper spray in an already tense derby, didn't do anything to calm the situation and indeed injured several fans. At half-time in the game against HSV, however, something remarkable did happen – Ultrà Sankt Pauli took a quick vote, via a show of hands, and USP, plus a number of other St. Pauli fans, some acting on principle, some just plain frightened by what they had experienced, decided that rather than be treated like criminals they would simply leave the stadium. It was a dignified response to the awful treatment they had received and it also meant that they missed Asamoah's winner. Of course, the fans that left early weren't free to leave the stadium complex and had to wait for the game to finish and for the rest of the St. Pauli contingent to join them before they were bussed back to town.

So even though the chant of 'Derby-Sieger' is sung with gusto in the away end in the run-up to kick-off against Dortmund, there is still a slight tension in the air, especially among those who had witnessed the events in the AOL Arena (again, eventually, I have to refer to it by its latest sponsor-approved 'brand' name.)

But things settle, and it isn't long before the St. Pauli fans are in full voice. Kick-off is preceded by a sing-along version of *You'll Never Walk Alone*, which, despite the piped-music accompaniment, is very atmospheric. Of course, being St. Pauli (and YNWA being one of 'our' anthems) we manage another verse and chorus once the music has stopped, before launching into my favourite chant of 'Aux Armes' that sounds great bouncing between the upper and lower tiers of the Nordtribüne. I really like the international flavour to the St. Pauli song book, appropriating YNWA from Merseyside and 'Aux Armes' from Marseilles, especially as my French is marginally better than my German so I can roughly work out what's being sung.

The game itself is unremarkable and the scoreline fairly predictable. Despite St. Pauli's recent run of form, most fans don't expect to be leaving the Westfalenstadion with more than a point. Dortmund go in at half-time 1-0 up and any hope St. Pauli have of staging a fight-back is ended early in the second half when Ralph Gunesch diverts a shot into his own net to give the league leaders a 2-0 lead. But I've not come looking for a win. I've come to stand and sing with the St Pauli faithful in this grand setting. And I've come to see and hear the Südtribüne in full flow. In true, away fan fashion, it feels like we are out-singing the home fans for much of the game. But, if the noise coming from the Südtribüne isn't especially impressive, the sight of 25,000 fans pogoing on the spot sure makes up for it. It is then I really appreciate the vast scale of the terrace. In the end it isn't the acoustics that blow me away, but the seething mass of bodies. Whether the fans are jumping up and down in unison or holding scarves aloft it provides a sight that takes me back to the great terraces of the 1970s. It is reminiscent of The Kop or the Stretford End as seen on old *Match of the Day* footage. And, just as importantly for me, it is done safely. Despite the early squabble between fans and stewards over where to hang banners, the stewarding has been excellent. I had to retain and show my ticket when I wanted to return to my allocated block after half-time, an excellent measure to prevent overcrowding, and the officials I spoke to both inside and outside of the ground were friendly and incredibly helpful. (I can't imagine your average Premier League steward conversing amiably with an overseas visitor in fluent German – but, I may be wrong!)

It finished 2-0. Fairly respectable when you consider we are missing derby hero, Gerald Asamoah, influential midfielder Fabian Boll and centre-half Carlos Zambrano. We also lost left-back Bastian Oczipka due to injury early in the first half, which meant another appearance from former *Times* columnist and Craven Cottage resident, Moritz Volz. But as the St Pauli players come to applaud the fans in the guest block my mind starts to wander to the long journey home.

Despite the bitter cold, I make all my train connections; in fact so efficient is the free U-Bahn service from the ground back to the main railway station, I manage to get a train back to Köln an hour ahead of schedule. When you consider how long it takes to get a similar number of fans out of Wembley, you can't help falling back on those old clichés of German efficiency. Over the course of the weekend, I had traversed parts of Germany, Belgium and France without a hitch, yet on returning home, there was the obligatory ten-minute wait 500m short of Milton Keynes station as they struggled to find a platform for us. You'd think they'd get the idea by now: a train generally requires a platform on which to deposit its passengers.

Still, I have finally made it to Dortmund and I've seen my team play there. The result is unimportant. Instead, I got to experience the atmosphere at one of the best stadiums in the world. I also met another really nice batch of UK-based St. Pauli fans, all of whom were prepared to travel halfway across Europe to watch their team and have a beer with like-minded supporters.

I still believe that if you brought back modern, safe and regulated standing to football grounds in England, the atmosphere at Premier League and Championship matches would improve almost overnight. There's nothing more I'd like to see than the Stretford End I remember from the telly of my youth, swaying and singing in unison, but I'm pretty sure it will never happen.

Not because it can't be done sensibly and safely – the Südtribüne at Dortmund, and terraced areas at countless other German stadia proves it's possible – but because you can charge more for seats.

Chapter 7
RETTER & THE REGIONALLIGA

Saving St. Pauli and returning from the wilderness

FC ST. PAULI'S three-season stay in the Bundesliga came to a dramatic close at the end of June 1991. The 1990–91 season had been one of struggle, punctuated by a couple of remarkable away victories. The first of these had come in Berlin on the opening day of the season, where St. Pauli hit two second-half goals to come from behind and beat Hertha Berlin in the Olympiastadion. The second victory, on an overcast Saturday afternoon in February, was also Olympian in its achievement, with St. Pauli recording a historic 1-0 win over Bayern Munich in their Bavarian Olympiastadion.

Ralf Sievers had fired St. Pauli into the lead two minutes before half-time, and a string of fine saves from legendary keeper Volker Ippig had kept Bayern at bay in a sparsely populated Olympiastadion (only 15,000 were in attendance) and St. Pauli held on for the win. At full-time, the players headed as usual to the guest block to celebrate the historic win with the St. Pauli fans. The Fanladen even produced special 'I was there!' T-shirts for those fans who had travelled to Munich (and quite possibly a few that hadn't).

These two away victories, coupled with just four wins at home, were the 1990–91 season's only on-the-pitch highlights. But by now, St. Pauli fans were starting to travel to matches in increasing numbers, taking their politics and fan culture with them as they travelled across the country. The Fanladen organised a special train for the final league game of the season, away at Borussia Dortmund. It proved so popular that extra buses had to be drafted in to get fans to the Westfalenstadion. Going into the game St. Pauli had a chance to avoid the drop, but they would need to beat Dortmund and hope 1. FC Nürnberg failed to win their final game (actually both sides could've won, and St. Pauli could still have stayed up as long as they won by three more goals than Nürnberg). In the end, it was academic: St. Pauli lost 5-2 to Dortmund while 1. FC Nürnberg grabbed a 1-0 away win at SG Wattenscheid 09. FC St. Pauli found themselves up against Stuggarter Kickers in the two-legged 'Relegationsspiel.'

The first leg was on Wednesday 19 June 1991 in front of just over 20,000 spectators at the Millerntor. The fight for Bundesliga survival got off to a good start when André Golke put St. Pauli ahead after 31 minutes, but after failing to convert a host of other chances the inevitable happened. With just two minutes left on the clock Marcus Marin equalised. FC St. Pauli had failed to make the most of home advantage and were forced to head to Stuttgart just four days later with the tie all-square. Once again, the Fanladen organised a special train. More than 3,000 fans travelled by bus and car as well as train looking to cheer the team to Bundesliga survival. The second leg in the Neckarstadion in front of 32,000 fans played out in an almost exact reverse of the previous game. Alois Schwartz put Stuttgart ahead on 25 minutes, but Golke levelled six minutes after half-time for St. Pauli. Matters had been made worse for the visitors as they played the entire second half with ten men after Dirk Zander's dismissal before the break. The game ended 1-1 (2-2 on aggregate). The two teams would need to meet again for a decisive third game at a neutral venue.

The game that would decide the issue was to be played in Gelsenkirchen at Schalke's Park Stadion. The stadium, built for the 1974 World Cup, could house upwards of 60,000 fans. The Fanladen was swamped with fans wanting tickets and transport. Queues wound round the block as fans waited patiently for the opportunity to travel on one of the two trains laid on. Around 15,000 St. Pauli fans made the trip. They were housed on the Nordkurve, underneath the giant scoreboard, separated from the players by an imposing metal fence and the running track. Three sides of this old-school stadium were open to the elements. Four towering floodlight columns stood guard, the running track adding to the vast oval bowl-like shape that was so prevalent among larger European stadia of the era – a stark contrast to Schalke's modern-day home, with its retractable roof and 'mothership' like qualities. The St. Pauli fans were in full voice and the terrace was awash with brown and white flags augmented by the now familiar Totenkopfs.

The less said about the game itself the better. Unusually the teams made the journey from the changing rooms to the pitch via an escalator, with FC St. Pauli wearing a combination of purple shadow-striped shirts, black shorts and white socks that could best be described as 'hard on the eye'. They were suffering from injuries and they found themselves 2-0 down with just 35 minutes on the clock. Peter Knäbel gave the fans hope two minutes later but Stuttgart scored again three minutes before the break through Dirk Fengler. Try as St. Pauli might they couldn't force their way back into the game in the second half. There were no further goals, and Stuggarter Kickers ran out 3-1 winners to earn themselves a place in the Bundesliga and relegate FC St. Pauli to the second division.

For fans of St. Pauli the scenes at the final whistle would be remembered for much longer than the match itself. A documentary by the NDR television network (part of it is available to watch on YouTube) captured the raw emotions of relegation on film. It was set to the music of Bob Dylan's lament *It's All Over Now, Baby Blue* and it documented the sheer devastation of players and fans alike. Volker Ippig's heroics couldn't save St. Pauli this time and he was seen leaving the pitch in tears at the end of the match. But it is the fans' reaction that is really moving. As we have come to expect from St. Pauli supporters, the team were cheered at the final whistle, engulfing the entire end of the stadium in a wave of emotion. When the players finally returned to the dressing room, the cameras lingered on scores of St. Pauli fans weeping openly on the terrace. Others embraced, seeking solace in each other. From the green-haired punks with their 'Gegen Rechts' patches sewn onto the sleeves of their jackets to the older fans smeared in brown and white face paint, the emotion was the same: devastation that St. Pauli's three-year spell in the Bundesliga was over. One banner hanging from the fence read, 'FC St. Pauli – Damn, I love you'. After what players and fans had just been through, it seemed just perfect.

The structure of the league for the 1991–92 campaign was altered to accommodate sides from the former East Germany in the wake of the reunification. The second division of the Bundesliga was divided into two groups: North and South. The season was further complicated by a preliminary round of matches that ran until the December, with each of the 12 teams in the league playing each other home and away. At this point the league split into two with the top six teams playing each other twice again in a promotion play-off, while the bottom six teams played in a corresponding relegation play-off. FC St. Pauli, who had made the cut in December and were playing in the promotion play-off, couldn't grasp an immediate return to the Bundesliga, finishing fourth in the play-off round with a record of: won four, drawn two, lost four.

The following season, the North and South groups of the second division came back together, but St. Pauli came no closer to regaining their top-flight status. In fact they came perilously close to being relegated to the Regionalliga. After a promising start to the campaign, they faded badly, finishing 17th, one point and one place above the final relegation spot, occupied by SpVgg Unterhaching.

Promotion back to the Bundesliga was finally achieved in the 1994–95 season. After a slow start, things began to pick up for Uli Maslo's men. An impressive 4-1 away win at FC 08 Homburg marked the end of the first half of the season and saw them starting the Rückrunde in second place. The season also produced a decent run in the DFB Pokal with two trips to Berlin, beating Union Berlin in the first round, before a dramatic 4-3 win against Tennis Borussia in the following round. Another away victory against Saarbrücken set up a quarter-final tie against Kaiserslautern in the imposing Fritz-Walter-Stadion. This time, St. Pauli were unable to pull off another away victory, losing 4-2 in front of 24,000 spectators. The excitement of the cup was just a precursor to the drama that was to follow in the battle for promotion to the Bundesliga. After a slight dip in form in the spring, St. Pauli mounted a final push. It was still tight at the top and St. Pauli went into the final game of the season, at home to the already relegated Homburg, in the second promotion spot (of three; there were no promotion play-offs at this time), but they knew they would have to win to be completely sure of going up. The game was all but over and promotion all but won as early as the 37th minute when Jens Scharping put St. Pauli 3-0 ahead. After the break it was 4-0, and Scharping was on the score-sheet again on 84 minutes to make it 5-0. The party at the Millerntor was in full swing. As the clock crept ever closer to the final whistle, hundreds of

St. Pauli fans massed around the edge of the pitch waiting to mount a joyous pitch-invasion to celebrate promotion.

On 87 minutes, referee Bodo Brandt-Chollé blew his whistle for what was originally intended as a penalty – and hundreds of fans poured onto the pitch, assuming it was the end of the game. There followed a period of confusion and bewilderment that had a typically St. Pauli feel to it. The stadium announcer, Rainer Wulff, broadcast 'the game is not finished yet', urging the supporters to leave the pitch. Still, many continued to party, while others were shouting 'Ihr seid doof!' ('you are stupid!') from the terraces fearing that failure to complete the fixture might result in the club missing promotion. After what seemed like an eternity but was in reality about 15 minutes, a visibly shaken vice president Christian Hinzpeter announced via the stadium microphone that the match was indeed over, allowing fans and players alike to begin a series of celebrations that would last long into the warm June night. In front of the TV cameras, Brandt-Chollé steadfastly refused to admit he had intended anything else than to end the game. It was not until ten years later that he publicly told the true story behind the early end of that legendary match. The fact that he knew beforehand that this was to be the final match before his retirement from refereeing might have contributed to his relaxed handling of things. Afterwards he celebrated with his linesmen among ecstatic fans and still remembers this 'wonderful day' fondly.

St. Pauli's return to the Bundesliga began in explosive fashion. A remarkable 4-2 opening day win over 1860 Munich at the Millerntor created a little bit of history. The following morning the tabloid sports pages contained a league table that showed FC St. Pauli top of the Bundesliga, ahead of the mighty Bayern Munich on goal difference. Nonsense, of course, with only one game played but something that made supporters smile and even gave them hope that the season could be something other than a long slog for survival. However, that's pretty much what the 1995–96 campaign turned out to be. St. Pauli clung to the upper echelons of the Bundesliga until the fourth round, then slipped steadily down the table, finishing 15th, just one place and two points above the relegation zone.

Trouble had flared during the away game with Hansa Rostock. St. Pauli fans were attacked both inside and outside the stadium, while legendary goalkeeper Klaus Thomforde was treated by paramedics suffering the effects of a smoke-bomb that was thrown in his direction. It was a game that certainly fuelled the bitter rivalry between the two North German clubs, which is also perceived as a clash of ideologies. In 1992, Rostock's Lichtenhagen district was the scene of the biggest racist riots in Germany's post-war history. In 1993, this rivalry inspired Bernd Schadewald's film *Schicksalsspiel* ('Match of Fate', official foreign title: *Soccer Love*), a slightly cheesy Romeo-and-Juliet-style love story between a male St. Pauli supporter and a waitress from Rostock set amidst rampant riots between their rival camps. However, on the pitch, it was a case of mission accomplished. Survival had been secured and FC St. Pauli had lived to fight another day in Germany's top division.

The 1996–97 campaign was a relegation battle almost from the outset. Despite a rare win against Bochum, followed by a draw at home with 1860 Munich, Uli Maslo was sacked after a disastrous 4-0 away defeat to fellow strugglers SC Freiburg. His former assistant, Klaus-Peter 'Ka Pe' Nemet, took over but he couldn't stop St. Pauli's slide towards the second division. The last seven games of the season were lost, including a 6-0 thumping in Bochum. St. Pauli finished the season in last place, 13 points short of safety.

The next two seasons were remarkable only for the number of managerial changes at the Millerntor. Ka Pe Nemet was replaced by Eckhard Krautzun in the summer of 1997, but he only lasted until the November of that year, replaced in turn by Gerhard Kleppinger. Kleppinger himself was only three months in the job when he was succeeded by former boss Willi Reimann in January 1999.

The 1999–2000 season was memorable, if only for the drama that ensued on the last day of the season. Willi Reimann had been relieved of his duties on 14 March 2000, to be replaced by Dietmar Demuth the next day, but despite another managerial change St. Pauli continued to flirt with relegation to the Regionalliga. They really needed a decent win against Rot-Weiss Oberhausen at the Millerntor in the final game of the season to be sure of survival. They were level on points with Stuttgarter Kickers going into the game, with just one goal superior goal difference. It was incredibly tight. Disaster struck early, with Oberhausen taking the lead after 31 minutes. The score remained 1-0 to the visitors at half-time, as news that Stuggarter Kickers were 1-0 up in Karlsruhe started to filter through. As it stood, St. Pauli were heading to the Regionalliga. Better news filtered through from Karlsruhe: they had equalised against Stuttgarter Kickers, St. Pauli just needed to find a goal from somewhere and hope the Kickers' score remained the same.

Time was running out and the tension at the Millerntor was unbearable. Incredibly, in the 90th minute the ball was launched towards the Südkurve and the Oberhausen penalty area, Ivan Klasnić refused to give up as the ball bobbled around the area and fired a shot-cum-cross across the penalty area that was fired into the roof of the net by the in-rushing Marcus Marin. The stadium went mental, then held its breath. The final whistle blew and the agonising wait for news from Karlsruhe began. Finally it was confirmed: Karlsruhe and Stuttgarter Kickers had also drawn 1-1, assuring St. Pauli's survival on goal difference. Another pitch invasion followed, mixing celebration and relief in equal measure. That last-minute goal by Marin was a moment many St. Pauli fans, Sven Brux among them, describe as their favourite in many years of watching their team. The club had stared down the barrel of the gun, but had somehow dodged the bullet and escaped demotion to the Regionalliga – for a few seasons at least.

Indeed, St. Pauli were heading in the exact opposite direction. The 2000–2001 campaign was something of a miracle. Off the pitch, the Fanladen celebrated their tenth birthday. The occasion was marked with a concert and party that included a set from Attila the Stockbroker, the English punk-poet, who had been told of St. Pauli at a Political Song Festival in East Berlin in 1989. He first watched St. Pauli the following year and had been returning to the Millerntor ever since. By the beginning of May 2001 St. Pauli were looking good for promotion. A trip to the Tivoli resulted in a win in Aachen and put St. Pauli within touching distance of promotion. The game also saw a protest by 100 or so St. Pauli fans who had purchased tickets for the seated section next to the guest-block and unfurled a banner that read 'Big Schily Is Watching You', a reference to Interior Minister Otto Schily, who had been tightening controls on football supporters through an increased police presence and the emergence of CCTV within stadiums.

St. Pauli had a chance to clinch promotion back to the Bundesliga at the Millerntor in the penultimate game of the season against Hannover

96. Frustratingly, they found themselves 2-0 down at the break. It took a goal from Holger Stanislawski to get them back into the game, and a point was saved eight minutes from time when Ivan Klasnić equalised. It meant that St. Pauli would have to travel to 1. FC Nürnberg on the final day of the season needing a victory to be sure of promotion.

Once again, the Fanladen organised two special trains as more than 5,000 St. Pauli fans made the journey to Nürnberg. Even more remarkably, a crowd estimated between 20,000 and 30,000 watched the match on a giant screen on the Heiligengeistfeld. In familiar fashion, St. Pauli found themselves a goal down, before Dubravko Kolinger equalised on the stroke of half-time, sending fans both in the Frankenstadion and on the Heiligengeistfeld into a frenzy. Better was to come with Deniz Baris heading home the winner as the ball cannoned back towards him off the crossbar.

Wild scenes ensued, with players celebrating with fans, while the already promoted Nürnberg fans spilled onto the pitch and looked on. It was truly 'the miracle promotion' – nothing in particular had been expected of the team the previous August, with the press seeing St. Pauli and its team of largely unknowns as the number one candidate for relegation. The return to the Bundesliga lived long in the memory and was immortalised in a partially ironic advertisement that ran along the length of roof on the Gegengerade stand. It read: '1954 The Miracle of Bern, 1966 The Goal of Wembley, 2001 The Rise of St. Pauli' – the advert comparing St. Pauli's promotion to the Bundesliga with two of the most iconic events in German football folklore.

The next two seasons can be classified as total disasters. The return to the Bundesliga would last just one season, with FC St. Pauli finishing bottom and recording just four wins during the entire campaign, all of them at home. The most famous of these victories was undoubtedly the 2-1 victory over Bayern Munich on 6 February 2002. A packed Millerntor watched an upset unfold, with FC St. Pauli scoring twice in three minutes during the first half. Thomas Meggle (Fussball-Gott) swivelled inside the area and fired St. Pauli ahead with a shot beyond the reach of Bayern's Oliver Kahn. Kahn was beaten again just minutes later when Nico Patschinski fired home from close range. Despite Bayern pulling a goal back three minutes from time, St. Pauli held on for a famous victory. After a 1-0 victory over Boca Juniors in Tokyo in the 2001 Intercontinental Cup the previous November, Bayern Munich were effectively the best club in the world. On the back of St. Pauli's victory over them, the club sold huge amounts of a T-shirt bearing the legend, 'Weltpokalsiegerbesieger' – translated somewhat clumsily as 'World Club Cup beaters'.

Off the pitch, during the winter break, the Fanladen moved premises the short distance from Thadenstraße to Brigittenstraße – a human chain of around 300 volunteers helping with the switch. A 4-0 defeat at the hands of HSV in the 'home' derby game played, once again, away from the Millerntor at the AOL Arena, was memorable for the impressive choreo organised by St. Pauli fans. The top tier was a sea of sparklers, the middle tier a collage of brown and white checks with the bottom tier depicting a pirate ship on a blue sea. The banner that spread across the width of the St. Pauli end read, 'FC St. Pauli is the honourable ruler of Hamburg and the seven seas.' In terms of creative, and passionate support yes; unfortunately, on the pitch the team were well and truly scuttled – much worse than in the 'away' derby, when St. Pauli had almost managed an improbable comeback: after 0-3 in the first half, the game ended 4-3, with one goal by Thomas Meggle and two by André Trulsen, who almost scored the equaliser with his third.

FC St. Pauli's relegation at the end of the 2001–02 season didn't come as a surprise to anyone. They'd been in the bottom two since the fourth Spieltag in early August. Yet few could've anticipated back then that the club would go into a tailspin that saw back-to-back relegations and a financial crisis that almost put them out of existence. It was hard to believe that salvation would come, in part, from another home fixture against Bayern Munich.

St. Pauli's relegation from the Bundesliga had obvious financial implications. Players signed to play in the top flight on high wages became a burden on finances in the second division. The club had already been hit by the collapse of a shirt sponsorship deal with 'World of Internet' a couple of years earlier. On several occasions during the 1990s the club had been helped out financially by then chairman, 'Papa' Heinz Weisener. But by 2000, Weisener himself had run into financial difficulties and had stood down from his role as club president. FC St. Pauli no longer had someone they could rely on to bail them out of a crisis. There would also be a longer-term headache for the club, resulting from Weisener's departure. In trouble financially, Heinz Weisener sold 50 per cent of the club's merchandising and marketing rights (which he owned) to a company called Upsolut. It was a deal that would have long-lasting ramifications for the club.

The 2002–03 season got off to a disastrous start. A 4-0 opening day defeat in the Waldstadion against Eintracht Frankfurt was followed by a 4-1 reverse at the Millerntor at the hands of LR Ahlen. A 6-1 thumping at VfB Lübeck in the third game of the season compounded a miserable start to life back in 2. Bundesliga. True, the next game saw FC St. Pauli record a 7-1 home win over Eintracht Braunschweig, but this was a rare bright spot in a season that saw the club record just seven victories. Just as it had been the year before, relegation seemed inevitable. Despite a late rally that saw St. Pauli beat MSV Duisburg at the Millerntor in the penultimate game of the season, relegation to the Regionalliga Nord was confirmed by a 4-1 defeat to Alemannia Aachen at the Tivoli on the final day. For the first time in 17 years, St. Pauli found themselves back in the third tier of German football. There was no guarantee the fall from grace would end there.

There remained the very real possibility of FC St. Pauli being refused a licence to play in the Regionalliga, triggering a further demotion to the Oberliga that would threaten the club's very future. Falling from the first to the third tier in successive seasons had devastated the club's finances. Television income was slashed, and coupled with over-spending on facilities and wages, FC St. Pauli found themselves in dire financial straits. The DFB demanded the books show a financial reserve of €1.95 million or they would refuse to grant a licence for the club to play in the Regionalliga, money that had to be in place by 11 June 2003. The club looked at selling key assets, including their youth training facilities, which were bought by the City of Hamburg for €720,000. However, this still left a huge hole in the accounts that needed to be filled – quickly.

The club launched a number of income generating schemes. Ticket sales were brought forward, and on the first day of sale more than 1,000 season tickets were sold, and over that summer, an incredible 11,700 season tickets were bought by fans eager to help save the club. However, this wasn't the most notable or financially beneficial aspect of the fund raising that occurred that year. The club launched their 'Retter' or

'Saviour' campaign. T-shirts were printed with the club logo (surrounded by the word 'Weltpokalsiegerbesieger') and 'RETTER' written beneath it. The implication was clear: each and every person who bought a T-shirt (priced at €15 and making the club a reported €10 per shirt) was helping to save the club. In *FC St. Pauli. Das Buch*, Corny Littmann reflected, 'As 25,000 were sold, there were no brown T-shirts left in Europe. So I said, okay, let's print black ones.' It was an incredible response. 'Retter' T-shirts were worn all over Germany, and were even spotted in the rest of Europe. Other clubs helped out too. Rapid Vienna bought five 'Retter' T-shirts and auctioned them on their website. Controversially, the 'Retter' T-shirts were also stocked and sold at local branches of McDonalds, leading to criticism from many fans. There were other initiatives too, including 'Drink for St. Pauli.' On Friday 6 and Saturday 7 June, local pubs and bars added 50 cents to the price of each beer they sold, with the extra money – in the region of €20,000 – going to the club. More money was raised from the 'Drink Astra – Save St. Pauli' initiative that saw €1 donated for every crate of Astra sold.

The fund-raising initiatives worked. On 10 June 2003, one day before the DFB's deadline, HSH Nordbank guaranteed the €1.95 million needed to secure the club's participation in the 2003–04 Regionalliga. On 12 July, Uli Hoeness brought his Bayern Munich team to the Millerntor for a pre-season friendly dubbed 'Retter Finale'. The match raised a further €200,000, and saw Hoeness don a 'Retter' T-shirt in front of the Nordkurve as he and Corny Littmann joined the players in a lap of honour at the end of the game. Before the summer was out, the Millerntor also hosted a fund-raising music festival.

If the summer had been eventful – and a close season doesn't get more dramatic than securing the club's future – the 2003–04 season was something of an anti-climax. There was no immediate return to the second division. In fact, after a 1-0 defeat against Rot-Weiss Essen at the end of April, St. Pauli slipped to 14th, just one position above the drop zone. The following Monday, manager Franz Gerber was replaced by Andreas Bergmann, who stepped up from managing the club's amateur side. One thing remained constant during a season that started with an unrecognisable team and included a change of manager – the fans.

Following on from the incredible volume of season ticket sales that formed part of the campaign to save the club, the support never waivered. Pre-match choreos were impressive and ingenious. There were also derby games, albeit against Hamburger SV's amateur side, and they yielded an impressive 3-0 win at the Millerntor, followed by a 1-0 reverse away from home. The game at the Volksparkstadion proved controversial from the supporters' perspective. The choreography for the guest block had been carefully prepared weeks in advance, but ended up being banned, leading to considerable ill-feeling among the St. Pauli support.

The following season saw FC St. Pauli again finish mid-table in the Regionalliga Nord. Off the pitch the club, in conjunction with the Fanladen, the Fanclub Sprecherrat and FARE (Football Against Racism in Europe), unveiled a plaque in front of the Südtribüne that read: 'In memory of members and fans of FC St. Pauli between the years of 1933 and 1945 who were persecuted or murdered by the Nazi dictatorship'. It was the club remembering the past and reaffirming its stance against racism and fascism in modern-day Europe.

Tensions continued to exist between elements of St. Pauli's fan base and Corny Littmann. 'Littmann Raus' banners were a regular feature in the USP's section of the Gegengerade, angered by police repression and stadium bans of its members. There was also continued dissatisfaction with on-going financial problems. During the winter break the club once again flirted with insolvency before reaching an agreement with the tax office.

On a happier note, the 2004–05 season celebrated the 15th anniversary of the Fanladen, an event marked with a party and numerous speeches. It also saw the publication of the excellent book, *15 Jahre Fanladen St. Pauli, 20 Jahre Politik im Stadion*, which has been an invaluable reference tool in the writing of this book. The team also visited Havana, Cuba, during the winter break, playing several friendly matches. The legacy of this was the effect it had on the squad, and one player in particular, Benny Adrion. Rather than staying holed-up in a training camp, the team visited local towns and villages, and Adrion was moved to help launch an initiative to provide clean drinking water to local schools and nurseries. When, the following year, injury brought a premature end to Benny's career, he decided to set up a charity to help provide clean drinking water in developing countries. In September 2006, *Viva con Agua de Sankt Pauli* was formally established.

The charity has raised money through a variety of cultural events, including football matches, concerts, fashion shows and marathons. Since its inception, the organisation has worked on projects to provide clean drinking water in Cuba, Ethiopia, Benin, Rwanda, Madagascar, Nicaragua, Tajikistan and Cambodia. Benny Adrion and his team have worked tirelessly to help improve the lives of people across the world, itself a pretty impressive benefit from a football club's tour of Cuba.

In 2009, the German President, Horst Koehler, awarded Benny Adrion the German Federal Cross of Merit in recognition of his work establishing Viva con Agua.

A third season in the Regionalliga Nord saw an increase in consistency but, ultimately, FC St. Pauli finished sixth, out of the promotion picture. However, the 2005–06 campaign is remembered for the epic cup run that saw the club reach the semi-finals of the DFB Pokal. It began, in late August, with a dramatic 3-2 win over Wacker Burghausen of 2. Bundesliga. Fewer than 10,000 fans were in the Millerntor to witness St. Pauli blow a 2-0 lead, pegged back by two late goals which took the tie into extra-time. Victory was secured in the 113th minute when Felix Luz stretched to head home the winner in front of the Nordkurve.

The next round saw a convincing 4-0 home victory over VfL Bochum under lights at the Millerntor, which included an incredible strike from Florian Lechner. Momentum was building. The next round, four days before Christmas, pitted FC St. Pauli against Bundesliga opposition, Hertha Berlin, at the Millerntor. It was a game packed with goals and drama. Hertha were 2-0 up on 40 minutes, before Michél Mazingu-Dinzey sprung the offside trap and pulled one back right on half-time. Four minutes from the end, a beautifully weighted corner from Mazingu-Dinzey was met by a flying Felix Luz and FC St. Pauli were level. Hertha took the lead in extra-time, before Lechner, with the aid of a slight deflection, made it 3-3. There was time for one more twist, with Robert Palikuca heading powerfully home at the far post from a corner to put FC St. Pauli 4-3 up and into the quarter-finals. The players had delivered an unlikely but very welcome early Christmas present and celebrated into the night with fans at the Millerntor.

The quarter-final took place on a freezing cold January evening. Snow had been falling throughout the day, and the pitch was blanketed with it. With hindsight, it is easy to say that Werder Bremen of the Bundesliga, packed full of stars including Miroslav Klose, Torsten Frings and former St. Paulianer, Ivan Klasnić, just didn't fancy it. However, footage of the teams lining up in the tunnel would appear to confirm this – the St. Pauli players look pumped up with Florian Lechner barely supressing a smile, while their counterparts from Bremen look like they'd rather have stayed in the warmth of the dressing room. Mazingu-Dinzey put FC St. Pauli ahead after just ten minutes on a pitch that resembled an ice-rink. Bremen levelled but goals from Fabian Boll and Timo Schultz gave St. Pauli a famous 3-1 victory. It was a game that would live long in the memory of the Millerntor faithful. In the morning, car owners across the district woke to '3-1' written on their snowy windscreens. Of course, FC St. Pauli now found themselves in the draw for the semi-final of the DFB Pokal.

Drawn at home, St. Pauli found themselves up against the reigning Bundesliga champions and DFB Pokal holders, Bayern Munich. By now, the Pokal had been renamed 'Bokal' due to the fact that the club had faced opposition from Burghausen, Bochum, Berlin, Bremen and now Bayern. A banner at the Millerntor added 'Bokal' and 'Barcelona' to the list, in honour of the final and a potential European tie with the mighty Catalan club. Sadly, FC St. Pauli didn't make the final. Owen Hargreaves opened the scoring for Bayern after 15 minutes. And although St. Pauli created numerous chances, they weren't converted, and eventually the German champions made them pay, with two late goals from Pizarro, giving Bayern a flattering 3-0 victory. The cup run had taken the club and its fans on an incredible journey, and crucially given them both renewed hope for a promotion push in the 2006–07 season and a much needed boost to their finances (it has been acknowledged that the Millerntor rebuilding programme which began in 2007 wouldn't have been possible without the funds generated by the cup run).

There would be no cup run to distract the team in 2006–07. In a twist of fate, the first-round visitors to the Millerntor were Bayern Munich. Timo Schultz fired St. Pauli ahead in spectacular fashion from a Mazingu-Dinzey pull-back, but Podolski levelled for Bayern just after the interval. Thanks to a string of incredible saves from Paddy Borger in the St. Pauli goal, the game went into extra-time, but in the 105th minute he was finally beaten, turning a cross-cum-shot from Philipp

Lahm into his own net. It was heart-breaking for Borger, who had done so much to keep his side in the tie until that point.

There was still hope that this would be the season that FC St. Pauli would end their exile in the wilderness of the Regionalliga. However, the first half of the campaign was blighted by draws, and after the seventh draw, at home to FC Rot-Weiss Erfurt, Andreas Bergmann was sacked and replaced with club legend Holger Stanislawski.

Stanislawski didn't get off to he best of starts, losing 3-0 in Dresden, but after the winter break St. Pauli found the knack of turning those annoying draws into victories. The club climbed the table, finding themselves top after an away win against Werder Bremen's amateur side after the 34th Spieltag. Thousands of fans had made the short trip south-west to Bremen, making it feel like a home game, and for many it was the moment that promotion became a real possibility. The celebrations at the end of the game in the Weserstadion were spectacular, with an emotional rendition of *You'll Never Walk Alone* living long in the memory of those that were there.

Important victories over Fortuna Düsseldorf at the Millerntor and away at FC Rot-Weiss Erfurt left FC St. Pauli needing just one point from their final two league games to secure promotion. Surely, St. Pauli, even with their knack of heroic failure, couldn't stuff this up? The penultimate game of the 2006–07 was on a Friday night at the Millerntor at home to Dynamo Dresden. The Millerntor was sold out with 15,500 fans (the capacity reduced as the old Südkurve had been demolished to make way for a new stand and facilities required for the club to maintain its professional licence). An estimated 10,000 fans watched the game on big screens on the Reeperbahn. Charles Takyi fired St. Pauli ahead from the penalty spot after 14 minutes to help calm an incredibly tense Millerntor. Dresden equalised on the stroke of half-time when a long-range effort squirmed through a mass of bodies in the penalty area, just to ratchet up the tension again. Seven minutes from the end, Carsten Rothenbach put 2. Bundesliga within touching distance when he headed home from close range. However, Dresden leveled on 90 minutes with a carbon copy of their first-half goal. The Millerntor held its breath. A draw would be enough, but Dresden couldn't snatch a last-minute winner, could they? As Dresden launched the ball into the penalty area for one last assault on Patrick Borger's goal, the ball was cleared upfield, leaving Michel Mazingu-Dinzey racing clear with only the keeper to beat. His low shot crashed against the upright, but it didn't matter. Seconds later the final whistle blew. FC St. Pauli were back in the second division with a game to spare.

The celebrations really did last all night. Eventually, the players left the pitch wearing 'Back from Hell' T-shirts, but the party continued in the dressing room and on the Reeperbahn for hours afterwards. Finally, after three seasons in the Regionalliga Nord, FC St. Pauli, under the leadership of Holger Stanislawski and André Trulsen, were returning to the second tier of the Bundesliga.

Chapter 8
ULTRA SANKT PAULI

Choreo, blockades and boycotts

THIS MAY COME as a shock to fans who visit the Millerntor from overseas, but Ultrà Sankt Pauli (USP) divide opinion. In one sense this shouldn't be surprising as for years ultra groups across Europe have courted controversy: there are those that disagree with the hold that certain ultra groups have over individual clubs, or the influence they exert inside stadiums; then there's the debate over the political allegiances of various groups and the assumption, in the mainstream press at least, that being an ultra is synonymous with being a hooligan.

However, the majority of criticism levelled at ultra groups in general can't really be applied to Ultrà Sankt Pauli. For a start, their politics are sound, and fit with the left-wing ethos of the majority of St. Pauli fan groups. They don't exert an undue hold over the club; in fact, they are often very vocal opponents of certain club policies, especially during Corny Littmann's time as president. They are also not a group that goes looking for confrontations with other fan groups or that advocates violence in any way. Indeed, watching FC St. Pauli for the first time, it is impossible not to be spellbound by USP. If, like many international fans visiting the Millerntor for the first time, you obtain your tickets via the Fanladen, there is a good chance you will find yourself with a ticket for the Südkurve, and, depending where you choose to stand, you could find yourself standing with Ultrà Sankt Pauli. Those people that have stood directly behind the goal on the Südkurve will know, first hand, what an incredible experience it is. The singing is incessant: from the moment the stadium announcer kills the music ten minutes before kick-off until long after the final whistle. Any lulls in support are soon quashed by the members of USP standing on the fence and starting a new song or urging fans to sing a little louder. If you have been really fortunate you may have witnessed, or more likely taken an active role in, one of the many impressive choreographies that Ultrà Sankt Pauli put together as the teams run out. And if you return to the Südkurve more than once hopefully you'll have dropped a few spare Euros into the collection buckets that help fund these stunning visual displays of support. Even if you've stood or sat elsewhere in the stadium, you can't have helped be impressed by the atmosphere and vibrancy that USP bring to proceedings, especially when comparing it with the lack-lustre support and distinct lack of atmosphere that dominates football matches in the UK.

However, the ultra style of support is not to everyone's taste, and there are fan groups within the Millerntor that feel Ultrà Sankt Pauli exert too much control over the nature of support and choice of songs. It is true that USP are unwavering in their support – to the point that what is actually occurring on the pitch is largely irrelevant. They will sing, working through their repertoire of songs regardless. To those of us that have chosen to follow FC St. Pauli from overseas this is part of the attraction, yet there are fans that hanker for the 'English model' of support, a model that is more reactive to what is going on in the match, the atmosphere in the stands being a reflection of what is being played out in front of them.

On occasion, Ultrà Sankt Pauli has also courted controversy with their actions inside the stadium, with some even arguing that their attempts to lead and direct other supporters are counterproductive and controlling. This chapter will go on to look in more detail at one specific example of controversial action by USP during the home game against Hansa Rostock on 28 March 2010, and how it divided fan opinion at the Millerntor. First, it would be prudent to sketch an outline of Ultrà Sankt Pauli, how they came into being and how far their influence on the St. Pauli fan scene extends.

Keen observers will have noted that the year 2002 often appears underneath the braun-weiss images of Che Guevara on Ultrà Sankt Pauli's badges and banners. This is a direct reference to the year of the group's foundation. Prior to 2002, the first fan group to openly model themselves on the Italian ultra model of support were 'Carpe Diem'. In turn, Carpe Diem (translated from the Latin as 'seize the day') had been formed by members of the 'Klaus Thomforde' fan group named after the popular goalkeeper of the late 1980s and early 1990s (Thomforde was voted as the all-time number one goalkeeper in a team chosen to celebrate St. Pauli's centenary celebrations in 2010).

The 'Klaus Thomforde' fan group changed its name to 'Carpe Diem' in 1999, on Thomforde's retirement. The group's banner hung in pride of place at the front of the southern corner of the Gegengerade, and as a group they took the lead in developing pre-match choreographies and were responsible for adding colour and noise to that particular area of the stadium. They may have shifted along the terrace towards the southern end of the stadium but in terms of noise, politics and enthusiasm, Carpe Diem, and then USP, followed a direct lineage from those original Hafenstraße residents who first gathered together behind the dugouts on the back straight.

In 2002, as a result of continued growth in membership, Carpe Diem and several other smaller, active fan groups came together to create Ultrà Sankt Pauli. As with any amalgamation of this type, the transition wasn't always smooth and there were disagreements between members. However, the over-arching aim was agreed: to create an organised and united fan group, rooted in the strong traditions of left-wing politics and anti-fascism that had been present among supporters since the mid-1980s. This point was confirmed by Martin from USP in an interview I conducted with him for the Yorkshire St. Pauli fanzine in October 2012: 'it's a fact that a small group of freaks nobody in the Gegengerade wanted to understand became one of the most formative groups of FC St. Pauli's fan scene. One of the reasons for that is the move to the south stand terrace. But what's important as well: we carry on and flesh out the values of the active supporters scene that make the club so special since the 1980s.'

Along with the club's flirtations with the Bundesliga in the mid-1990s and again, for one solitary season in 2001–02, came concerns that St. Pauli's fan base was losing its radical edge; that the number of fans prepared to actively support the team was dwindling. As we have seen already, and will return to in the 'Sozialromantiker' chapter, concerns over the dilution of fan culture and the loss of atmosphere are reoccurring themes among St. Pauli's reflective fan base. United under the Ultrà Sankt Pauli banner, members hoped to revive the ailing fan scene and inspire a new generation of active fans. While some existing fans expressed concerns, perhaps happy with how things were at the Millerntor, Ultrà Sankt Pauli continued to grow and began to extend its influence.

Today, Ultrà Sankt Pauli has around 50 to 60 active members, although the number of people who identify and associate with the group is much larger, swelled by those who hold a 'Südkurven-Card' which gives them access to USP merchandise and discounts. With the completion of the new South Stand in 2007, USP relocated from the corner of the Gegengerade to the terrace of the Südkurve. Although relationships between USP and the club have often been frayed, it is widely accepted that this stretch of terrace is the home of USP, and as such they are allowed to organise and direct choreography and place what is commonly referred to in ultra circles as a 'capo' (loosely translated from the Italian as 'leader') but that USP prefer to call a 'Vorsänger' (which translates as 'leading voice' or 'choir leader') at the front of the terrace armed with a megaphone imploring the crowd to sing as one. This grants USP a degree of autonomy and is an acknowledgment of the atmosphere that they help provide.

Ultrà Sankt Pauli offer an open membership and encourage those people considering getting more involved in their fan scene the opportunity to attend regular Wednesday evening meetings at the Fanladen. Although the number actively involved with day-to-day activities is much smaller than the overall membership, the group still adopt a democratic and non-hierarchical structure to decision making. Perhaps the most obvious example of this democracy in action came during the derby game against HSV in February 2011: after police stormed the away supporters block causing a crush in the tightly packed terrace area, injuring several fans in the process (the police action was in response to St. Pauli fans letting off flares and a smoke bomb – at precisely 19.10) members of USP took a show of hands from the crowd as to whether to stay inside the stadium or to walk out in a peaceful protest against the reaction of the police. Between 40 to 60 fans (mostly USP members) walked out of the stadium, missing one of the most famous victories in the club's history on a point of principle. It is one example, but it highlights how much emphasis USP places on the values they stand for.

During Corny Littmann's presidency, Ultrà Sankt Pauli were often at odds with the club in general and the president in particular. The 'Littmann Raus!' banners mentioned elsewhere were a regular feature on the Gegengerade as USP (and other supporters) clashed with the president over banning orders handed out to fans as well as the increased commercialisation of the club. However, after Littmann's departure in 2010, relations between the club and the group improved. USP also had one of their own on the playing staff in the shape of goalkeeper Benedikt Pliquett. Indeed, it was Pliquett, given a starting place by manager Holger Stanislawski, for the 2011 derby against HSV, who produced a number of fine saves to help the club achieve a first league win over their bitter rivals since 1977 – particularly ironic as many of his most ardent fans in USP had taken the decision to leave the stadium.

As mentioned at the start of this chapter, USP are not universally popular with other sections of St. Pauli's support, although it must be said, the majority of fans inside the Millerntor recognise and value the role they play in generating atmosphere. In recent times, one particular action went a long way to polarising opinion about Ultrà Sankt Pauli.

In advance of the 28th Spieltag of the 2009–10 season at home to Hansa Rostock, despite opposition from the Ständiger Fanausschuss – a panel of fan representatives from around 13 different fan groups, that meets every four to six weeks to discuss key issues with the club – St. Pauli decided to reduce Rostock's ticket allocation from the usual 1,900 to just 500. The decision to limit away fans was a result of trouble the previous season that had seen violent clashes with police outside the Feldstraße U-Bahn and outside the ground. The match itself, a dramatic 3-2 win for St. Pauli, was stopped for a few minutes as the ground was engulfed in smoke caused by Rostock fans setting the guest block ablaze with a series of flares and fireworks. There had also been trouble at the game in Rostock earlier in the 2009–10 season with many St. Pauli fans being attacked as they left their chartered train.

Despite Hansa Rostock being bitter rivals, St. Pauli fans were outraged by the reduction of tickets for away fans. Ultrà Sankt Pauli issued a statement on their website that said: 'Rostock today, tomorrow us?' This was a ground-breaking decision, an attack on supporters' rights and there was general agreement that this could signal the start of away fans being limited or prevented from attending games that the authorities viewed as 'high-risk'. Supporters felt particularly let down by the club itself; they felt that it was FC St. Pauli that was driving the decision, rather than the police. The USP website stated that it was the club who had made a representation to the German Football League with regard to banning away fans or limiting the ticket allocation, and it was only when this suggestion was dismissed that they sought the backing of the police to request a reduction in Rostock fans. USP stated: 'Although the police issued the injunction, it corresponds exactly to the interests of the Presidency of FC St. Pauli. It is the club's management which creates an unparalleled precedent.' Never before had FC St. Pauli sought to ban or reduce the number of away fans attending a game at the Millerntor. As USP stated this was unprecedented, and despite it being Hansa Rostock fans that would suffer, they were totally opposed to this course of action.

In the end, Rostock refused their entire ticket collection, leading to a piece of Millerntor history: a game taking place without any away fans. Despite the ongoing rivalry and the questionable politics of some Rostock fans, various St. Pauli supporters' groups continued to lobby the club to change their minds and, when it became apparent there was to be no reversal, they met to agree a course of action.

The outcome of that meeting was the organisation of what subsequently became referred to as the 'blockade'. Various fan groups lent their support for a five-minute boycott of the game by fans on the Südkurve in solidarity with the locked-out Rostock fans and as a stand against the infringements of supporters' rights. The boycott would send a very visual message to the club, the police and the football authorities: here were one set of supporters prepared to put aside their differences and show solidarity, over the exclusion of rival fans. The teams would take to the field with large swathes of terracing left deliberately empty.

It is important to note that, although USP were widely portrayed as being the sole instigators of the blockade, the action had actually been approved by the Ständiger Fanausschuss. This was not unilateral action agreed and carried out solely by Ultrà Sankt Pauli.

As spectators made their way up the steps leading to the Südkurve on that overcast Sunday lunchtime in March, they were greeted by banners informing them of the intention to boycott the first five minutes of the match in protest at the club and police decision to exclude away fans from attending the Millerntor. As previously mentioned, there is no love lost between the fans of FC St. Pauli and Hansa Rostock, yet here a significant group of St. Pauli supporters were acting in solidarity with their rivals from near the Baltic; in turn they hoped and expected a similar level of solidarity from the rest of the home fans making their way into the ground. Of course, it wasn't just about the fans of Hansa Rostock, it was about the club's decision and the police response too. But it was also about the bigger picture: if the authorities could decide one week that fans of Hansa Rostock couldn't visit the Millerntor because of the risk of trouble, who was to say that a few weeks or months down the line, St. Pauli fans wouldn't be prevented from visiting the likes of Dynamo Dresden on a similar pretext. Extrapolating this theory further, if it was allowed to happen once then the same ruling could be applied to fans of any club at any time on the whim of the police or the football authorities.

As kick-off approached, both the away terrace and the Südkurve were eerily silent. A group of Rostock fans had been allowed into the stadium to hang their protest banners but had since vacated the terracing in the far corner of the ground. The Südkurve was also deserted aside from a huge banner that read, 'Stell dir vor es ist fussball und keiner darf hin' (which translates roughly as, 'imagine if there's football on and nobody is allowed to go.') Even with 20 minutes to go until kick-off, the sight of the players warming up in front of totally empty stretches of terracing was striking. This is what USP and others were hoping for, the dramatic impact of an empty home terrace beamed across Germany (and around the world, at least to those watching on live internet feeds). A clear message to the police and football authorities: without us the game means nothing. The plan was for the terrace to remain empty for the first five minutes and then for fans to enter the terrace and pick up the time-honoured chant of 'Aux Armes!' On their website, USP called upon the rest of the stadium to take up the chant 'with all its might'. As we shall see, the reception wasn't quite as triumphant as USP had hoped for.

With kick-off approaching rapidly, the mood on the concourse underneath the Südkurve was beginning to change as it filled with spectators and it became apparent that their entrance to the terrace itself was being blocked. The film-maker Felix Grimm was recording the scene on the Südkurve for his documentary *Das Ganze Stadion*. The footage, included as an extra on the DVD, captures the mood change. Perhaps there was a significant body of fans that were simply unaware of the boycott, although this is unlikely as it had been well publicised before the game in the media and online. The film footage clearly displays the banners alerting fans to the boycott and also shows leaflets being distributed to fans approaching the Südkurve. Perhaps, the balance between active, politically aware St. Pauli fans and those who just come for the football had shifted more emphatically in favour of the latter than even the most cynical 'radical' fan could have envisaged.

Either way, the atmosphere changed as people were prevented from taking their space on the terrace and, as a result of the crowds in the concourse, were also unable to make their way to their seats above. As USP were at pains to point out, blocking access to the seats had never been part of the plan.

Undoubtedly, conditions in the concourse weren't ideal. There was a degree of pushing, shoving and jostling as fans disgruntled at being denied entrance to the terrace lost their patience with those barring their way. But tabloid reports of 'crying children in the terrifying crush' were typically sensationalist. In the aftermath, the organisers freely admitted they got elements of the organisation of the protest wrong, but the situation inside the stadium did not put spectators at risk. While the frustration of individual fans being barred from taking their place in the South Stand was understandable, the obscenities directed at those organising the blockade was far from acceptable.

In a statement regarding the blockade, the Fanladen reported that abusive, racist and homophobic language was directed at both USP and members of the Fanladen. This abuse shouted at fellow St. Pauli fans shocked many people, and reminded people that despite all the good work to rid the club of racism, homophobia and intolerance, these opinions could still be found among supporters on the Südkurve.

Those watching the game on television were totally unaware of the ugly atmosphere on the concourse under the Südkurve. Instead, the visual impact of a totally empty Südkurve had achieved what it set out to do: it sent a powerful message to the football authorities, a message that fans have rights. It was also an impressive show of solidarity with the fans of Hansa Rosock. Later, during the course of the game, a banner was unfurled on the terrace that summed up the delicate nature of the protest with considerable humour: it read: 'Even arseholes have rights!' – yes, some Rostock fans have 'questionable' political viewpoints, but even they don't deserve to be banned from travelling to watch their team.

Watching the events unfold on a live internet stream of the match, the action made me proud to be a St. Pauli fan. It marked us out as different; fans prepared to take a stand against the decisions imposed upon them. Once again, St. Pauli fans were capable of looking at the bigger picture. It was only as the five minutes of the blockade came to an end and fans started to stream onto the Südkurve that I heard the strains of 'Scheiß USP' being chanted by sections of the crowd, and I realised that this action wasn't universally popular.

The debate over the blockade raged for weeks, threatening to cause real fissures in the St. Pauli fan scene. Unfairly, it seemed to be USP who shouldered the majority of the blame. Perhaps the blockade gave those who disagree with USP's style of support something tangible to moan about. It is worth remembering that those standing on the Südkurve are aware that Ultrà Sankt Pauli exercise a degree of autonomy on what occurs on the terrace. USP believed, correctly, that they had the support of those supporters' groups that form the Ständiger Fanausschuss and from this they assumed that they had the tacit support of the majority of people who regularly stand on the Südkurve. Sadly, this wasn't the case. It was a shame that such a well-intentioned show of supporter solidarity caused such controversy. Mistakes were made, and in hindsight USP themselves admitted that while they had only intended to blockade the terrace the protest also stopped fans from reaching the seats above. To my mind, the blockade was a bold and just protest. It is also worth remembering that it was also largely symbolic: fans weren't prevented from watching the whole match; the blockade was only ever intended to last five minutes. It is a shame that those St. Pauli 'fans' that shouted racist and homophobic insults at those organising the blockade couldn't be identified and banned from the Südkurve for a great deal longer.

With FC St. Pauli spending the 2010–11 season in the Bundesliga, the issue of Hansa Rostock fans' right to travel to the Millerntor to watch their team didn't rear its head again until April 2012. The outcome was no less controversial. However, it did show that some of the interested parties had learned from the mistakes of the 2010 blockade. The Hamburg police decided that the only course of action was to once again ban Rostock fans. However, this time, to their credit, rather than accepting the police verdict the club decided to appeal against the decision. Sadly, the appeal against the provisional injunction wasn't successful and once again, away fans were excluded from the Millerntor (the club are continuing the battle to overturn the ruling in the longer term). Fans of Rostock decided to stage a march in Hamburg to protest against the decision. This, too ,was banned on the grounds that it might spill over into violence. However, on appeal, Hansa Rostock fans were allowed to march in protest through nearby Altona.

This time, rather than repeat the tactics of the blockade, Ultrà Sankt Pauli called for a boycott of the game by home supporters. As this idea gained momentum, the police began to panic. Suddenly, there was the possibility of large numbers of both sets of supporters on the streets while the match was being played. In draconian fashion, the police declared the whole district of St. Pauli a 'special zone'. This meant that from the docks and the Fischmarkt on the Elbe to Sternschanze in the north the police could use a range of special powers, that included the right to detain anyone without the correct ID or anyone they thought looked suspicious. The atmosphere in the days leading up to the game was tense, mostly due to the actions of the authorities.

The march through Altona by the Hansa Rostock fans passed off peacefully. It is important to remember that although Rostock have a minority hooligan element with distinct right-wing tendencies, they also have a majority of normal fans, who felt justly aggrieved at being deprived of a chance to watch their team play an important game against St. Pauli in their own club's fight against relegation. At the Millerntor, the protest started at around 11.00am with fans taking part in a funeral procession, carrying with them a coffin marked ' Fankultur' to signify the death of fan culture that a banning of away supporters represented. The procession ended at the Südvorplatz outside the stadium and the coffin was placed in front of the concrete FC St. Pauli logo and surrounded with red candles and flowers. As kick-off approached it became clear that a sizeable number of supporters were supporting

USP's boycott. It is estimated that between 1,500 and 2,000 fans remained outside the stadium, listening to the game on the radio, drinking beer and chatting peacefully with friends around the AFM container. They joined in with the chant of 'Aux Armes' and the mood was relaxed, with those boycotting the game in good spirits. It wasn't just USP; fans from all parts of the stadium had joined the boycott.

In many ways, it worked much better than the blockade of 2010, as fans were given a choice in how they wished to protest. It wasn't even a simple case of 'for or against' as many fans who didn't take part in the boycott still supported the protest from inside the stadium through a mixture of banners and chants. On the pitch, FC St. Pauli dispatched a weary Rostock side 3-0 to bolster their promotion hopes while at the same time further damaging Hansa's survival chances. Outside the stadium the first two goals had been joyfully celebrated but as the third goal went in things took an unexpected turn. Police sirens wailed and there were reports of a disturbance outside the Jolly Roger fan pub on Budapester Straße. Subsequent newspaper reports laid the blame for the disturbance with bottle-throwing 'ultras'. However, the accuracy of this claim remains in considerable doubt. USP had called for a peaceful boycott and up until this point the demonstration had been exactly that. It would seem incredibly strange for USP to then take part in a direct confrontation with the police.

It is more likely that the disturbance was started by a group of 'anarchist troublemakers' (as the tabloids are so fond of labelling them) with no link to USP or the football club but who saw the declaration of a 'special zone' and the heavy police presence as an opportunity for trouble. The police response was predictable: water cannons were deployed and large numbers of riot police were quickly on the scene in what looked from the video footage shot by fans standing on the Südvorplatz as a massive, almost comical show of strength by the authorities. Tensions were high as the stadium emptied and the crowds tried to make their way home after the match. Fortunately, despite the huge numbers of riot police, the majority of fans were allowed to leave peacefully. Unfortunately, a water cannon was still used fairly indiscriminately by the police, and later in the day a minority of idiots did get into further scuffles with the police and also used the occasion to launch an unprovoked attack on the HSV fan pub, smashing windows and causing damage. These actions were quickly condemned by the Fanladen.

The declaration of a police 'special zone', and the isolated incidents of trouble (perhaps connected, perhaps not?) were the low points of an otherwise successful protest. Although elements of the local media continued to demonise USP, inaccurately laying the blame for the violence at their door, the idea of a boycott had been a success. Just as in 2010, the boycott, like the blockade, hadn't been exclusively USP's doing. This time, however, the group came under far less criticism from other elements of the St. Pauli fan base. But once again, USP had shown that they were prepared to act on a point of principle. They were prepared to take part in a boycott for the greater good, in an effort to preserve fan culture both at the Millerntor and in German football in general.

There have been other successes. In October 2011, Ultrà Sankt Pauli were one of three organisations to be awarded the Hans Frankenthal Prize, awarded by the Auschwitz Committee Foundation, in recognition of USP's work fighting against fascism, racism and homophobia. Hans Frankenthal. and his brother Emil, survived the Holocaust and imprisonment in Auschwitz and Hans wrote about his experiences in the concentration camps – where both his parents died – and his post-war return to the small village of Schmallenberg, aged just 19, in a book, *The Unwelcome One: Returning Home from Auschwitz.*

USP were awarded the prize for establishing the Alerta Network, an international alliance of fan groups, all committed to fighting fascism. USP, via the Alerta Network, helps to organise the highly regarded and well-attended annual anti-racist football tournament, which attracts fan groups from all over Europe. In addition, two or three matchdays a year are devoted to promoting the Alerta Network inside the stadium, with pre-match choreos being devoted to spreading the anti-fascist, anti-racist message. The group also run workshops to educate and raise awareness among fans. The award was not only well-deserved recognition for USP's hard work fighting fascism, but also provided them with prize money that would continue to subsidise travel and material costs for networking and choreos, as well as enabling them to set up a website for the Alerta Network, raising its profile and making interaction with like-minded fan groups easier.

In addition to the prize money, USP were also given a bunch of flowers to celebrate their success and the next morning a small delegation laid them on the grave of communist resistance fighter Fritz Bringmann, who had been arrested and tortured for painting the slogan 'Down with Hitler' on a roof in 1935. Bringmann had spent the majority of his time in prison during Nazi rule. He once managed to escape, from the Neuengamme concentration camp on the outskirts of Hamburg, before being captured some seven weeks later. He died in April 2011, so the flowers were a fitting way for him to be remembered by USP.

Of course, while standing up for fan culture, making links and supporting other like-minded groups across Europe is part of USP's core-values (a recent collection for fans of MTZ Ripo in Belarus raised more than €2,000) Ultrà Sankt Pauli remain committed to improving the atmosphere at St. Pauli games. And whatever you think of the 'ultra' style of support, the ambitious choreographed displays on the Südkurve as the teams emerge from the tunnel are often spectacular. None more so than the choreo produced to celebrate ten years of Ultrà Sankt Pauli for the game against Eintracht Braunschweig in February 2012. As *Hells Bells* rang out, signifying the arrival of the teams, banners depicting a variety of freaks were unfurled across the length of the Südkurve. Along the entire length of the terrace at the front was a banner that read 'Wir Sind Ooooooh-Oh Sankt Pauli!' Fans waved brown and white flags in blocks either side of the centre-piece – a giant freak, eyes shut, head poking over the top of a fence. As the teams emerged, the eyelids slowly opened and revealed giant, blood-shot whites, which were soon replaced by swirling psychedelic eyeballs, being rotated by hand behind the choreo. It was mind-blowing. The attention to detail was spectacular. The entire choreo was soundtracked by a repetitive, low rumbling chant of 'Wir Sind Ooooooh-Oh, Sankt Pauli!'

As Martin from USP commented, 'It's difficult to say how long it took to prepare the choreo; it must have been a couple of weeks. Large, impressive and difficult displays are created based on ideas of many people at USP, it's like a constant, creative brainstorming. To plan and implement such actions we have a special group called "Choreogruppe". Everybody else can give suggestions and other input as well, naturally.'

It was another example of the incredible lengths to which USP go to demonstrate their support for the club and to add to the atmosphere inside the stadium. Sadly, the impressive choreo also attracted the attention of the DFB and resulted in a fine for the club, as the banners depicted a freak wearing a T-shirt with the legend 'ACAB' (All Cops Are Bastards) on the front while another held a scarf that said 'Bullenschweine'.

Despite the banners being largely satirical, they prompted a charge of 'unsporting behaviour' from the DFB. Commenting on this reaction, USP said, 'It is not tolerated to criticise institutions such as the DFB or the police. The punishment for the FC St. Pauli is absolutely ridiculous and shows once again how massive the conflict between active fans and DFB is. The supporters of FC St. Pauli, especially, are a thorn in the flesh of the DFB as they don't conform to expected behaviour, but communicate their critique openly and publicly.' It is hard to disagree.

In September 2012, for the home game against SV Sandhausen, USP ran another breathtaking choreo to further mark their tenth anniversary. There was no controversy this time, just a stunningly choreographed display, including an additional display as the teams re-emerged after half-time. The 10-year celebrations continued after the game, as Martin explained: 'At 3.00pm we met up in the district to start into the evening with beer, good music and fantastic food. By nightfall, more than 600 ultras, St. Pauli supporters and friends of the group went to Knust, a club close to the Millerntor ground where the actual party was to take place. It would be inappropriate to even try to describe how much fun we all had at that party, how much joy could be seen in the faces, how emotional the atmosphere was and how much we are still happy about it. To sum it up: it was perfect.'

As, can be seen from the examples above, the fan group Ultrà Sankt Pauli are often (unfairly) drawn into controversy, controversy that is usually the product of an overriding misunderstanding of USP's role in the St. Pauli fan scene. True, you might not agree with all their actions, you might also not approve of their unwavering style of support, but anyone that has stood on the Südkurve or with St. Pauli fans at away games can't have failed to notice that it is USP demanding fans sing their hearts out that adds to the unique atmosphere at matches involving St. Pauli.

USP are also sometimes misunderstood, and occasionally resented, by other supporter groups, but it is hard to disagree that the Millerntor in general and the Südkurve in particular would be a lot less atmospheric without them. They know that not every action they have taken in the last ten years has been a success. This capacity for self-reflection and self-regulation is another excellent feature of Ultrà Sankt Pauli. It is perhaps fitting to leave the last word to them. 'We discussed a lot, we made mistakes, but we never tried to avoid the dialogue with those that criticise us. Especially when considering the pre-conditions stated above, ten years of USP at the Millerntor are a downright success story, to the profit of everybody at the club.'

However, it is also worth remembering that despite a willingness to engage in dialogue with the club and other fan groups, USP has its own ideals and identities. As Martin stated, 'We cannot please all of the supporters and that is not the intention of an ultra group. We have our ideals, our values and our dreams, and we live them.'

And that is exactly how it should be.

Chapter 9
SOZIALROMANTIKER

THE RECORD BOOKS for FC St. Pauli's 2010–11 Bundesliga campaign deal exclusively with the facts: 34 league games that yielded eight wins, five draws and 21 defeats, finishing bottom of the league with 29 points and a goal difference of minus 33.

Make no mistake: it was a dismal return to the top flight. The low points were plentiful: a 13-game winless run, that stretched from February to the end of the season; the number of goals conceded in the last few minutes that turned wins into draws and draws into defeats; the humiliating 8-1 defeat at the hands of Bayern Munich in the last home game of the season. It was no way for the Millerntor faithful to say goodbye to manager Holger Stanislawski. The highs, meanwhile, were few and far between: that opening day win on a balmy summer's day in Freiburg promised so much; three wins in a row in January and February that saw FC St. Pauli climb to a respectable 11th, that culminated, of course, with Gerald Asamoah's winner in the Volksparkstadion against HSV on 16 February.

But what happened on the pitch wasn't the real story – a backdrop, yes – but the season will be remembered not for the on-the-pitch shortcomings, but the events that occurred off it, in the stands, on the terraces and elsewhere, in bars, cafes, homes, offices and out in cyberspace.

That the club was back in the top flight of German football for its centenary season had a certain fairytale quality to it. Unfortunately, one of the main things promotion back to the Bundesliga inadvertently achieved was to bring to a head long-running differences of opinion between those that run the club and those that support it.

Sozialromantiker

Perhaps the most obvious manifestation of these differences was the Haupttribüne, the new stand completed over the summer of 2010, with its business seats and executive boxes. As the Sozialromantiker (more of them shortly) commented: 'The old main stand (Haupttribüne) at the Millerntor was a bit different from many others in that it used to be the home of supporters with a variety of backgrounds, a relatively small hospitality section and even an informal support group.' The implication was clear: the old Haupttribüne, although not a hotbed of support like the Gegengerade or the Nord and Südkurve, was still a special place for those fans who chose to sit there. Despite offering arguably the best seats in the Millerntor, the old Haupttribüne wasn't the home of corporate 'guests' but a meeting place for ordinary fans, those who preferred to sit rather than stand.

As mentioned previously, by the start of the 2010–11 season, the Millerntor represented a perfect visual dichotomy of old and new, the dividing line a clear diagonal between the new South Stand and Haupttribüne and the down-at-heel Nordkurve and Gegengerade. Of course, things were not as clear cut as this architectural division between the smooth pre-cast concrete of the new stands and the crumbling, weather-beaten steps of the old suggests. The terracing on the Südkurve had already been appropriated by the fans through a series of stickers, artwork and spray-paint; while the Haupttribüne isn't entirely comprised of business seats and plays host to some active, albeit slightly older fan groups, among them the wonderfully named St. Pauli Oldtras.

There were certainly issues with the new Haupttribüne that weren't clearly identified when the new Südkurve was constructed. For a start, the rebuilding of the Südkurve was necessary in order for the club to retain the professional licence issued by the DFB. In addition, the new south stand, although containing a similarly high proportion of business seats and executive facilities, also included a new terrace that offered cheap standing for 3,000 spectators. The Haupttribüne, on the other hand, was designed to be the stadium's 'main' grandstand, the posh bit, with around half of the 4,800 seats sold as 'business seats' to corporate clients. Another flashpoint with its construction was the installation of double the number of proposed executive boxes, or Séparées (an ironic nod to the booths in the strip clubs of the Reeperbahn). Constructing twice the amount of boxes angered many fans, especially those who thought the balance of the new stand was already tilting too heavily in favour of the corporate event, or 'mode' fan.

Then, fanning the flames of an already delicate situation, the club decided to let one of the new executive boxes to Susi's Showbar, a local strip bar. To the fans of FC St. Pauli, who for many years had fought sexism in football as hard as they'd fought racist, fascist and homophobic attitudes, this was a kick in the teeth. It was further compounded by the fact that the box rented by Susi's Showbar had scantily dressed women pole-dancing during the match. To all but those who had signed the contract with Susi's Showbar this was an abhorrent stain on FC St. Pauli's reputation. The Sozialromantiker (social romantics) commented on this in an interview I conducted with them in September 2012: 'Susi's Showbar was inappropriate for many reasons, but in addition, they used it extensively to get media coverage that was worth much more than what they paid for the box while damaging (or changing) the"image" of the club. Similar to *Kalte Muschi* (see below), they misused the club as a vehicle for personal gain in a way that was contrary to the values and ethics of the club while profiting more from that than they put back into it.'

There were other concerns too. There was a general consensus that the tentacles of commercialisation were starting to get a stranglehold on the club itself. Although most fans accepted that the club needed to generate revenue to survive – the spectre of the 2002 'Retter' campaign still lurked in the background of the club's Bundesliga promotion celebrations – there was an increasing feeling of unease among fans.

Pre-dating the letting of an executive box to Susi's Showbar, fans had been angered by the club's decision to award the title of 'official club drink' to the Kalte Muschi brand (which translates as 'Cold Pussy'). Fans saw this as another affront to the idea of FC St. Pauli being anti-sexist and lobbied hard to get the club to reverse its decision. There were other quibbles, things that are accepted with a resigned shrug of the shoulders inside English football grounds, like a sponsor's logo adorning the wall of the club crèche at the juncture of the South stand and Haupttribüne or the announcement of the team line-ups being preceded by a sponsor. The building of the crèche was widely lauded by fans as a progressive step but many wanted the concrete wall painted with children's artwork rather than be used as additional advertising space.

Once again the club and the fans were finding that simply being St. Pauli was like walking a tightrope. The club, although attempting to maximise revenue, were finding that things accepted as the norm in the rest of football are simply not St. Pauli.

As the season progressed, the tensions continued to bubble under. There was dissatisfaction with the support from the fans in the business seats, partly for their failure to join in vocally with the call and response chanting driven by USP on the Südkurve, but more for the swathes of empty seats at the restart after half-time. Much like the scenes at the new Wembley or the Emirates in London, many of these 'mode' fans were reluctant to leave the warm enivrons of corporate hospitality to return to their seats for the second half. Again, this was the sort of issue that annoys fans the world over, yet in most cases, these same fans feel powerless to do anything about it. Not so at St. Pauli.

As with most high-wire balancing acts, it took only a seemingly insignificant breeze and a particularly icy day to knock the participants off balance. In the final home game before the winter break, against Mainz, the club, in conjunction with its 'official wireless partner', gave what it no doubt thought would be a quirky Christmas present to the fans: scrolling LED screens, mounted high in the new stands, capable of displaying SMS text messages from supporters. No doubt, it was conceived, as so many marketing ideas are, as a bit of fun, the chance for fans to interact with the action on the pitch by sending messages of support to the team. Messages of encouragement were mixed with personal greetings and even texts from the away fans' section, 'Greetings from the away section.'

However, many fans' patience simply snapped. Whatever metaphor you favour: falling off the tightrope, or the straw that broke the camel's back, the implementation of the LED screen was seen by many as the act that finally fractured the fragile equilibrium between club and fans. Yes, scrolling SMS messages are a staple of 24-hour news and sports broadcasters, but many felt it had no place at the Millerntor during a game of football.

The winter-pause gave fans the opportunity to reflect, to gather their thoughts and to organise. On 22 December, just six days after the debut of the LED screen, a group called 'Sozialromantiker Sankt Pauli' published a statement and launched a petition on their website entitled, simply, 'Enough is Enough'. The Sozialromantiker took their name from a seemingly disparaging comment made by Corny Littmann when referring to the group of fans who opposed the 'Millerntaler' currency designed to replace money at catering outlets inside the Millerntor. To be a 'Sozialromantiker' implies that you have an outdated, romantic, unrealistic view on events, a view which often runs contrary to modern business models for generating revenue. The implication was clear: there is no place for these romantic ideals if you want to run a successful, commercially viable football club. With a nice twist, the Sozialromantiker saw it as a positive label for a group of people who believed that these old-fashioned, romantic ideals were precisely what FC St. Pauli should be about.

Sozialromantiker Sankt Pauli were able to mobilise enough support to stop the 'Millerntaler'. Replacing cash with 'stadium currencies', usually delivered through a payment card system, had been introduced to a number of German stadia. The 'Millerntaler' took this one step further, proposing that cash be exchanged for poker chips, sponsored by an online poker website. As the Sozialromantiker themselves commented, 'instead of adding just another card to the bulk of plastic in the wallet, it was supposed to consist of coins of varying denominations, so a real alternative currency. This would have had quite a few additional drawbacks: the supporters would need a second wallet or any other way to keep the coins, and as they'd be very impractical they would be left at home and most likely forgotten for the next match or even get lost, giving the club a healthy extra profit or at least interest-free loan.' In the end, thanks to the work of the Sozialromantiker, fans were successful in halting the deployment of the 'Millerntaler'.

In 2010, prior to the posting of the 'Enough is Enough' article, there were concerns not only with the direction the club itself was heading, but also the unity of the fan scene. Fissures and disagreements between different groups were starting to call into question the very nature of supporting FC St. Pauli. Yet within a matter of weeks these same fans were to come together in a show of incredible unity and solidarity.

The statement from Sozialromantiker Sankt Pauli started simply by stating that: 'It won't go on like this any more. We say stop.'

They believed the time had come to speak out, that simply remaining silent was no longer an option. The Sozialromantiker felt that the time had come to mobilise resistance to the changes occurring at the Millerntor: 'many supporters were unhappy but there was no sole big scandal that would have sparked off protests by itself. So we decided to provide a bit of an analysis and a call for resistance to give the worried and dissatisfied supporters a voice. Every fire needs a little bit of help and we thought it was time to hand out some matches.'

They, too, chose a metaphor, talking of two pedestals: one belonging to the club and its need to generate revenue, the other belonging to the fans, symbolising their idea of how football at St. Pauli should be experienced. Sozialromantiker Sankt Pauli talked of the 'deep canyon of insignificance' that lay between these two pedestals – the very real threat that FC St. Pauli could fall into the abyss and become just another football club. They referenced the list of ideals that had been drawn up at the previous year's fan congress which highlighted St. Pauli's uniqueness: the close social and political links between the district and the football club; the refusal to sell the stadium's name to commercial sponsors; the refusal to engage in contracts with sponsors suspected to have fascist, racist or homophobic sympathies; and the desire to keep the 90 minutes of football free from excess commercialism.

The Sozialromantiker went on to discuss how, through a succession of small steps, the pedestals had moved further apart, listing the many reasons highlighted above: the executive boxes, the business seats, the sponsorship deals, the LED display. They continued the metaphor by stating, 'You really moved your pedestal so far that the balancing act is hurting every bone, every tendon, every nerve. And you have asked us in the last month to "be so kind" as to move our pedestal, too... in your direction. BUT THIS IS NOT WHAT WE ARE GOING TO DO! BECAUSE THIS IS NOT WHAT WE AGREED!'

They then listed the following demands:

- No further advertising during the agreed times (i.e. in the 5–10 minutes before kick-off)
- No additional advertising on the concrete of the new stands
- Cancellation of the executive box contract with Susi's Show Bar
- No LED displays in the stadium and no audiovisual adverts during the match

- Transformation of sections of the business seats into affordable seating
- Painting of the walls of the club crèche
- No more lip service from club officials

Should these demands not be met, the Sozialromantiker promised 'open resistance', They threatened to throw a spanner in the works and begin activities the club wouldn't even dream about. They threatened to boycott food and drink outlets in the stadium, to spam sponsors' email inboxes, to call an extraordinary general meeting of club members, and most dramatically to boycott matches. They concluded by stating: 'We will do everything until you realise how many we are!'

It was a bold stance by Sozialromantiker Sankt Pauli and it caught everyone off guard. For a start, nobody could be sure exactly 'how many' they were. The online petition grew steadily but the club had been here before with petitions against the Millerntaler. At first it seemed unlikely that the protest would develop much beyond the relative anonymity of the internet but things quickly snowballed.

By the new year, the Sozialromantiker petition had more than 3,000 signatures. Moreover, the protest had really caught the imagination of FC St. Pauli fans. The protest had also developed it's own iconography. In a clever subversion of the club's official (and trademarked) symbol, the 'Jolly Roger', fans started producing a homemade appropriation, the 'Jolly Rouge'. This black skull and crossbones on a red background had history too: it was the symbol pirates chose to fly when they intended to take 'no quarter' or no prisoners. It was a perfect symbol, a twist on the original Jolly Roger brought to the Millerntor by Doc Mabuse all those years earlier, the same Jolly Roger that had itself been appropriated and trademarked in complicated licensing agreements for corporate gain. An image that had been repackaged and sold back to the fans as a symbol of 'rebellion' and 'counter-culture'. It felt like something had been taken back, and soon homemade 'Jolly Rouge' flags, posters, stickers and flyers were being produced by fans all over the city. It was as if someone had awoken the DIY ethos of punk, a simple act of symbolic subversion, enthusing the entire fan scene with a desire for change. Nobody had been quite sure who exactly the Sozialromantiker were, or indeed how many of them were out there. Now it was becoming abundantly clear that the entire fan scene was 'Sozialromantiker'.

On 4 January 2011, Sozialromantiker Sankt Pauli called for a day of action at the first home game after the Rückrunde, which was against Freiburg. Under the banner of the Jolly Rouge and the slogan 'Bring Back Sankt Pauli', they urged fans to turn the Millerntor into a sea of red in protest at the club's continued refusal to meet the demands of the fans. Momentum was building. In the build-up to the game, the internet was alive with photos and blogs detailing the flags and banners being created. Stickers started appearing on lamp posts and signs around the district and the Jolly Rouge was spotted hanging from numerous apartments and buildings in the neighbourood. It felt like something special was about to happen.

As matchday approached, there was still a sense of nervousness among the fan scene. Yes, it appeared, looking at the plethora of blogs and social media sites on the internet, that the campaign to 'Bring Back Sankt Pauli' had real momentum. But the internet can be misleading, a place where information can be streamed so selectively that the work of a dedicated group of activists can seem greater than the end result. However, as kick-off grew nearer, it became apparent that this wasn't the action of a select few, that under the banner of the Sozialromantiker movement and the flag of the Jolly Rouge a united force was emerging.

Approaching the stadium across the Heiligengeistfeld, red Jolly Rouge flags, T-shirts and banners abounded. Fans dressed in red, some with their hair dyed, congregated at the AFM container as a real sense of common purpose filled the air. Even the supporters' pub, the Jolly Roger, had been given a temporary change of signage to Jolly Rouge. Inside the stadium, the scene was even more dramatic. The Südkurve and Gegengerade were swathed in red, the 'Nord Support' fan group on the Nordkurve had swapped their giant brown/white and white/brown heart flags for two equally impressive flags: one with a black skull and crossbones on a red background, the other a red skull and crossbones on a black background. The 'Oldtras' hung a banner bearing the slogan of the day, 'Bring Back St. Pauli To Me' on the Haupttribüne.

In the moments before the teams came out, the whole stadium took up the Oldtras' mantra, singing 'Bring Back St. Pauli To Me!' to the tune of the traditional Scottish folk song, 'My Bonnie Lies Over the

Ocean'. It was a moment of high emotion, the whole stadium singing in unison, the stands turned bright red by 10,000 printed cards and thousands more homemade flags and banners. As *Hells Bells* began, the sea of flags lit up an overcast day like a poppyfield in an unseasonal winter's bloom. It was a truly heartwarming sight, not just for those inside the stadium, but also for those following the game all over the world over a variety of erratic internet streams.

The match itself almost seemed like an irrelevance, and perhaps would've been had it not been for the team's need for points to aid Bundesliga survival. A headed goal from Marius Ebbers sent St. Pauli in 1-0 up at the break. The half-time break, usually an excuse to chat to friends, nip to the loo, or to get a re-fill of Astra, prompted an emotional mass sing-along of Thees Uhlmann's *Das hier ist Fussball*. The second-half saw St. Pauli give away their 1-0 lead, score again to make it 2-1, before shipping another of those costly late goals to share the points.

However, 15 January 2011 had never really been about the result on the pitch. Instead it would be remembered as the day the fans of the club came together, in a way that really wasn't thought possible just six weeks before, claiming a little bit of the club back for themselves. The way the Sozialromantiker movement had flourished had taken even the most devoted fans by surprise. A fan base that seemed to be splintering with alarming ease was united again under the banner of the Jolly Rouge. In pirate terms it would be classed as a mutiny by fans against the leadership of the club, with the supporters wresting back the identity of the club from the money men. In the short term at least, the day had exceeded all expectations.

After the game somewhere between 500–1,000 fans defied the wintry rain to march in solidarity with the district of St. Pauli through the streets. The movement had expanded beyond football. Under the banner of 'Bring Back Sankt Pauli – Reclaim Your District', fans and residents gathered on the paved area outside the Südkurve to protest against the creeping gentrification and unsightly urban regeneration that was not only depriving residents of social spaces but that continued to force rents in an upward spiral, thus forcing out those people at the very heart of the St. Pauli community. In one way it was a familiar tale, one that harked back to the demonstrations on the Hafenstraße and the protests against the Sport-Dome. Nearly 20 years had elapsed but still fans and residents alike were coming together to preserve the St. Pauli way of life as it came under threat from outside sources.

Following the Freiburg game, one thing was certain – the Sozialromantiker movement wasn't limited to the 4,000 or so people who'd signed the online petition, it wasn't limited to the most active members of the fan scene, nor was it exclusive to USP on the Südkurve. This was a movement that had the support of everyone inside the Millerntor.

The Sozialromantiker movement, initially dismissed by the club as 'just another group of supporters that has to whinge about our decisions on the internet', had caused quite a stir. They claimed that 'reports from the hospitality sections of the ground told us about very urgent meetings of club officials at half time (in the Freiburg game)'.

Certainly, after the match, events moved quickly. A scheduled meeting of the Fan Committee and the club was dominated by the demands of the Sozialromantiker petition (although the Sozialromantiker group themselves were not present at the meeting). The club announced that it was going to set up a working group of officials to review all new advertising campaigns, to ensure new companies adhered to the existing criteria, although Sozialromantiker Sankt Pauli continued to insist that the committee would only move towards true objectivity if it contained a fan representative. Many of the other issues, including the continued renting of an executive box to Susi's Show Bar, remained unresolved. Pole-dancing during the match was banned, but still allowed both before and after. The Sozialromantiker group also continued to call for the dismantling of a number of business seats. However, despite the strongly worded rhetoric that 'the time for meetings and talking is over', the real success of the 'Bring Back Sankt Pauli' campaign was precisely that: to re-open meaningful dialogue between the fan base and the club. For club officials, it was a timely reminder that any commercial activity has to be carried out with the broad consent of the fans.

The Jolly Rouge continued to be flown at home games for the rest of the 2010–11 Bundesliga campaign, but it was the show of strength and unity at the Freiburg game that sticks in the minds of everyone present. The were other tangible signs of success too. The LED screen displaying SMS messages never returned, and the following season it was announced that the two-season contract with Susi's Show Bar would not be renewed. FC St. Pauli hadn't been won back in a day – that just wasn't possible – but the fans had come together in the biggest show of collective solidarity since the 'Retter' campaign almost a decade earlier. And in doing so, they had shown that together they could still exert significant influence on the club they loved. To borrow a metaphor from Sozialromantiker Sankt Pauli themselves, considerable pressure from the fans had caused club officials to gently push their pedestal a little closer to the pedestal occupied by the fans. Of course, for us, outdated romantics and unrealistic dreamers, it wasn't close enough. It was a start, though. And, more importantly, it showed two things: first, that the fans still cared; and second, that the club still noticed – for all its faults the commercial entity of FC St. Pauli hadn't sailed off into a sea of corporate greed, perhaps it didn't quite dare, as it knew to get to those waters it had to outflank and outgun a collection of pirates, flying a flag that indicated they would give no quarter.

In a season that ultimately ended with the inevitable, yet no less crushing disappointment of relegation, that dank January afternoon represented a high point. For those lucky enough to be inside the Millerntor, it was one of those life-affirming moments, when you remember why you fell in love with the club in the first place. Even for those who witnessed the event second-hand, through video clips or via press cuttings or blogs, it was an emotional occasion with everyone united under the reclaimed flag of the Jolly Rouge. Football fans by definition are social romantics, reluctant to accept change, and St. Pauli fans, more than most, have good reason to protect their legacy. As Sozialromantiker Sankt Pauli themselves state: 'This club is a gem. The best thing you can find in German football. This club has fans that will go to hell and back. Fans for whom the club is a pure labour of love.'

It is is hard to disagree with that.

The Jolly Rouge flew over the Millerntor some 18 months later, on 25 September 2012 for the game against VfR Aalen. Once again, the stadium reconstruction played its part, but this time the argument wasn't about business seats or executive boxes, it was about the proposal to site the new police station underneath the new Gegengerade, right next to the proposed home of the Fanräume and other fan spaces, including the Fanladen. In one sense the club had been true to its word.

After the construction of the Haupttribüne, the popular Gegengerade terrace was next in line for redevelopment. The iconic status of the Gegengerade as the birthplace of 'the mythos of St. Pauli' meant that fans would not tolerate a similar gentrification of the new stand. As a result, the new stand was to be built with an impressive 10,000 standing places plus a smattering of regular seats (i.e. no business seating) above the huge terraced area. It had long been the plan to dedicate a significant amount of space underneath the new Gegengerade for fan projects.

Since 2007, the Fanräume (fan rooms) project had been raising funds to create a fan-centric space in the rebuilt Gegengerade. The Fanräume needed to raise €400,000 in order to complete the project. This self-financing was due to the club not being able to finance the space itself, but also provides the Fanräume with independence from the club. The idea was to make various fan projects accessible under one roof. The Fanladen was to be relocated from its base in Brigittenstraße, while the AFM also agreed to rent space from the Fanräume. The space would also eventually hold an archive of fan-related culture and media, that would be open to the public to view.

Thanks to the hard work of those involved (even occasional international visitors will have noticed their matchday stall selling merchandise) this fan space at the southern end of the Gegengerade was designed to act as a central point for supporters. The problem wasn't with this allocated space, it was with their potential neighbours – the police.

It had been proposed that the new police headquarters – which were in a cheerfully painted if somewhat run-down building on the Heiligengeistfeld on the corner of the Nordkurve and Gegengerade – were to be located next door to the Fanräume in the new Gegengerade. It was accepted that the upgrade to the police HQ, which would include holding cells for any fans arrested in the stadium or its immediate environment, was a necessity of the DFB's licensing agreement. But what angered fans was the decision by the club to locate it next to the fan space. The supporters uneasy relationship with the Hamburg police would make their close proximity to each other at best a folly and at worst a downright insult.

As work on the Gegengerade advanced (it was opened with a significantly reduced capacity for the first home game of the 2012–13 season, despite the old stand being demolished only a couple of months before) fan opposition to the police HQ became more vocal. The club argued that its location in the Gegengerade made financial sense as it would save the cost of financing an additional building. Fans favoured the building of an external police station, possibly on the site of the old HQ, but they were also accepting of it being located underneath the Nordkurve after that stand's eventual redevelopment. These seemed like reasonable suggestions for a police station that would not only serve FC St. Pauli on matchdays, but would also be used when the Dom funfair was in residence on the Heiligengeistfeld.

The fans were searching desperately for alternatives but one thing was clear: the Gegengerade was sacrosanct. The very idea of a police station located on the spiritual birthplace of the 'Black-Bloc' was abhorrent to a significant number of fans. Not only this, but the supporters of St. Pauli wanted the space which was to be given over to the police to be developed into a museum, charting the history of the club. Given the success of the temporary museum created out of shipping containers that stood on Südvorplatz for much of the club's centenary season this seemed like a sensible request, one that further encouraged the space under the Gegengerade to be used for a communal purpose.

A meeting was called at Centro Sociale on 14 September 2012 and from it the campaign for a museum instead of a police station quickly intensified. Word spread that the home game against VfR Aalen 11 days later would see the Millerntor once again turned red with the Jolly Rouge. The DIY ethos kicked back in, and as kick-off approached (at the fan unfriendly time of 17.30 on a Tuesday afternoon – it was English week!) the Millerntor was a sea of red flags, banner and placards. The death of one their members, Jan Hoppe, saw USP turn the Südkurve black in the build-up to kick-off as they paid their respects to a friend. But after that, despite the sadness at the loss of one of their own, USP, too, joined in the protest. Photographs from the game show a stadium bathed in red pro-museum banners visible in every corner of the ground. The speed at which the DIY nature of the protest was mobilised was, like that for the Freiburg game, simply staggering. There was a report of a couple of fans in the business seat section of the Haupttribüne rudely refusing to have anything to do with the protest but this was very much an isolated incident. Elsewhere, flags and banners even hung from the executive boxes.

Once again the fans had spoken. The message was clear: the fans wanted a museum not a police station. They wanted a space in which to celebrate the club's unique culture and history, not a space swarming with police officers that would totally undermine the concept of a fan-centric environment. Once again, and in no uncertain terms, they had told the club how they felt.

The following day a press conference was called. Not to directly respond to the overwhelming message sent by an entire stadium flying the Jolly Rouge the night before, but to sack the manager, André Schubert. The game against VfR Aalen had seen St. Pauli slump to a 1-0 defeat, compounding a poor start to the 2012–13 campaign. Schubert, who had dodged the bullet at the end of the previous season – he had attended a similar press conference, called the day after the 5-0 end-of-season victory over Paderborn, expecting to be fired, but instead Sporting Director Helmut Schulte had been axed – was finally fired as coach.

However, in among the questions about the sacking and the search for a new manager, a journalist asked about the location of the new police HQ. President Stefan Orth responded by saying that the police HQ would be built outside of the stadium and that 'We have to combine our efforts, fans, amateur divisions, AFM ...' to make this a reality.

The issue of funding the external police station was still unresolved, but the implication was that the club – at last – had understood the fans' concerns and were willing to work with them to find an acceptable solution. Until the matter was resolved, and the police HQ built elsewhere, there would still be an element of doubt and concerns that the club might change its mind, but that aside, Orth's response seemed like another victory for fan power and the Jolly Rouge.

Chapter 10
BEER CUPS, TILL ROLLS & GHOST GAMES

Ongoing challenges facing the St. Pauli fan scene

IF THE 'JOLLY ROUGE' home game against Freiburg in the January of 2011 had been the highlight of St. Pauli's 2010–11 season in the German top flight, then the low point can be accurately attributed to the 87th minute of the home game against Schalke on 1 April 2011. The incident certainly felt like an April Fool.

To give the game, and the incident, some context, FC St. Pauli went into the fixture on the back of six straight defeats. The remarkable win over local rivals HSV in the Volksparkstadion was starting to feel like a long time ago, with St. Pauli in free-fall and heading for a relegation scrap.

A goal from Raul after 26 minutes had put Schalke ahead at the break, but things only really started to get interesting in the second half. As the game wore on, referee Denis Aytekin's insistence on blowing for every conceivable incident disrupted the flow of the game and began to grate with the home support. Then, on 65 minutes, Gerald Asamoah was fouled about 40 yards out, over towards the Haupttribüne. Max Kruse swung a ball into the area, it deceived everyone – including Neuer in the Schalke goal and the onrushing Fabian Boll – and flew into the corner of the net. St Pauli were level. Game on. Only they weren't.

The linesman on the Haupttribüne side of the ground had flagged for offside. Aytekin and his assistant, Thorsten Schiffner, had a brief conflab before disallowing the goal. TV replays showed what a close call it was. Boll may have started his run a split second too early yet, although he cut across Neuer's line of vision briefly, he certainly made no contact with the ball. To those fans inside the stadium, without the benefit of television replays, it appeared to be an awfully bad call, the sort of decision that changes seasons, especially – if like St. Pauli – you are embroiled in a relegation battle and in desperate need of a change in fortune. To make matters worse, as the fall-out from the offside decision raged in the stands and on the touchline, Schalke went straight up the end and Jefferson Farfan made it 2-0. From 1-1 to 2-0 in a matter of seconds. Now the entire Millerntor was seething.

At this point, with the Millerntor close to boiling point, the referee might have opted to take a little of the heat out of the situation. Instead, just two minutes after Schalke's second goal, he chose to pour oil on burning waters by sending off Jan-Philipp Kalla for a second yellow. By the letter of the law he was right: Kalla had got himself stupidly booked early in the first half, and did jump in when attempting to win the ball. To make matters even worse, on 78 minutes, Fin Bartels, a forward pressed into service at right-back due to injuries, took a real golf-swing of a challenge at Farfan and was – quite rightly – shown a straight red. Not a malicious challenge, but a stupid one, especially considering the circumstances. St Pauli were down to nine, and in total disarray. However, none of this can excuse what happened next.

On 87 minutes, linesman Thorsten Schiffner was hit on the back of the head by a full cup of beer lobbed by a fan seated in the Haupttribüne. The assistant referee collapsed to the ground as everyone in the stadium looked on in disbelief. Once Schiffner was back on his feet, Aytekin consulted both him and the other assistant referee (who appeared to empty his pockets to show the ref a variety of other objects that had been thrown in his direction) and abandoned the match. It was a bold decision, but ultimately, if he feared for the safety of his officials, the referee was left with no choice.

There was a period of confusion as players and fans alike tried to establish what on earth was going on but soon the match officials were heading to the dressing room. Emotions were running high; the yellow umbrellas offered little protection to Aytekin and his assistants, and even the presence of St. Pauli keeper (and passionate Sankt Paulianer) Bene Pliquett walking in front of the officials didn't seem to quell the torrent of abuse and further projectiles being aimed in the officials' direction. It was a grim end to the evening, the only positive being the fact that, thankfully, the linesman suffered no lasting damage. The same couldn't be said for St. Pauli.

It didn't take long for the culprit to be identified and arrested in conjunction with the incident. However, this wasn't a one-off. The referee mentioned post-match that a range of coins and lighters had been directed at his officials during the game. This wasn't just one nutter. And it wasn't just one game. The implications didn't just concern what penalty the DFB decided to hand out: a heavy fine; banning of beer; ground closure; or points deductions were all possible, but irrelevant compared to the long-term damage the club's image suffered.

It's an image that portrays St. Pauli fan culture as different from the rest of German football. In many ways it's true, but more than anything this incident forced St. Pauli fans to do some soul-searching and realise that they – like a significant number of other German clubs – had a problem with projectiles being thrown onto the pitch. It was not a new problem either, it went back years. Bayern boss, Jupp Heynckes, had been pelted with bottles and beer cups at the Millerntor in 1988. Even discounting the popular pastime of lobbing your beer cup up in the air to create a celebratory beer shower whenever a goal is scored, the Millerntor has had an ongoing problem with fans throwing objects onto the pitch in frustration or anger.

The incident against Schalke was significant for a number of reasons. First, because the beer cup actually *hit* the linesman. Second, because, in 2011, unlike 1988, with the advent of 24-hour news media and the increased popularity of football, the game was constantly in the media spotlight. This was evidenced by the fact that news of the incident made the front page of the BBC Football website by 11.13pm the same evening. Finally, and fortunately, society had moved on a bit, and there really was no excuse to be throwing missiles at people who are just trying to do their job. Sporting Director, Helmut Schulte succinctly summed up the incident saying: 'We have just got to face up to the consequences, this is a bad day for FC St Pauli.'

There was perhaps the smallest sense of relief that the beer cup had been thrown from seats in the new Haupttribüne stand. It was easy to imagine the level of tabloid hysteria had it come from the direction of Ultrà Sankt Pauli on the Südkurve. At least, this time, the incident couldn't be blamed on fans standing on the terracing. However, it was clear that the DFB punishment would be severe regardless of where it came from or who had lobbed it – be it a gnarled veteran of the wilderness years in the Regionalliga or upwardly mobile newbie attracted by the glamour of the Bundesliga.

Either way it was a blow for the fan scene at the Millerntor. FC St. Pauli prides itself on standing up for what is right. Its fans might well be anti-fascism, anti-racism, anti-sexism and anti-homophobia. Yet there appeared to be an increasing need to be 'anti-idiot' as well. Sure, the club or its supporters can't legislate for every nut-job who takes it upon themselves to lob something at the officials, but they can collectively make it clear that this sort of behaviour is just as unacceptable as shouting racial or homophobic abuse. Fortunately, one of the greatest attributes of St. Pauli fans is their self-reflection and this was evident in the frenzied dialogue that dominated their various internet forums over the following days and weeks.

The DFB quickly decided that the 2-0 win for Schalke would stand, but they took a little longer to confirm St. Pauli's punishment. The gut feeling among supporters was that there would be a heavy fine and the possibility of a game behind closed doors, popularly referred to as a 'ghost game' due to the total lack of spectators and the eerie silence that would echo through the deserted stadium. And indeed the DFB's ruling was that the home game against Werder Bremen on 23 April 2011 must be played in an empty stadium.

It seemed that supporters' fears had been confirmed: the Millerntor was to host a 'ghost game'. While not a shock, the punishment carried with it a sense of injustice, much like a class detention used to punish one or two unruly pupils, especially as tickets for the Werder Bremen game had already been sold, and the punishment would also impact on fans travelling from Bremen. With this in mind, the club decided to appeal. President Stefan Orth sounded hopeful when he said: 'We will try with the DFB to find a solution that avoids a ghost game at the Millerntor.'

Eventually, a compromise of sorts was reached. The Werder Bremen game was allowed to go ahead as usual with 24,487 spectators watching St. Pauli suffer another home defeat (3-1). But the club were ordered to play their first home game of the following 2011–12 season at a stadium at least 50km from Hamburg. This was not the first time the DFB had chosen a punishment with a geographical restriction. In 1995–96 Hansa Rostock were forced to play their home game against Fortuna

Düsseldorf in Berlin's Olympic stadium, the punishment backfiring when more than 50,000 turned up to watch the game in Berlin. To avoid a repeat of a punishment becoming a payday for the club in question, the DFB added a caveat to the 50km restriction: a maximum of 12,500 St. Pauli fans could attend the game.

Over the following weeks, right up until the fixtures for the 2011–12 season were announced, there was much speculation as to where the first home game would take place. St. Pauli's relegation to 2. Bundesliga narrowed the field, and it was widely thought that it would be in Lübeck up on the Baltic coast (those UK-based St. Pauli fans who have flown into Hamburg–Lübeck airport will be aware of the considerable coach journey that's required before you are finally deposited in Hamburg). And once the fixtures were confirmed, it was announced that FC. St Pauli would host FC Ingolstadt 04 at VfB Lübeck's Stadion an der Lohmühle.

The 'ghost game' had been avoided, but the punishment was still a considerable inconvenience for St. Pauli fans. In the end, despite packing trains and buses for the journey north the game did not sell out. Only 10,093 watched St. Pauli, and new boss André Schubert, get the season off to a winning start, defeating Ingolstadt 2-0. This meant that nearly 2,500 tickets went unsold. The early start to the league campaign – the season started in mid-July so that it could finish early to accommodate Euro 2012 – played a part in the lower than expected attendance (there had also been a great deal of consternation over who would and would not be able to secure tickets for the game – the attendance was supposed to be limited to season ticket holders) as did the gloriously hot July weather, but mostly it was the hassle and annoyance of having to play a 'home' game 50km from Hamburg that stopped the game selling out. In that regard, the punishment had been 'successful'.

Not only had staging the game in Lübeck cost the club around €400,000 in lost revenue and additional costs, it had dissuaded a number of fans from attending the first home game of the season. However, it could also be argued that the club (and the fans) had taken their punishment (no matter how unfair on the majority of supporters) and could look forward to the new season with a clean slate, having benefitted from a period of self-reflection and having put its house in order. Unfortunately, things weren't to be that simple.

FC St. Pauli's fourth home game back at the Millerntor after the 2011–12 season opener in Lübeck was marred by another cup-throwing incident. A stoppage time strike from Mahir Saglik wasn't enough to avert a 3-2 defeat at the hands of Erzgebirge Aue and at the end of the match a beer cup (albeit empty this time) was thrown from the Südkurve, hitting referee Christian Leicher. There were reports from the crowd that two drunken men had been causing a nuisance for much of the game, with one throwing a beer cup onto the pitch with 20 minutes remaining. It seems the stewards tried to apprehend the man who threw the first cup but for some reason couldn't. Then, at the end of the game, the second man threw the cup that hit the referee. This time the stewards quickly intervened and managed to apprehend the perpetrator.

Perhaps it wasn't such a shock this time. In a crowd of nearly 25,000 people there are always going to be one or two idiots, the sort of people who think it is amusing to copy a previous incident. Although, having seen the impact this action had on the fan caught for throwing the beer against Schalke you would think they would have thought twice. Reports suggest the man lost his job and he also faced the possibility of being made liable for the costs the club incurred by the game being moved to Lübeck.

Again, there was talk of a 'ghost game', especially as St. Pauli were now repeat offenders. This time the DFB chose to fine the club €8,000 and insist that they improve the infrastructure inside the stadium to include a caterpillar-style extendable tunnel, to afford both players and officials extra protection from projectiles as they entered and left the pitch. Again, there was much soul-searching on internet forums about the problem of objects being thrown on to the pitch. Most fans seemed to agree that while things had improved dramatically since the Schalke game, with fans realising the damage such incidents did to the club's reputation, it remained really hard to legislate against the actions of one or two individuals. Surely, that would be that?

Sadly not. The last game before the winter break saw St. Pauli at home to Eintracht Frankfurt in one of the universally unpopular Monday night fixtures. The evening had begun in high spirits with USP creating a choreo that depicted a giant joint being rolled by a cartoon St. Pauli freak. The completed joint even 'worked', with smoke bellowing out from the end. This inventive, tongue-in-cheek choreography was a direct response to Frankfurt's previous visit to the Millerntor, when their Ultras created a choreo entitled 'High Again' replete with green smoke. St. Pauli won the fixture 2-0, but again the drama focussed on the stands. Early in the second half with St. Pauli about to take a corner in front of the Südkurve an object thrown from the crowd hit Frankfurt's Pirmin Schwegler. There was confusion in both the penalty area and the stands. Fortunately, Schwegler wasn't hurt. The referee then issued a message over the tannoy, threatening to abandon the game if another object was thrown onto the pitch.

It turned out that the object thrown had been a till roll – usually used in great numbers at the start of games to create a barrage of streamers – that had failed to unfurl. Immediately after the incident, the culprit was helped by fellow fans on the Südkurve to change his clothes, so that he could avoid identification and slip out of the ground without being caught.

Once again there was considerable online debate over spectator behaviour at the Millerntor. The discussion was so intense it even led top the moderators of the fan-forum closing the site for a period to allow people to cool off. This angst was also reflected inside the stadium. With the incident over, and St. Pauli still leading 1-0, the Südkurve tried to lift the atmosphere by starting up the familiar call and response chanting with fans standing on the Gegengerade. Instead of responding with a chant a number of supporters on the back straight answered with boos and catcalls. They were venting their fury, not just at the thrower of the till roll but the whole Südkurve. It seems unlikely, at this point, that they would've known about fans on the terrace helping the protagonist to get changed and escape arrest, so it can only be assumed that the Gegengerade were directing their anger at the Südkurve in general and USP in particular. It was another low point for the St. Pauli fan scene, and also a little unfair on the vast majority of supporters, USP or otherwise, who stand in that particular part of the stadium.

After an appeal on the club website, the offender came forward. He turned out to be a 20-year-old student, who had not meant to cause any harm; his till roll had simply failed to unfurl. The club and fellow fans were moderately appeased by his honesty, both hoping that the DFB would see that this was different to the previous two cup-throwing incidents. Unfortunately the football authorities did not agree. The DFB chose to order a partial closure of the Millerntor for the game against Karlsruher SC on 2 March 2012. Both the Südkurve and, inexplicably, the Nordkurve would be closed, stopping 5,800 fans from attending the game. It seemed a strange punishment even by DFB standards. It was almost possible to accept the decision to close the area of terracing from where the till roll had been thrown, but to close the Nordkurve, and yet leave the standing area of the Gegengerade open? There was no real reason or logic that could be applied to the decision. Once again, a large number of fans had to pay the price for one individual's foolishness. Of course, the partial closure also had financial implications for the club, who expected to lose around €63,000 because of the reduced spectator numbers.

Fans were furious with the DFB for the closure, the randomness of the punishment making them even more partisan. There was a lot of pressure for the club to appeal, especially as the more radical suggestions from fans included blocking the team buses' access to the stadium, storming the stadium and staging a sit-in protest, or even digging up the pitch so that the match couldn't take place. Although fans had initially been divided over the till roll incident, the DFB's response had united them in anger against the governing body. The club decided to appeal.

Then, strangely, the DFB had a change of heart. It may have been a result of events at the game between Union Berlin and Eintracht Frankfurt on 26 March 2012. Around a thousand Frankfurt fans had been banned from attending the fixture but they travelled regardless. At the stadium, with encouragement from the Union fans who had helped them get tickets for the home end, they jumped the fence into the empty guest block to take their places. In the end, the police and stewards opened the gates to the away section. Both sets of fans continued their vocal and visual opposition to the DFB's treatment of fans throughout the game. Fans of various different clubs were coming together in their opposition to the exclusion of supporters.

In another incident, despite being ordered to play their game against Ingolstadt behind closed doors, Dynamo Dresden sold more than 40,000 'tickets' to the match, raising thousands of Euros for the club. It seemed, at last, that the policy of punishing the majority for the actions of the minority was coming to an end. It is worth mentioning here that no Dynamo Dresden fans were officially present at the Millerntor for their game in November 2011. Following trouble at Dynamo's cup tie in Dortmund, the club refused the option to take up their ticket allocation for the visit to St. Pauli, but plenty still made it inside the stadium.

Indeed, the morning after those Eintracht Frankfurt fans gained access to the guest block at Union Berlin, the DFB issued a statement, declaring that partial or full ground closures would no longer be used as a punishment, seeking instead to look for different sanctions against clubs and fans guilty of misbehaviour.

The ramifications for St. Pauli were obvious: the forced closure of both the Südkurve and Nordkurve did not come to pass. Instead, the club was punished with a fine of around €50,000. It was another minor victory for German football fans although none were foolish enough to think that this was a turning point for fan culture in Germany. Indeed, following further incidents in the second leg of the play-off between Fortuna Düsseldorf and Hertha Berlin for promotion to the Bundesliga at the end of the 2011–12 season, media hysteria prompted the DFB to act. Flares had been thrown but what had most shocked the watching media was the pitch invasion by Fortuna fans before the match had finished. The fact that this invasion was purely celebratory – and included the slightly ludicrous sight of one fan digging up the penalty spot to take home the turf as a souvenir – were totally overlooked in the tabloid frenzy that followed. Apparently, the very future of German football was balanced on a knife-edge. Something just had to be done to stop these pesky football fans returning the sport to the dark ages. The German Interior minister Hans-Peter Friedrich mooted the possibility of all-seater stadiums to counter the perceived threat of hooliganism and suggested that convicted football hooligans should be electronically tagged.

In the end, the DFB, the DFL and the German Interior Ministry called a 'Security Summit' in July 2012 and outlined a Code of Conduct designed to eliminate violence at football grounds. No violence would be tolerated, stadium bans for offenders would be increased from three to five years, and they also confirmed the blanket ban on supporters' use of pyrotechnics in the stadium, that had been announced, much to the chagrin of the pro-pyro campaigners, at the start of the 2011–12 season. All 54 member clubs of the Bundesliga, 2. Bundesliga and 3. Liga were 'invited' to sign up to the plan. This despite there being no consultation with supporters' groups or fan projects. The clubs themselves only received the Code of Conduct 20 hours before they were due to sign it. The lack of dialogue with supporters shocked football fans across Germany. Despite this, 53 of the 54 clubs signed up to the plan. Only Union Berlin refused, attracting a great deal of admiration from fans of other clubs.

These were clearly interesting times for fan culture, not just in St. Pauli but for German football in general. On the one hand, the solidarity shown by various supporter groups has overturned the unjust use of stadium closure, but on another level the screw seemed to be turning ever tighter regarding punishment for any behaviour the DFB thinks contravenes their Code of Conduct.

Chapter 11
RIOTS & ROCKETS

THE PREVIOUS CHAPTER touched upon the German football authorities' perception of an increase in hooligan activity. It is fair to say that, while incidents of violence are frequently over-egged by a sensationalist media, and are nowhere near the levels of the late 1980s and early '90s, problems with hooliganism are still very real. Indeed, beer cups and till rolls weren't the only problems facing St. Pauli fans in the season that followed the club's sojourn in the Bundesliga.

Trips to the Baltic port of Rostock have always been risky affairs for St. Pauli fans. There is absolutely no love lost between fans of St. Pauli and Hansa Rostock, the divide being political as well as geographical, with St. Pauli representing the left and Rostock the right. Since the early 1990s, the game has taken on an unpleasant edge, with fans clashing with each other and the police. During the 2009–10 promotion season, St. Pauli fans were attacked as their train arrived in Rostock, and as a result, as the teams got ready to meet again on 19 November 2011 at Rostock's Ostseestadion, the prospect of violence hung heavy in the air. The night before the game, Hansa hooligans attacked a police station in the town with stones and bottles, causing considerable damage. It is thought that the attack was in response to one of the Rostock hooligans being taken into custody as a preventative measure prior to the arrival of St. Pauli the following day. On the day of the game, a huge police presence escorted the St. Pauli fans – who had arrived on two special trains – to the ground (St. Pauli fans took the precaution of taping the inside of the windows of their shuttle buses to avoid the glass shattering from the expected onslaught of rocks and stones. Once at the stadium, around a hundred or so St. Pauli fans stormed the guest block to gain access to the ground. This probably happened, not because the fans didn't have tickets to the game, but because they wanted to get flares and smoke bombs into the stadium without being detected.

As kick-off approached, it seemed like the whole stadium had joined in with a protracted chorus of 'Scheiß St. Pauli!' It turned out they had. The Rostock fans had taken up the chant, but the St. Pauli fans in the guest block returned the chant with gusto, prompting looks of bewilderment and some head scratching. Sometimes, the best way to deal with prejudice is through humour. As the stadium announcer read out the Rostock team, leaving a theatrical pause for the home fans to chant the player's surname, St. Pauli fans responded with a huge shout of 'NAKI' after every Hansa player – they did this in honour of Deniz Naki, who had scored in the last encounter and endeared himself to St. Pauli fans for all eternity by ceremonially planting a St. Pauli flag in the Rostock pitch during the post-game celebrations. Once again, a touch of humour to lighten the mood.

Just before kick-off, the Rostock fans threw a huge quantity of bananas on the pitch – an action which in England would have immediate racial connotations, but was in fact the Rostock fans mimicking a sticker that St. Pauli fans had produced to wind up the Rostock supporters about the apparent scarcity of bananas in East Germany before the wall came down.

The game got off to a fiery start, with Rostock's Weilandt being shown the red card after just seven minutes for elbowing St. Pauli captain Fabio Morena. Not surisingly this did nothing to ease the tension in the stands, but it was Max Kruse's goal on 40 minutes that, if you'll pardon the pun, really lit the fuse. For those watching the game on television or on the internet, the screen first went blank, and then began showing endless replays of Kruse's goal. A flare was let off in the away section, undoubtedly one that had got into the ground during the storming of the away entrance, but that is fairly standard behaviour for away fans, especially during such a keenly contested derby. At the same time, however, explosions were heard. Fireworks were launched at the away section from both the end containing Rostock's 'Suptras' and the stand running along the side of the pitch. This was pretty shocking. The use of flares in football is subject to the long-running legalisation of pyrotechnics debate but this was different – the actual firing of rockets at opposition fans. More chillingly, and this is clearly audible on the YouTube footage of the incident, a significant number of regular Rostock fans were cheering this attack, before launching into another chorus of 'Scheiß St. Pauli!' A handful of idiots firing rockets is one thing, but virtually the whole stadium cheering them on is something else entirely – a rivalry that has gone too far: to misquote Orwell, 'football as war *with* the shooting.'

The referee took the only sensible course of action and took the players off the pitch. For those watching on television or on live internet streams, the break in play was spent frantically trying to piece together what had gone on, and then praying that no one was seriously hurt. Fortunately, no one was injured in the rocket attack. There was a 13-minute pause before the game resumed, and then after five minutes of play the ref blew for half-time.

More insults were traded in the stands at the interval and about ten minutes in, a mistake by Philipp Tschauner presented Rostock with an equaliser. However, the man advantage started to show as the half wore on, and on 79 minutes, St. Pauli regained the lead. Substitute Mahir Saglik (on for cult hero, Naki) was fouled on the corner of the penalty area. Florian Bruns cleared bananas out of the way before swinging in a free-kick which was duly headed home by Saglik.

In the crowd, Hansa's Suptras took much delight in burning stolen banners and scarves (the latter probably expensively purchased via eBay) but another Saglik strike in injury time sealed another victory for St. Pauli against their rivals. The victory was most welcome as it maintained St. Pauli's promotion push and kept Hansa confined to the lower reaches of 2. Bundesliga, but the events off the pitch over-shadowed everything. Due to the massive police presence most of the travelling fans made it back to Hamburg safely, although a small number were injured when they were pelted with rocks and stones on leaving the stadium. This was a rivalry that was out of hand. It was clear that the majority of the blame lay with the fans of Hansa Rostock, although the storming of the guest block, letting off flares and reports of one particularly foolhardy St. Pauli fan positioning himself in the Rostock end (and attempting to fight his way out) meant that St. Pauli fans weren't totally perfect. It was going to be very interesting to see how the DFB reacted.

Rostock were ordered to play their match against Dynamo Dresden on 18 December 2012 behind closed doors, thanks to the DFB's fairly predictable 'ghost game' punishment, although the club was able to reduce the financial impact of this verdict by selling 'tickets' for the match to those supporters willing to pay not to watch the game. St. Pauli's punishment was a €20,000 fine awarded because the DFB had mistaken the St. Pauli fans' repeated response of 'NAKI' for 'NAZI' as the stadium announcer read out the Rostock line-up. You almost couldn't make it up.

What is clear from this incident, and the countless other examples over the years where St. Pauli fans have been attacked by rival fans at games, is that being a St. Pauli fan can make you a target for other hooligan groups. The violence isn't just confined to football matches either. In May 2011, a 24-year-old man was badly beaten up by a mob of Rostock hooligans because he was wearing a St. Pauli jacket. The hooligans had wanted his jacket so they could burn it; when he tried to escape he was heavily beaten. The hatred runs deep, and for many right-wing hooligans, St. Pauli's defiance of their twisted value system makes their fans legitimate targets for violence and abuse.

It is not just right-wing hooligans that make supporting St. Pauli a risky business. For many years, fans have also had what could be best described as a strained relationship with the local police.

St. Pauli fans' mistrust of the authorities goes back a long way. It has its roots in the battles over the Hafenstraße, or the treatment at away games from the late 1980s to the present day. Many of the concerns mirror those of football fans the world over, and it boils down to the way football fans are frequently viewed as and treated like criminals or animals. These concerns are universal. However, the remainder of this chapter will look at a couple of specific situations where police actions, regretfully, reinforced many St. Pauli fans' perceptions of their local force. Of course, it is easy to deal in sweeping generalisations and football supporters are as guilty as anyone. You don't have to look to hard around the Millerntor to find plenty of 'ACAB' stickers (All Cops Are Bastards) although the popular acronym has been subverted for St. Pauli purposes to 'ACABEB' (All Cops Are Bastards Except Boll – Fabian Boll, the long-serving midfielder, is also a part-time policeman). While the generalisation is unhelpful, the twist adds a dash of wry humour.

On the evening of Saturday 4 July 2009, violence flared at the popular Schanzenfest street festival, in neighbouring Sternschanze. The festival had attracted around 10,000 visitors and offered the usual eclectic mix of stalls, live acts and music. As night fell, there were running battles between the police and youths. There are mixed reports on who started the trouble: some reports claim that around 600 Autonomen and a mix of local youths started the riot by throwing bottles and Molotov cocktails at the police, while others mention that heavy-handed police tactics provoked the crowd into action. There were repeated clashes between rioters and police. Stones and bottles were thrown and rubbish set on fire, while the police responded with water cannon. So far, these events had very little directly to do with FC. St. Pauli. All this changed at around 1.30am on Sunday morning. There were reports that some of the rioters had fled in the direction of the Millerntor stadium and more particularly Budapester Straße, home of the St. Pauli fan pub, The Jolly Roger.

Despite none of the rioters actually taking refuge inside the Jolly Roger, the police surrounded and then stormed the pub, using pepper spray and wielding batons. Inside were nearly 100 guests, celebrating a birthday party. None of them had had any involvement with the disturbances at the Schanzenfest. The attack was totally unprovoked and used a disproportionate amount of force. Guests were forced to flee towards the back of the pub, taking refuge in the toilets and the cellar to try to escape the effects of the pepper spray. One guest, a freelance journalist and St. Pauli fan, known to many as 'Hossa', took a baton full in the face and lost four teeth. The attack was completely nonsensical and widely condemned by all in the days that followed. FC St. Pauli supervisory board member, Tay Eich, stated: 'The police operation in and around the Jolly Roger is completely unacceptable and must be clarified completely.'

Peaceful partygoers had been terrified, many suffered the effects of the large quantities of pepper spray and tear gas used in a confined space, and Hossa, in particular, was badly assaulted and would face extensive surgery and dental bills totalling nearly €25,000 (with €5,000 covered by his health insurance and the remaining €20,000 covered by donations).

As the days passed, a theory began to emerge that might have helped to explain the randomness of the attack on the Jolly Roger. The theory linked the attack to previous disturbances on the street outside the Jolly Roger after the home game against Hansa Rostock, in March 2009, when a police officer was badly injured. The injured officer was from a police unit brought in from Eutin in Schleswig-Holstein to help police the Rostock game. St. Pauli fans had felt unjustly targeted by police from that area after the U23 St. Pauli team had secured promotion to the Regionalliga in Kiel. It was rumoured that officers from Eutin, again drafted in to police the Schanzenfest, had used the opportunity to retaliate against St. Pauli fans by attacking the Jolly Roger. In response to widespread criticism of the attack, the police launched an internal investigation. Police spokesman, Ralf Meyer denied the link between the attack on the Jolly Roger and the police unit from Eutin, saying: 'That is complete nonsense, particularly as many of the police officers involved in the operation were from Hamburg.' Whether the retaliation theory is true or not remains uncertain.

One positive that did emerge from the attack was the way in which St. Pauli fans rallied round and organised a collection for Hossa, so that he would be able to afford the surgery he needed. Various events in bars and clubs around St. Pauli were organised and included a charity match between the women's teams of St. Pauli and Altona. The flip side, of course, was that the attack provoked a lot of anger among St. Pauli fans, who felt that it was another example of the police singling them out in violent attacks. The following Friday, after a pre-season friendly against Hearts, a demonstration was organised to protest against police violence and raise awareness of the incident. There was also a further demonstration after the first home game of the season against Rot Weiss Ahlen attended by about 5,000 people.

The events of 4–5 July 2009 deepened the already shaky sense of trust between the police and St. Pauli supporters. It wouldn't be the last high-profile example of police using considerable force against St. Pauli fans guilty of no more than being in the wrong place at the wrong time.

During the Bundesliga's annual winter break it has become something of a tradition for clubs to participate in a variety of indoor tournaments across Germany. Sometimes these tournaments are glitzy affairs played on astroturf and featuring a selection of clubs from the top two divisions; other tournaments have a more regional flavour, mixing local amateur outfits with professional sides. For many years, FC St.

Pauli has sent teams to the Schweinske Cup held in the Alsterdorfer sports hall in Hamburg. The competition has been running since the late 1980s and has regularly featured two teams from St. Pauli, one containing players from the first team squad and the other made up of players from the Under-23 side. In the past the tournament has also featured Hamburger SV, smaller teams from around the region, local amateur sides and guest teams from overseas. The tournament was popular with supporters, perhaps desperate for their football fix during the winter break, perhaps grateful to escape the cold of a Hamburg winter by seeking shelter in the warmth of the sports hall.

Thanks mostly to the loud and colourful support led by the USP, the Schweinske Cup had become an event that many fans looked forward to – even those miles away from Hamburg could watch the action, as it was often televised on the internet. In 2010, the FC St. Pauli first team squad had triumphed with a 6-4 win over Holstein Kiel in the final. A year later, in January 2011, St. Pauli won the Cup for the ninth time with a 4-2 win over Danish side Brøndby IF. Again, it was the atmosphere generated by the St. Pauli fans bouncing up and down in the hall that really made the tournament. Expectations were high for another good tournament in 2012, although a few eyebrows were raised when it was announced that Hamburger SV were scheduled to compete. In the end, concerns over potential crowd trouble prompted HSV to withdraw. However, the 2012 version also included VfB Lübeck, a club with a known minority of fans with far-right connections. Again, there were mutterings of discontent on the internet. The tournament was supposed to be fun, a chance to sing and support the team during the winter break. People wondered why instead of inviting VfB Lübeck, a club like SV Babelsberg 03 with links to the St. Pauli fan scene and a like-minded political outlook weren't chosen, thus ensuring a festival atmosphere. That said, no one expected the tournament to turn out the way it did

Following events from afar is never ideal when trying to work out exactly what is going on – it often takes a while for a reliable version of events to emerge. For example: when the plug was pulled on the TV coverage of the game in Rostock, those watching online had no idea that rockets had been fired at the away fans or that the referee had halted the game. On the night of Friday 6 January 2012, getting an accurate report of what occurred during the opening games of the Schweinske Cup was similarly difficult. More worryingly, thanks to a considerable amount of inaccurate reporting of the evening's events in the media it took several days before what really happened came to light.

Instead of the usual internet stream of matches from the Schweinske Cup, reports started to seep through of trouble between rival fans early on Friday evening. Initially it seemed that a number of VfB Lübeck fans, complemented by hooligans from HSV, had attacked a section of St. Pauli fans in the hall, possibly stealing some flags belonging to St. Pauli fan groups. It then seemed that the police responded by attacking the St. Pauli fans with batons and pepper spray. The first reports that filtered through in the media turned this situation into a riot by St. Pauli fans, apparently intent on retribution over their rivals from Lübeck but also determined to clash with police. It was widely reported that St. Pauli fans not only clashed with police but also ransacked the tournament's VIP area. Violence was also said to continue outside the venue with fans throwing bottles, paving slabs and flares at the police. In the midst of all this, at around 11.00pm on the Friday evening, the organisers, at the request of the police, cancelled the tournament, which had been scheduled to continue the following day.

For the next day or so, various branches of the German media ran with stories that seemed to place the St. Pauli fans at the centre of the violence. But how could this be? How could a tournament that had traditionally been not just peaceful but a showcase for loud, vibrant, positive support turned into something so ugly? There had to be something more to this story.

As usual, the internet provided a useful, if not entirely reliable barometer of St. Pauli fans' experiences of the evening. It was clear that many fans were angered by what was generally perceived as the heavy-handed policing of events (and that is putting it mildly). There was also a reasonable amount of criticism directed at the organisers of the competition.

The club themselves were quick to react, demonstrating solidarity with the version of events recounted by many St. Pauli fans. The club issued a statement laying the blame for the trouble at the door of the police and the organisers (although they were also quick to acknowledge that not all St. Pauli fans' behaviour had been exemplary). A statement, issued the Monday after the trouble, clearly set out their version of events – a version that differed considerably from the one provided by the police.

The club's statement, drawn from the experiences of fans and officials who had been present at the Alsterdorfer sports hall (a number of club officials had experienced the police's aggressive tactics first hand), recounted their version of events in chronological order. It began by explaining how a group of around 200 St. Pauli fans were escorted from the nearby Lattenkamp train station to the Alsterdorfer venue. Some fans at the back of the group let off flares and this prompted the police to halt the progress of fans on three occasions. In contrast to the police report, the use of flares wasn't linked or in any way a precursor to the violence that would follow, it was just fans creating some atmosphere as they walked to the arena. The club, after consultation with fan groups, also established that there had been no prior 'agreement' with fans from VfB Lübeck (or other clubs) to organise a fight between fans. Indeed, the statement indicates that the St. Pauli fans were looking forward to an exciting, atmospheric evening, like the ones they had experienced in previous years.

Fans of FC St. Pauli, despite delays getting into the hall caused by only two entrances being open, made their way peacefully to their allocated section. In the seats opposite about 120 fans, mostly from VfB Lübeck, took their seats. It was pretty clear from the chants that began to emerge that they were more interested in goading the fans of St. Pauli rather than supporting their own side. There were repeated chants of 'Faggots, Faggots', 'Jews' and 'Gypsies' directed at the St. Pauli block. The club noted that neither the organisers nor the police did anything to stop this chanting. There was no tannoy announcement and no police action was taken. At this point in proceedings the club statement made it clear that they disagreed with the police's version of events, reiterating that at this point no St. Pauli fans tried to attack their counterparts from Lübeck.

Trouble started at the end of the first match in the group stage of the competition between FC. St Pauli's Under-23 side and VfB Lübeck. Many fans left their seats and headed to the concourse under the stand to use the toilets. A low barrier separated the two sets of fans. Robust, verbal exchanges took place between the VfB Lübeck supporters, and interestingly a number of HSV fans, and their counterparts from St. Pauli. As things got more heated (there had been no violent exchanges between the rival sets of supporters at this point) the police intervened. They had been standing between the two groups facing the St. Pauli fans. They then decided to push the St. Pauli fans back toward the entrance to the hall. In doing so they used considerable force, including batons and pepper spray. One 20-year-old man was hit so hard he was knocked unconscious, his crime seemingly queuing for the toilet. Other fans were injured in the baton attack and many more fell victim to the liberal use of pepper spray. Police reinforcements arrived and forcefully drove the St. Pauli fans back into the east side of the hall. At no time during this action did the police or the hall announcer issue any instructions or explanations over the loudspeakers. Instead, a sense of panic spread through the hall as hundreds of innocent fans, including children and pensioners, were caught up in the pandemonium.

At this point, the VfB Lübeck fans managed to get to the St. Pauli section behind the goal and steal three banners belonging to prominent St. Pauli fan clubs (Ramba Zamba, Hinchas, and Kein Mensch ist illegal). It is worth noting, that the stealing of banners, scarves and flags of opposing fan groups is considered as a badge of honour among certain ultra-stye groups in German football. It was undoubtedly an act of provocation on the part of the VfB Lübeck fans and their allies. A couple of St. Pauli fans had tried to prevent the theft by confronting the Lübeck fans and this prompted further use of pepper spray on the St. Pauli block by police, a move that injured many St. Pauli fans totally uninvolved in the trouble. Around 25 St. Pauli fans did try to get to the Lübeck block, but again they were blocked by a combination of stewards and police.

Groups of St. Pauli fans then vented their frustrations on the police, who returned with more baton charges and indiscriminate use of pepper spray. The club were quite open about the fact that a number of St. Pauli fans sought violent conflict with the police but were also concerned about the way in which the police responded. As mentioned previously, reports in the media had indicated that a mob of St. Pauli fans had ransacked the VIP area. The club's view was somewhat different: far from attacking the VIP area, these were desperate fans trying to evade the police charge. In this phase of the conflict, a 72-year-old man was treated for exposure to pepper spray and a member of the club's Supervisory Board was hit with a baton.

The trouble rumbled on, with many St. Pauli fans effectively kettled inside the hall. Interestingly, it appears that the 120 or so VfB Lübeck fans were allowed to leave of their own accord, taking the stolen banner with them. After an hour and a half the St. Pauli supporters were allowed to leave through a single exit. Outside the hall trouble flared again, with more St. Pauli fans being kettled or arrested. The trouble continued at the station where there were reports of pepper spray being used in one U-Bahn carriage.

The club statement was a strong one. It directly contradicted the statement issued by the Hamburg Police Department and clearly sided with the fans' version of events. The club acknowledged that a minority of St. Pauli fans had contributed to the violence. However, they were quick to point out that it wasn't St. Pauli fans that instigated the trouble. The statement concluded: 'The police operation in the venue was excessive, not just by our judgement, but by that of many eye witnesses and bystanders as well. Many respectable and innocent football fans were injured and not just physically... A spiral of violence was started, but not by the behaviour of supporters of FC St. Pauli... FC St. Pauli has participated in the tournament for decades with joy and our supporters contributed massively to the success of this event. We reject the accusation that because of the behaviour of our supporters the tournament cannot take place in the future. If individuals or groups showed misconduct, the club bears a share of the responsibility. But we call on the public to look at the events in an objective and differentiated manner and refrain from hastily or generalised conclusions.'

The statement further strengthened the bond between the club and its supporters. Rather than take the easy option of going along with the police version of events and issuing a bland condemnation of the violent behaviour of fans, they wanted an independent inquiry into the organisation and policing of the event. The club simply were not prepared to go along with the police (and media) version of events. Sven Brux, the club's security officer, who had also been caught up in the trouble, getting hit with a baton, went even further in his press conference. He appeared to advocate direct action against Nazi hooligans: 'We also have to look at the reality when it's about confrontations with let's say

Nazis or right-leaning hooligans. We (St. Pauli) are praised all over the country for being "against Nazis" and for standing up to them. Well, then that has to be implemented in reality at some point. If a Nazi thinks he could use such phrases in a St. Pauli section, then he must get the feeling it might not be that good for his health.'

Brux knows the St. Pauli fan scene better than anyone, and that one of the central tenets of supporting the club is to be anti-fascist. He appeared to be suggesting that, if suitably provoked, there comes a point where you have to stand up to the fascists. It was the sort of statement that wouldn't be made at any other football club in Germany, perhaps in Europe.

Of course, the authorities were quick to rebut the club's claims, with Hamburg's Senator Michael Neumann defending the actions of the police and shifting the blame back onto the shoulders of the fans.

The difference in the accounts of the incident underlines the level of mistrust that exists between St. Pauli fans and the police. It is probably fair to say this mistrust is mutual.

Beyond the headlines of a cancelled tournament (it was later announced that there would be no Schweinske Cup in 2013 with the city council ordering a ban on professional teams' participation in indoor events), 80 injuries and 77 arrests, there remain two prominent issues facing St. Pauli fans. First, that they continue to be at risk of attack from far-right hooligan groups; second, that there has been a breakdown of trust between fans and the police.

In response to the different versions of events put forward by the police and the club, the Ständiger Fanausschuss commissioned an independent inquiry into the events at the Schweinske Cup. The report was chaired by Professor Dr Thomas Feltes, a Professor of Criminology and Police Science at the Law Faculty of the Ruhr-University in Bochum. In May 2012 Feltes published his findings. The report criticised the police heavily. Firstly, police preparation was criticised. It was reported that they were well aware of HSV hooligans' plans to 'crash' the tournament, as well as having knowledge of around 30 to 40 'problematic' VfB Lübeck fans that would be attending. The report also highlighted police reluctance to deal with the supporters of VfB Lübeck as they chanted obscenities, instead allowing them free rein to move around the hall. There was also criticism of the way the police, instead of dealing with the VfB Lübeck mob, positioned themselves in front of the St. Pauli fan-block, obscuring the view of the pitch, serving to heighten the tensions between the fans and the police. The excessive use of force directed towards the St. Pauli fans, especially the use of pepper spray at close quarters, which saw innocent bystanders including people of all ages being injured, was also roundly condemned.

This independent report concurred with the view of the club and its supporters that much of the blame for the escalation of violence lay with the police and the organisers. Of course, no one was suggesting that the St. Pauli fans were completely innocent but the report showed that they were not the instigators of the trouble. This stance was supported by previous experiences at the Schweinske Cup, which for many years had been a highlight of the football calendar for genuine St. Pauli fans. It seems obvious that these fans were targeted by a handful of right-wing hooligans from VfB Lübeck and HSV and that the police response to this attack, bizarrely, assumed that the St. Pauli fans were the aggressors.

This returns us to the central premise of this chapter, that being a St. Pauli fan – and being proudly anti-fascist, anti-sexist, anti-homophobic – can make you a 'legitimate' target for misguided right-wing hooligans. It also, all too frequently, places you at odds with the police and the authorities.

MATCH

NO PLACE LIKE HOME

FC St. Pauli 5 SC Paderborn 07 0
2. Bundesliga
Sunday 6 May 2012, 1.30pm, Millerntor Stadion

THERE WAS A reasonable amount riding on St. Pauli's last game of the 2011–12 season at home to Paderborn. A win for either team offered a sliver of hope of claiming third place in 2. Bundesliga (the 'relegationsplatz' – which offered the chance of promotion via a two-legged play-off against the team finishing third from bottom in the Bundesliga). However, in the race for third place it was Fortuna Düsseldorf who held all the cards, as a win in their last match at home against Duisburg would mean they'd claim third, not St. Pauli or Paderborn. A draw for Fortuna would also do, as long as FC St. Pauli didn't beat Paderborn by nine clear goals.

However, this wasn't why I so desperately wanted to be at the Millerntor. I wanted to say goodbye to the Gegengerade, the ramshackle, outdated but downright lovely stand that ran the length of the pitch on the Heiligengeistfeld side of the ground. The stretch of terrace that was lovingly referred to by fans as 'the back straight'.

It's probably fair to say that the Gegengerade is up there with Dortmund's Südtribüne as one of Germany's most iconic football terraces. In terms of cultural significance it is probably even more important. As we have seen, it was on the Gegengerade that the 'mythos of St. Pauli' was born. It was from here that the group of punks and anarchists from the Hafenstraße first watched St. Pauli back in the mid-80s. It was on the same shallow terrace, just behind the dugouts, that this 'Black-Block' grew in number and helped establish FC St. Pauli as a 'Kult' phenomenon. In the quarter of a century that followed, the Gegengerade established itself in German football folklore as somewhere truly special to drink, make friends, talk politics, talk nonsense, sing (or not sing) and occasionally watch football – a proper communal space, for many fans an extension of their living room or their local pub. Or, put more simply, it was home.

Although the myth of the back straight took hold in the mid-1980s, the shallow terracing of the Gegengerade was first laid in 1961, when the club moved a few hundred yards from its previous home at Ernst-Thälmann-Straße to the Millerntor as the land where the previous stadium stood, itself only built in the aftermath of the Second World War, was required to host the IGA – International Garden Exposition of 1963.

There's a lovely photograph in *FC St. Pauli. Das Buch* which shows five boys standing on the corner of the terrace where the Gegengerade meets the Südkurve. They are looking out over the Millerntor as the construction work draws to a close in 1961. From that photo and other pictures dating from the period, you can see that not a lot changed over the intervening 50 years. Save for the addition of a security fence and the construction of the 'temporary' seating of the Gegentribüne, the back straight retained most of its original features.

I wanted to be a part of this farewell. Although a relative newcomer to the Millerntor, the Gegengerade holds special memories for me as well. As you'll recall from the opening chapter of this book, nearly five years earlier, my father and I had stood at the north end of the back straight in the baking hot sun watching St. Pauli defeat Bayer Leverkusen in the first round of the DFB Pokal. Quite simply the experience had reignited my love of football. Or more specifically my love of being part of a crowd watching football.

My Dad and I loved it: we'd been showered in beer, embraced by total strangers and made to feel incredibly welcome. And, although I've returned numerous times since, I'll always hold that first experience dear. As a result, I just had to be there for the Gegengerade's curtain call.

I'd been looking forward to the trip for weeks, especially as my mate Shaun was coming along and we were making a long weekend of it, courtesy of a handily-placed Bank Holiday Monday in the UK. Shaun and I have been friends for more than 20 years, and he's like family to me. He'd been through a hell of a time, losing his wife Helen in a road accident. He's held himself together admirably since, looking after his two children. It's hard to put into words the respect I have for him and the way he has coped with the tragic hand that fate has dealt him. This trip fell a week or so short of the second anniversary of Helen's death, and we hoped it would give him an opportunity to put things to the back of his mind for 48 hours or so. We certainly planned to enjoy it.

We get into Hamburg at lunchtime on the Saturday and, as we can't check in to the hotel until three, decide to visit *Beatlemania* on the Reeperbahn. The museum is a delight – spread over five floors and covering everything from their arrival in Hamburg to their eventual split. It is surprisingly quiet, perhaps due in part to the countless other 'attractions' the Reeperbahn offers, even at three in the afternoon!

It is FA Cup final weekend back in England with Chelsea taking on Liverpool, and with Shaun being a Liverpool fan, we then have to find somewhere to watch the cup final. We settle on the Copa Cabana Sportsbar on Clemens-Schultz Straße. Again, it is far from crowded, with just a sprinkling of British football followers, although it is great to briefly bump into Malcolm from the UK St. Pauli messageboard, and (whisper it) another Watford fan.

That evening, we decide to spurn the tawdry sleaze of the sinful mile, heading instead for Sternschanze, where we stumble across an excellent anti-Nazi gig at Rote Flora. Crowds are out in numbers, the atmosphere is relaxed and we spend the evening sitting outside drinking Astra. It is the perfect way to spend the night before a game, and as neither of us are massive drinkers, it isn't long past midnight before we are back in our hotel room with a supply of chocolate talking football, politics and gibberish into the small hours.

Sunday morning starts slowly, but we soon make it to the Fanladen, where I am able to catch up with another Watford fan, Chris. We'd first met on the platform at Coventry station in 1990 when we used to get the train down to Watford for home games. But due to me officially renouncing my support for the Hornets when Tory party supremo, Lord Ashcroft became chairman, I've not seen Chris for a good six or seven years. It is good to catch up, and interesting to find out that Chris has been working on the excellent *Sporting Statues* project, documenting and mapping statues of sports stars in the UK (and beyond). Of course, it is also good to see Stefan and the Fanladen crew, as without their continued assistance and good cheer these trips wouldn't be possible.

Not being ready to get back on the Astra, Shaun and I head out in search of something to eat – and you just can't beat a currywurst for breakfast – and then make our way into the ground. We take up a spot on the Südkurve, to the right of the goal and near enough to the Gegengerade to get some good photos of the back straight's last stand (since the redevelopment of the Südkurve, the Fanladen's ticket allocation for international fans tends to be for that part of the stadium). Before long the familiar chimes of *Hells Bells* are ringing out and all eyes turn to the Gegengerade to witness the choreo. The fans in the Gegentribüne seats light sparklers while those on the terrace below conjure up a confetti-storm (at our end) and twirl black flags. Large plywood freaks and a tombstone with the legend 'RIP Gegengerade 1961–2012' are raised at the front of the terrace by the fence and complete the show. It is an impressive and emotional start to proceedings.

The game gets under way and I'm never much good at keeping track of what's happening on the pitch. I am more interested in the trading of songs between the backstraight and the Südkurve. It seems that for the first 15 minutes it is the back straight who are leading the chanting and not the USP – now, that may've been down to our location, but the USP guys on the fence don't look too happy. Yet, it seems only fitting that the fans on the Gegengerade are giving the terrace a rousing send-off, and before long both stands are belting out chants in unison.

At some point in the first half we go a goal up through a Lasse Sobiech header; hell, it may even have been the result of a corner – and we never score from corners! Then, Max Kruse bursts through the centre and makes it 2-0. We are doing our bit, but what is going on in

Düsseldorf? There is a lot of checking of mobile phones and it seems that Düsseldorf and Duisburg are drawing 2-2. This is confirmed at half-time as the latest scores are displayed on the big screen.

Paderborn still looked shell-shocked as they emerge for the second-half; at 2-0 down they are all but out of the promotion race, but despite St. Pauli being in front, no one really expects Fortuna to stuff it up at home. There are some nice exchanges between the stands in the second half, including the whole of the Südkurve attempting to sit down in unison, in response to the fans in the Haupttribüne standing up to acknowledge our support – this is no easy feat on a packed terrace, especially for Shaun with his newly replaced hip.

Florian Bruns finishes coolly on 60 minutes, and then something bonkers happens. Reports start to trickle through that Duisburg are 3-2 up in Düsseldorf. In the blink of an eye it is 4-2, prompting wild celebrations, the hugging of total strangers and genuinely acting like loons. With 20,000 people trying to get confirmation via their mobiles, the data network locks out, but who cares? There are further unconfirmed reports of a fifth goal for Duisburg and suddenly we are surfing an adrenalin rush as huge as the TV tower looming in the distance. It is five minutes of pure ecstasy that only football can provide. Unfortunately, some time after Moritz Volz adds a fourth with a delicate chip over an out-of-position Paderborn keeper, the wave crests and we are brought crashing back to reality by a rather sheepish man in an official tracksuit top who emerges from the tunnel (where they must've had the 'conference' showing on a TV) and reluctantly holds up two fingers on each hand. The comedown is momentary. We are 4-0 up on the last day of the season; this is no time to get weighed down by trivial things like promotion – and, anyway, another five goals will see us overturn Düsseldorf's superior goal difference regardless!

Deniz Naki comes off the bench on 78 minutes to a rapturous reception. The pint-sized striker is being released at the end of the season and this is his chance to say goodbye. Right on the final whistle (and I mean right – there is no time even for a restart) Deniz pops up at the far post to bundle home a fifth goal for St. Pauli, sparking more crazed celebrations in the stands. It is a fitting final cameo for a modern-day cult-hero, a player with the capacity to dazzle and frustrate in equal measure, but a man the fans had taken to their hearts.

And so with the game over, and a 2-2 draw in Düsseldorf confirming Fortuna's place in the 'relegationsplatz' play-off with Hertha Berlin, it is time to start saying our goodbyes. The team assembles for a photo against the backdrop of the Gegengerade, as fans continue to trade songs in the stands. Soon, an emotional Deniz Naki recreates his goal celebration against Hansa Rostock by ceremonially planting a flag in the pitch right in front of us. Fellow departee, the dependable Carsten Rothenbach follows suit. Naki is visibly moved by his reception and sheds the first of the afternoon's many tears. At some point he is handed a microphone and makes an impassioned speech in front of the Südkurve. The match has finished a good 45 minutes earlier, but no one is leaving. Eventually, after more tears, Naki disappears reluctantly down the tunnel.

With the players finally gone, attention once again shifts to the back straight. Seats are being ripped out, planks of wood snapped off and there are even attempts to dislodge the crush barriers from their concrete foundations. We hear of one fan who had gone on the stadium tour the day before and hidden a hacksaw on the Gegengerade, so that his mate could have a go at sawing off a crush barrier. Unfortunately the barrier was so thick that the hacksaw snapped. Other fans appear to have bolt cutters and are snipping away at sections of the perimeter fence. The back straight will stay open for two hours after the end of the game, but stewards are trying to chivvy us out of the Südkurve, so reluctantly we shuffle out and head for the Gegengerade, but not before Shaun's forest green corduroy jacket has attracted much attention from a young dreadlocked chap on the concourse. An obligatory group hug follows, along with prolonged stroking of said corduroy. It is another typically St. Pauli moment, one you can never imagine being replicated in the football grounds of Britain.

Round the back of the Gegengerade stewards are refusing to let fans from other parts of the ground on to the back straight. We decide that it is a good time to get back on the beer and observe fans' increasingly ingenious attempts to get their seats out of the ground without paying the controversial €19,10 for the privilege. We see one man carrying a couple of seats opt for out running the stewards, while others have short-term success lobbing seats out of the back of the stand to friends waiting the other side of the fence (the fluorescent jacket mob soon put a stop to this).

As mentioned earlier, Shaun and I aren't the biggest of drinkers, but we decide now is the time to go for it and continue on the Astra, making our way round to the AFM container, which has been temporarily relocated to the paved area outside the Südkurve. Here, buoyed by the alcohol and armed only with the phrase, 'Hi, we've come from England?' (no, we don't know why we adopted this line of enquiry either) we begin our mission to be photographed with as many St. Pauli players as possible as they head for their cars. This was the first time since a Junior Hornet Open Day in 1985 that I've been photographed with a professional footballer, but I've got to say, despite being a good few years older than most of the players, it is enormous fun. By this time, we have again bumped into Mark and Claudia, who we met earlier and who have been standing behind us during the game – Mark had spectacularly managed to spill his beer all over my jeans – and they are kind enough to get the scoop of the day: a photo of me and Shaun with Deniz Naki.

We stay drinking outside the ground until about 7pm. The game has finished nearly four hours earlier, but no one is in a hurry to leave (another fantastic difference between football here and back home). We desperately need something to eat to soak up the beer, so wimp out of further end-of-season celebrations at Knust, as by then we are starting to contemplate the 4.45am start needed to catch our plane home. With one final walk past the Gegengerade, we make it back to the hotel in good time, where there is some totally unexplained and unprecedented dancing round the room in our pants to *Livin' Thing* by ELO as we attempt to pack (apologies for the mental image, I've no idea why this happened, and the tune's certainly not very punk rock – although I do blame that final Astra).

Despite all the frivolity, our plane is caught and we make it home, bleary-eyed, early doors on Bank Holiday Monday. Like always, it has been a hell of a trip. The match itself, although incredibly entertaining and with bags of goals, is once again just the backdrop.

I'm still incredibly sad that the Gegengerade has been demolished (as I write the stand has already been reduced to rubble). Even though I only stood on its shallow steps a handful of times, the loss of such an atmospheric, old-school terrace resonates deeply. Perhaps it reminds me of all the lost grounds of my youth that have been replaced by the perfunctory, soulless stadia that now dominate English football. I hope we don't end up looking back on the Gegengerade's demolition in the same way as I look back on the changes in the English game. For me the destruction of our old grounds, our sporting heritage, is intrinsically linked with British football losing its soul.

In one way, it is stupid to have such an attachment to some crumbling concrete steps and an assortment of steel girders, but in another way the sentiment is entirely justified: the Gegengerade is where I rediscovered that watching football really could be everything I wanted it to be. It was a space where thousands of others stood every fortnight, supporting their team, drinking beer and forging friendships. One of the first video tributes to the passing of the Gegengerade posted on YouTube was set to *In My Life* by The Beatles, and no song seemed more apt: 'There are places I'll remember all my life...' The back straight is one such place.

Of course, it is too easy to be both consumed by nostalgia and resistant to change. The back straight I fell in love with has gone, but in its place will be a new, steeper terrace with a capacity of 10,000 on the terracing and 3,000 seats (about 5,500 more than the old back straight). It will not be a stand consisting of padded seats and executive boxes – we have the Haupttribüne for that. And, if my trips to St. Pauli have taught me anything, it's if there's one thing more important than the team, the stadium or the club itself, it's the supporters. They'll return in August, renew friendships, drink, watch football and welcome, with open arms, us 'foreign' fans who make the trip over to share the occasion with them. The old Gegengerade may be gone, but those people who made it their home will return. And with them, the legend of the Gegengerade and the 'mythos of St. Pauli' will live on, evolve and permeate through the pre-cast concrete and steel of the new back straight.

MATCH

HAMBURGER WETTER

Offenburger FV 0 FC St. Pauli 3
DFB Pokal
Saturday 18 August 2012, 3.30pm, Karl-Heitz-Stadion

IT'S FIVE YEARS since my first ever game, St. Pauli's 1-0 win over Bayer Leverkusen in the DFB Pokal on that hot August afternoon. So, it seems fitting to mark the anniversary by attending another game at exactly the same stage in the competition. In 2007, with promotion just secured from the Regionalliga, St. Pauli were the underdogs, and as such were guaranteed a home draw against a team from the top two divisions. This time, as established residents of 2. Bundesliga, the roles are reversed, and we are drawn away against Offenburger FV, one of the lowest ranked teams in the competition. They secured their place by winning the Südbadischer Pokal at the end of last season with a 2-0 victory over SV Linx. Plying their trade in the Oberliga, the fifth tier of German football, they are such minnows that for a few moments after the draw was made they are confused on Twitter with the more illustrious Kickers Offenbach of 3. Liga.

A quick squint at Google Earth reveals Offenburg is just across the French border, about 30 minutes from Strasbourg, which makes the trip eminently possible by train. A further bit of research shows that they play in a wonderfully basic-looking stadium that is predominantly terracing. Despite St. Pauli's appalling recent record in the DFB Pokal (crashing out two years running to lower ranked opposition) this looks as if it has the potential to be a great trip.

So, once again, train timetables are consulted, tickets purchased and I am on my way to Germany. I decide to base myself in Strasbourg, as I can get there in good time the night before the game and leave myself with a short train ride over the border on match day. I have to admit that, although I quite enjoy the solitude of these long train trips (it's an only child thing) I'd much rather be making the journey with friends or family. Journeys are better shared, and my most memorable experiences have come when I've travelled with my Dad, my family or mates.

Strasbourg, more chocolate box than I expect, is already bathed in early morning sunshine as I leave for the station. By the time I arrive in Offenburg the predicted heatwave is in full effect; temperatures are forecast to be over 30 degrees by kick-off. The city itself is picturesque, the central street bustling with a Saturday morning market. One thing I can't quite work out is the predominance of nautical statues dotted around the main street. Offenburg seems just about as landlocked as you can get, but I spy what looks like Neptune and the Loch Ness monster immortalised in bronze.

It isn't quite midday, but there are a fair number of St. Paulianer milling about, instantly recognisable in an assortment of black and brown shirts, which do absolutely nothing to reflect the building heat. The ground is a 20-minute walk from the town centre, and with nothing much else to do, I am on my way. The stadium looks as simple as it did on the internet, the shallow curves of terracing looking like they'd been cast from the same stone and laid to the same plan as the original terraces of the Millerntor back in the 1960s. The only thing slightly spoiling the ambience is the addition of temporary (I hope) security fencing around three-quarters of the stadium. The guest block has higher, maximum security fencing, which I am led to believe will remain, to allow the club to fulfill any safety requirements in the event of promotion. It's a shame, as it does spoil the look of the ground and I am pretty sure there is no real need for it, not for this game at least.

I meet Stefan from the Fanladen about two hours before kick-off, fresh from a minibus journey from Hamburg that began at 5am. By now the area around the stadium is starting to buzz with fans eager to get into the ground when the gates open at 1.30pm. The vibe is very relaxed, with the air and charm of a pre-season friendly or a particularly well-organised school fête. With just 500 seats in a tiny main stand, corporate hospitality (oh yes, even in the first round of the DFB Pokal) consists of a giant wedding marquee and trestle tables, with parasols to deflect the sun.

Rather than do the sensible thing of finding some shade to sit in for the two hours before kick-off at 3.30pm, I opt to get into the ground early. Maybe it is our abject summer that prompts me to soak up as many rays as possible, but after about half an hour baking in the heat, I regret not going for the shady option (Stefan has very sensibly based himself under a large bush, as he hands out tickets and passes for the game).

The 'home' sections of the ground seem to be fairly full already, although there is a high proportion of St. Pauli fans mingling with the locals. The guest block fills up gradually as people make their way either from the town centre bars or from their coaches after the long journey from Hamburg. The noise levels and the colour perk up as Ultrà Sankt Pauli arrive carrying with them the usual variety of flags and banners for this afternoon's choreo. One that catches my eye (it might not have been USP's, I can't be sure) is an excellent portrait of Woody Guthrie augmented with the legend 'All you fascists are bound to lose' – a great piece of artwork. I wonder if it has been produced to coincide with the centenary of Woody's birth?

It also makes me reflect on another of the many differences between British and German fan culture. On the internet that morning I'd read a report of the Cardiff v Huddersfield game from the previous evening. The main photo accompanying the piece referred to Cardiff's decision to ditch their traditional blue kits for red ones and depicted a homemade banner proclaiming that Cardiff fans 'bleed blue'. I don't have a problem with the sentiment or the protest against this particular strand of ludicrous commercialisation, but the banner itself looked like it had been hastily painted by enthusiastic primary school kids. The British Trade Union movement has a long tradition of beautifully crafted protest banners, but unfortunately this ethos has not quite made the transition to our football fans, where an old bed sheet and some emulsion are still the norm.

The sun beats down as kick-off approaches; teams of volunteers are wandering the terraces with buckets of water, splashing it enthusiastically over anyone who requests it, but it doesn't really make much difference. It is a case of refilling buckets of water while we burn. Then something highly unexpected happens: they bring out the water cannon. Normally, when we associate St. Pauli and water cannon, it spells trouble, usually a result of some over-zealous policing. Not this time. The local fire brigade have decided to turn their jets on the fans. It is pretty spectacular and a first for me. The chant of 'Hamburger Wetter' spreads across the terrace as everyone dances in the deluge. Within minutes the entire terrace is totally drenched, literally soaked to the skin. Fortunately, the heat is such that by kick-off we are just comfortably damp.

The surprises continue as the teams come out to the polite applause of a sold-out stadium. There has been debate leading up to the game about St. Pauli's oft ill-fated 'cup-kit'. In recent years, the club have taken to producing a special kit for the DFB Pokal, an act of total commercialism that has had its impact massively undermined by the fact that St. Pauli have taken to crashing out after just one game. Perhaps, with this in mind, no 'cup-kit' was released this year, but as the teams emerge St. Pauli are wearing their popular camouflage kit, last worn during their march to the semi-finals in 2005–06. Whether this is an inspired piece of retro marketing or just a case of the manufacturers, Do You Football, having a stockpile of old kits isn't clear. Either way, it is back to the future and though former striker, Felix Luz was conspicuous by his absence, my Facebook stream does indicate that Do You Football got St. Pauli legend, Michél Mazingu-Dinzey, in for the press shots (and by the time I returned home the shirt was available for purchase from the club shop for a whopping €59.95).

The heat is such that the game never really rises above walking pace (even the ICE trains that pass along the track behind the home fans on the Nordkurve slow to a crawl). And, aside from an early chance for Offenburger FV well blocked by Tschauner, the action is almost exclusively in Offenburg's half. They have parked the bus, and possibly the fire engine too (after it had returned to give us another soaking early in the first half). It is down to us to find a way through their 11-man defence. Eventually, Mahir Saglik, starting instead of Marius Ebbers, shows neat footwork to create enough space to get his shot away; it beats the keeper and finds its way into the bottom corner. One-nil up. Perhaps the camouflage cup-kit is going to bring us back some luck? That's how it remains at half-time after outstanding reflex saves from pint-sized Florian Streif in Offenburg's goal.

Despite USP's best efforts, the atmosphere has been distinctly muted, with the usual selection of songs sung at reduced volume. The heat doesn't help either and by now there are a large number of sunburned necks and faces. The second half is even more pedestrian than the first, Saglik scoring again on 68 minutes with a neat header to put the game beyond doubt, Offenburger haven't really looked like scoring one, let alone two. And on 78 minutes, substitute Daniel Ginczek gets off the mark with a simple tap-in. It finishes 3-0. After a couple of seasons where the second round of the cup had seemed like some unobtainable promised land, we are in the hat for the next round. And it is all down to the camouflage cup-kit. Well, mostly.

While the game itself has never really been a fair contest, St. Pauli winning without ever having to get out of first gear, it has been a delight to take in another DFB Pokal game, especially in such old-school surroundings. The only thing left to do is to rightly applaud the opposition on their well-deserved lap of honour and then leave for the station to begin the journey in reverse. Five years on: another sweltering hot afternoon of cup football, and no sign of my love affair with FC St. Pauli starting to wane. I still wouldn't swap these three or four trips a year for a season ticket in the Premiership. There'd be no water cannon for a start.

Chapter 12

REMEMBERING THE PAST, SAFEGUARDING THE FUTURE

A museum with a difference

THE HISTORY OF both FC St. Pauli and the district in which it resides is complex and continually evolving. Yet there is also a degree of continuity – or at least a number of recurring themes handed down through the years. The history of St. Pauli is the history of the outsider: the district always down at heel, never really sharing in the wealth of the City of Hamburg generated through hundreds of years as a busy, bustling commercial port; the club, trophy-less and always in the shadow of Hamburger SV.

In terms of recurring themes, some of the issues that the district faced in the late 1980s – issues that contributed to FC St. Pauli's 'Kult' status – are just as relevant today. The battle fought over the squatted houses on the Hafenstraße continues to resonate to this very day. Sure, some of the original punks and anarchists who congregated on the terraces of the Gegengerade are long gone, but the spirit of defiance and belief in social justice lingers on inside the stadium. More than that, the battle to defend community spaces is just as relevant in Hamburg today as it was 30 years ago. December 2013 saw massive protests at plans to redevelop the Rote Flora cultural centre in the neighbouring Schanzenviertel area. The former theatre, one of the few to survive intact from World War Two, has been squatted since 1989 and has become a hugely significant and symbolic centre for the leftist groups in Hamburg. For years the contract between the owner of Rote Flora and the council prevented a change of use from a social centre but since 2011 the owner has been free to sell the land for redevelopment. It is part of the wider issue of gentrification that haunts the district and has also recently seen the eviction of tenants from the so-called 'Esso' houses on the Reeperbahn. At the heart of these actions lies the future shaping of St. Pauli and its surrounding areas. Opposition to gentrification has been strong, with more than 7,000 people taking to the streets on 21 December 2013 to protest about the proposed eviction and redevelopment of Rote Flora. The mood of protest was reflected inside the Millerntor with banners and a show of solidarity for Rote Flora in evidence the previous evening at the last home game before the winter break against Karlsruher SC.

As we have seen, St. Pauli fans know the risk presented by the gentrification of football. They are also well aware that this isn't just a football issue, that the very district the club represents could be transformed forever if rents continue to rise, redevelopment continues and the very people who make the area special are forced to leave. St. Pauli fans are part of the fight against this desire to maximise profit and commercial gain; they understand what the club represents and that, like the district itself, they remain a thorn in the side of the establishment, a reminder that not everything has to be polished, pristine and soulless.

Part of safeguarding both club and district in the future stems from remembering and understanding the past. Understanding that – perhaps – without the squats on the Hafenstraße, without those squatters and their friends first setting foot on the Gegengerade there would be no modern-day 'Kult' club, and thus no focal point for those wanting to fight fascism, racism, homophobia and commercialism in football and society.

Remembering the past is vital in shaping the future, and this is why I decided to donate my authors' royalties from this book to the '1910 – Museum für den FC St. Pauli e.V.' (1910 e.V.) project. It is the biggest voluntary project ever started at FC St. Pauli, both in terms of the funding and the amount of voluntary work required to get the museum operational. It seems fitting then that the fan-led proposals to build a museum should focus on finding a home in the space under the newly-built Gegengerade stand. It is a case of closing the circle: commemorating the rich and diverse history of the club on the spot where Doc Mabuse and his friends from the Hafenstraße first stood a quarter of a century before.

We have already seen that in principle – and subject to funding being found – all sides have agreed that the controversial police headquarters (partly a prerequisite of the DFB's licensing agreement) can be built elsewhere, making it possible for the space under the Gegengerade to house a permanent club museum. To celebrate the club's centenary in 2010, the club put together a temporary exhibition on the Millerntorplatz, housed in a set of 31 interconnected shipping containers. It was a popular attraction; the use of the containers gave the exhibition an authentic and atmospheric feel and was a fabulous nod to the importance of the docks and the river Elbe to the history of both the district and the club. The centenary exhibition covered all aspects of the club's past and brought together many artefacts and exhibits for the first time (a personal favourite being the 'Save Football, Smash Bu$ine$$' banner that I'd first seen in video footage of games at the Millerntor). However, the centenary exhibition was only temporary and at the end of October 2010 the containers were removed, most probably relocated back to their natural home in the docks.

Then, in 2011, Michael Pahl, one of the authors of the club's centenary book, and Roger Hasenbein, a member of the supervisory board, put their idea for a permanent museum to a working party of supporters. Things moved quickly from there as fans mobilised themselves. One thing emerged from the early discussions: the museum couldn't just be a collection of old shirts and ephemera, it would need to be interactive – a place that would at once entertain and inform but also promote discussion and reflection on the past. The space will be right next to the communal areas of the Fanräume. It will not just be confined to the physical space under the Gegengerade. Stadium tours and links to the wider district will broaden the museum's remit and appeal.

Until the dream of a permanent museum can be realised, 1910 e.V. continue to organise a series of temporary events and exhibitions. The biggest event organised so far was the 'Football And Love' exhibition that took place in September 2013. The title was set in direct contrast to the usual association of football and violence by politicians and in the media. This was reflected in a panel discussion featuring – among others – the managing director of the DFL, Andreas Rettig, Daniela Wurbs, CEO of Football Supporters Europe and top sports journalists. Another panel covered sexual discrimination and homophobia in football. A 'street party' included bands, readings, and entertainment for the children. An extremely successful workshop about how to make flags and banners attracted both the youngsters and adults, introducing them to the DIY culture of being a St. Pauli fan. Overall, at least 2,500 people showed up. This mixture of football, pop and politics was a very deliberate strategy, reflecting perfectly the ethos of the club's supporters, as Christoph Nagel, curator of the exhibition stated: 'The fact that we did not begin with a "classic" museum exhibition, presents a very conscious decision... FC St. Pauli is more than a football club and has greatly influenced not only football and fan culture, but also pop culture.'

Prior to 'Football And Love', the museum project had organised a series of events to celebrate the 25th anniversary of the club's promotion to the Bundesliga in 1988. The team that clinched promotion was predominantly made up of players who had grown up in Hamburg or the north of Germany. Many knew each other from local youth teams. As a result, they formed an incredible bond, not just with each other but also with the fans, drinking together in the Clubheim after matches, regardless of the result.

Sönke Goldbeck, one of those working hard to make the museum a reality, outlined the wide aims of the project: 'The museum will be much more than the exhibition anyway. Like the visible part of an iceberg, the museum should be the brain or memory of the club. It will collect not just "real" objects, but digital items as well and preserve them for later generations. For the objects to have real value they have to be put into a context – something that requires further research. The museum archive will be available to interested parties for study. And it will be more than the rooms in the Gegengerade. With tours of the stadium and the district, the whole ground will become part of the unfolding story. Street art in the Gegengerade and the south and main stands are already examples of that, as is the wider St Pauli district which has played such an important role in the development of the club.'

Reflecting the number of people interested in FC St. Pauli from around the world and the inspiration supporters drew from outside

Germany, content will be presented in both German and English wherever possible.

There is a lot of hard work required for the museum to become a reality. It is anticipated that the cost of getting the project off the ground will run into six figures. When the museum opens its doors, it will not only be another victory for the collective spirit of the fans of FC St. Pauli. It will also help safeguard the future by celebrating the past. It's a future that – as evidenced by the Rote Flora protests – is still being fought for on the streets of Hamburg. It is a project in which, through this book, I am proud to play a small part.

MATCH

HOMAGE FROM CATALUNYA/REFUGEES WELCOME

FC St. Pauli 3 SG Dynamo Dresden 2
2. Bundesliga
Sunday 28 October 2012, 1.30pm, Millerntor Stadion

FC St. Pauli 0 SV Sandhausen 0
2. Bundesliga
Friday 25 October 2013, 6.30pm, Millerntor Stadion

ALMOST EXACTLY A year before (at the start of the October half-term) I'd spent an enjoyable couple of nights in Hamburg with my family, and my mate Shaun and his kids, celebrating my 40th birthday. We'd watched St. Pauli win 2-1 against FSV Frankfurt, and both Shaun and I had been a bit giddy on the three Astras we'd had before kick-off (so much so, that I'd missed Max Kruse's opening goal because of a trip to the loo). This time I am travelling alone, but the forecast promises more of the beautifully crisp autumn weather that we'd experienced 12 months earlier. I am looking forward to the match against Dynamo Dresden, but more importantly, I am looking forward to seeing the progress of the new Gegengerade first hand – I've been religiously following its construction via the club webcam and the constant stream of photographs posted on various blogs on a daily basis. I am also excited by the prospect of meeting up with several groups of St. Pauli fans that I've got to know via Twitter. However, it is also a trip tinged with worry. Not my usual paranoia about flying, nor the worry of attending what the police would call a 'high-risk' game against Dynamo Dresden; it is a very real, deep-seated worry about the future of German football.

As mentioned in a previous chapter, back in July the German football authorities had held a 'Security Summit' and released a Code of Conduct. But just a week or so before this trip to the Millerntor, the DFB and the DFL had published (or more accurately, had published for them – it had been leaked) a document entitled 'Sicheres Stadionerlebnis' or 'Safe Stadium Experience'.

On the surface, the document could be seen as a continuation of the authorities' tough stance on the perceived increase in football violence (despite statistics confirming that this is actually on the decrease). In truth their obsession with 'safety' is probably more to do with moving the Bundesliga 'brand' and German football in general to more closely replicate the English Premier League model. Scratch beneath the surface of the thinly-veiled threat of 'you'd better behave all or we will take away your terraces' is the idea that if you make your stadiums all-seater, you can charge people more money for the privilege of watching football in 'comfort'. Not only that, but taking away the terraces and putting up prices should rid the game of those pesky ultras and their pyro, flags and culture. Without going into the minutiae of the Safe Stadium Experience, it seems the clubs, and by implication the supporters, are being dealt with by the use of an awful lot of stick and not very much carrot ('carrots' being an apparent increase in funding for fan projects and the prospect of clubs taking their own stewards to away games). The list of sanctions was much more substantial. In addition to the threat of converting terracing to seats was the threat of removing a club's licence if rules were not adhered to, and the mooted withholding of TV money to pay for any fines that may occur during the season (clubs are heavily fined every time fans use pyrotechnics in the stadium). There were also very real threats to civil liberties, including ridiculously stringent searches of supporters entering the stadium: again ostensibly to improve the 'safety' of spectators but really to try to put a stop to pyro being smuggled into the ground. Under the proposals, supporters would have to sign up to a 'Fan Charter', effectively making them totally compliant to the stadium rules at all times. Failure to adhere to the charter would, of course, trigger a series of punishments, such as reduced ticketing and the continued use of stadium bans for those fans deemed to have caused an offence.

At first glance the Safe Stadium Experience document smacks of the authorities using a sledgehammer to crack a nut, i.e. the overstated problem (blown out of all proportion by a sensationalist tabloid media, sound familiar?) of violence at football games. This is a problem that most supporters from various fan scenes agree would be better solved through more compassionate, low-key policing and sensitive self-regulation by fan groups themselves (not enforced from above).

However, as someone who lived through the gentrification of English football, driven by the Premier League 'brand' and delivered through all-seater stadia and television money, it is hard not to believe that these changes are born from wanting to ape the Premier League. Unfortunately, the German football authorities can't see the wood for the trees. They don't seem to realise that they already have a successful, distinct 'brand'. The Bundesliga might not be populated with the biggest names in world football (Pep Guardiola's appointment at Bayern might change that) but it can certainly boast the best attendances, figures that put the Premier League to shame. Very rarely at a Bundesliga game would you see the swathes of empty seats that you might get at somewhere like Wigan, and this is precisely because tickets are affordable and fans have the option to stand. It makes you feel like shaking the nearest Bundesliga official (not that I'd recognise one) and telling them, your 'brand', 'product' or plain old 'football league' is already one of the most admired in the world. The last thing you want to be is a cheap clone of the Premier League.

My weekend is living proof of this. In the morning, I plan to meet with two groups of fellow St. Pauli fans who have travelled from England and Spain to watch a game. Why? Well, partly because of the unique social and political conditions in St. Pauli, but also because watching football on a terrace in Germany is so bloody good. Every week, the Fanladen handles numerous requests from overseas fans wanting tickets. It's not just St. Pauli; you only have to log on to a website like *European Football Weekends* to be bombarded with accounts of fans travelling across Europe to watch German football. And they travel precisely because of the fan culture and atmosphere that the authorities seem hell-bent on destroying.

Perhaps, because I've seen the soul sucked out of English football, the threat to the future of the German game seems even more painful. I stood by and watched as the club I loved for most of my life was reduced to an empty shell, frequently passed between owners, who seemed to care far less than us, like a second-hand car. I stood by (unless you count a few ranting fanzine articles) as the game itself got sold down the river, divided into a world of haves and have-nots, its heart ripped out and replaced with cheap plastic seats and corporate hospitality. But I was lucky, I found St. Pauli and got a second chance, and truth be told I'm really scared I'm going to lose it.

Still, if there's any group of football fans I'd want fighting my corner, it would be the intensely motivated, organised and politicised fans of German football. And I haven't flown all this way to depress myself, I have the excitement of an afternoon at the Millerntor to look forward to.

A combination of my flight being delayed, and me going the long way round on the U3 U-Bahn (the same principle as London's Circle Line) means I don't make it to my hotel until after 11.00pm, not being helped by the fact that I walk straight past it on a couple of occasions. There is a crowd outside the Jolly Roger as I walk from the station, and before I've even unpacked I've texts from Scott from Yorkshire St. Pauli fanclub encouraging me to venture back out into the night. However, showing my age, the prospect of a decent night's sleep and a chance to finally read a copy of *World Soccer* I bought a couple of weeks previously is too much to resist, even with the bonus of gaining an hour's extra sleep via the clock change. And I think I'd been so clever here, by not putting the clock on my phone forward an hour on arrival in Hamburg, so that I won't then have to put it back an hour again later that night (more of that genius plan shortly).

I wake up to find that the forecasters had come good on their promise of a beautiful autumn morning. Pulling back the curtains and opening the window I am greeted by a wonderfully pale blue sky and a rush of cool morning air. Footage from the German equivalent of *Match of the Day* the previous evening shows Freiburg and Dortmund playing their fixture in the Black Forest in a blizzard, a convenient reminder of what a huge country Germany is. I wake refreshed, and thinking I've got loads of time until my 10.45am rendezvous with the #FCSP twitter folk at the Jolly Roger. It takes a quick call home, and some triangulation of time zones via the internet to realise that my phone has actually out-smarted me and has automatically rewound an hour to accommodate for the end of British Summer Time. Thus it is 9.30am not the 8.30am showing on my phone. Man, it is confusing.

I want to wander around prior to meeting the others, mostly to get a good look at the Gegengerade. Last year, I went for an early morning run around the district. It's a great way to get your bearings, even if I had to body-swerve some less than sober revellers making their way home from a night out. I took my camera and was able to get great shots of the area around the stadium in the beautifully soft early morning light. This time it is only a short walk to the Millerntor and before long I am on an otherwise deserted Heiligengeistfeld taking pictures of the new stand. The Dom is either setting up or dismantling, I'm not sure which, but the sleepy caravans and battered trucks are a suitable counterpoint to the hulking pre-cast concrete of the new stand. From the outside, it is pretty impressive, if largely unlovable at the moment due to its plain grey concrete exterior. If I'm honest, I am not sure about these pyramid roof supports either (both structurally – how the hell do they keep the roof up? – and aesthetically they give the stand the appearance of an airport terminal). I also stand there frantically taking photos of the three remaining floodlight pylons, hoping there's a campaign to keep them as part of the stadium, even if they no longer serve a practical purpose (something about them being to expensive to maintain). To me, the floodlights are iconic, as important to the St. Pauli skyline as the bunker, the cranes on the harbour or the TV tower.

Of course, in recent weeks there's been good news, too, with the 'Goliathwache' police station looking likely to be externally sited, rather than sharing the back straight with the Fanräume, Fanladen and the AFM. The success of fans once again mobilising under the banner of the Jolly Rouge to ward off this particular threat to the St. Pauli fan scene has been the lone highlight of an otherwise dismal start to the 2012–13 season.

I get my photos of the Gegengerade redevelopment and make my way back towards the Jolly. It isn't open yet but there are already a number of subdued, hungover looking people hanging about outside. Looking more sprightly than most (I think they retired to their hotel at a sensible hour too) are the guys from Catalunya, unmistakable because they are carrying a couple of yellow, red and blue Catalan flags. Before long, we are joined by a slightly bleary-eyed contingent from Yorkshire St. Pauli who'd been in the Jolly the previous night until 3am or 4am, depending on how you view the clock change. The guys exchange fanclub stickers, and for my part, I pass round what is left of the Cherry Drops I'd bought at the airport the day before. They are something of a hit, giving a short-term sugar boost to bloodstreams still feeling the effects of a long night drinking.

As the Jolly Roger opens we opt for a seat inside (believe it or not, despite this being my umpteenth trip to the Millerntor, it was the first time I've been inside). It is smaller than I imagined, but the furnishings are just what I expected. Soon Catalunya and Yorkshire St. Pauli stickers are added to the tables already plastered with those from various fan groups and campaigns. It is still pretty quiet, with not much beer being consumed, but before long we're joined by Dave (the singer and guitarist with the band Swearing at Motorists) and his young son, Ludwig. Then, it is time to head down to the Fanladen to see Stefan and pick up our tickets. As we are leaving the Jolly I collide with a couple of fans I'd met on my last trip over to the Millerntor in May, who are out early looking for tickets and are already on the beer. These random happenings all add to the haphazard, mental, yet totally absorbing nature of matchday at the Millerntor.

The morning holds one more surprise. After queuing for an age in a packed Fanladen, and after being ribbed by a young drama student (studying in Dresden but a follower of St. Pauli) about the British obsession with queuing – apparently she was almost lynched in London by ignoring a queue at the bus stop – we go over to the AFM container for a pre-match beer. There we've arranged to meet a genuine FC St. Pauli legend, Michél Mazingu-Dinzey. Michél had two spells at the Millerntor and was part of the team that reached the semi-finals of the DFB Pokal in 2005–06; indeed it was his strike that opened the scoring in the amazing quarter-final game against Werder Bremen in the snow at the Millerntor. Having already done an interview in the YSP Fanzine, and being a member of the extended #FCSP Twitter family, he's volunteered to meet us prior to the game. I'm not sure I've ever met a nicer, more genuine footballer. He talks fondly of his time at the Millerntor and his plans to meet up with fellow ex-Paulianer Ian Joy and Florian Lechner over in the States. We even manage to get everyone captured on camera in a group photograph.

The morning has flown by, and before long we are climbing the painted concrete steps (rotated through 90 degrees since my last visit, due to the construction of the Gegengerade) of the Südkurve, enmasse and heading for the terracing. Since my trip over at the end of last season, the concourse under the South Stand has been considerably pimped up with some great bits of St. Pauli art. They include a tribute to local graffiti artist, Oz and an amusing and apt Rolling Stones pastiche that reads: 'Südkurve Rolling Stoned.' Slowly but surely, the sanitised concrete concourse of the rebuilt South Stand is being re-St. Paulified – hundreds of stickers adorn every free space, from the toilet walls to the crush barriers on the terrace – it's the sort of look that would give any UK stadium manager a heart attack, but again the sheer variety of stickers is a simple visualisation of the strength of German fan culture, the same culture that the authorities seem to want to crush.

We take our places to the far left side of the terrace (the opposite side to my normal hang-out) so that Ludwig has a fighting chance of seeing the action, but not before I sneak off to capture a few shots of the Gegengerade as it fills up. Mighty impressive it looks too. The three temporary TV towers, made from scaffolding and tarpaulin, currently restrict both numbers and the view, but even with 6,000 out of the 10,000 standing places filled it is an impressive sight. I look forward to the day when it's full and absolutely rocking. I have a feeling if the fan groups on the back straight get loud and co-ordinated, they could probably blow the roof off its suspended pyramid supports.

The Südkurve choreo is a mixture of confetti and till rolls, prompting USP to reprise their 'Photo Love-Story' instruction leaflet on how to unfurl and throw a till roll, and thus avoid a repeat of the Eintracht Frankfurt game. Prior to kick-off the bin-bags full of confetti and shredded paper are passed back through the crowd and the till rolls distributed. The results are pretty spectacular, as a wall of streamers explodes over the safety netting and onto the pitch, draping over the goal nets and causing the stewards to earn their money clearing the goalmouth and delaying the kick-off ever so slightly.

It is as close as I am going to get to recreating one of my earliest football memories, watching the ticker-tape explosion that greeted the teams at the start of the 1978 World Cup final in Argentina. Up the other end, the Dynamo fans are working through a smart two-stage choreo, that ends with the away end blocked out by a wall of yellow cards with thick, yellow smoke escaping through the cracks. To my mind, it is a nice use of pyro (have they obscured everyone's faces with the cards, to avoid people being identified and picking up a stadium ban?). Regardless, I'm sure Dynamo will get fined for it. Indeed, there appears to be a small ruckus between fans and stewards shortly after their choreo, something to do with the removal of banners from along the front fence, although it is hard to tell from our position and with the far end of the stadium bathed in bright sunlight.

I'm not sure I want to dwell on the game, not the first half-hour anyway. I've yet to warm to the majority of this team (there has been a big clear-out and an influx of new faces over the summer) and my fears are confirmed when we find ourselves 2-0 down with two-thirds of the game to play. At this point, I can see it finishing four or five-nil to Dresden and, despite it being October, the spectre of relegation and the disastrous financial implications that would follow loom large. Fortunately, one of the few remaining members of the old guard, Fabian Boll, swivels and fires in a low shot to bring it back to 2-1 just seconds before the break. Then, just the other side of half-time, Christopher Avevor powerfully heads home from a corner to bring us level. The game is in the process of being turned on its head. The lively youngster, Joseph-Claude Gyau, brought on at the break, causes the Dynamo defence all kinds of problems, but it is a surging run by Fabian Boll that sets up Daniel Ginczek to fire St. Pauli ahead.

It is a hell of a turn-around from 0-2 to 3-2 in the space of 15 minutes. But there are still 35 minutes left to play, and frankly I don't think this will be the end of the scoring. But somehow it is. A combination of Dynamo running out of steam and some good defending by the St. Pauli backline sees us hold out for a much needed three points. The celebrations at the end seem born more from relief than joy, but hopefully the nature of the victory will inspire the team to climb the table.

New boss, Michael Frontzeck, in his first game at the Millerntor, is cheered off (to be fair, he might be bald, but he has differentiated himself from previous managers, Stani and Schubert by wearing tracksuit bottoms instead of jeans) and long after the rest of the team has disappeared down the tunnel Bene Pliquett wanders over to the front of the terrace for a chat and to accept his Yorkshire St. Pauli membership card. Again, this is not something I can imagine happening too often in the UK, but Benny, who's also done an interview for the YSP fanzine, is a St. Pauli fan, someone who if he isn't out on the pitch or sitting on the subs' bench will be in the stand with us lot.

Everyone makes their way back to the AFM container, but after an interesting chat about the political situation in Spain in general and at Espanyol in particular (the FCSP Catalunya Supporters are working hard to rid the club of its small fascist following – a hangover from the 1980s and '90s hooligan scene) I have to say my goodbyes and head back to the airport. I tag onto the back of USP's 'Diffidati Con Noi' march for a short while as I walk to the U-Bahn, leaving them to return to the Fanladen as I leave for home (I'm led to believe the police weren't too 'helpful', blocking or altering the route of the march.)

I've only been in Hamburg 18 hours, and I slept for the first eight or so, but it has been another excellent trip – one that is testament to the allure of German football and the experience its supporters create. Thanks in part to the power of social media – I'd never have met any of these like-minded people without Twitter – fans from all over Europe have come together to watch St. Pauli. The trip on my own would still have been enjoyable (I've been over 16 times now, and have never failed to enjoy myself) but it was incredible to meet a load of really good people, each doing their bit to spread our love of St. Pauli and to fight against the fascism and consumerism that remains a blight on the game we love.

As I mentioned above, German fans aren't just going to roll over and let the authorities shaft them, the way we did. A week and a bit before the Dresden game, Union Berlin published their own comprehensive response to the 'Safe Stadium Experience'. And once again, this was the club itself issuing a joint statement alongside their fan liaison office and various supporters' groups, including the umbrella group of Union ultras. The document, which ran to nine pages, offered a counterpoint to every issue raised by the DFB/DFL. It even used a wry line in humour to disarm the authorities over the perceived issue of football violence. In a nutshell, they pointed out that, statistically, arrests and injuries were far higher at that bastion of German cluture, the Oktoberfest in Münich than they were at football matches. It was one in the eye, not just for the DFB and DFL but also for the increasingly judgemental tabloid media.

Fan reaction began to snowball, both via the internet and among organised fan groups. There was an additional problem for St. Pauli fans: club vice president, Dr Gernot Stenger had been on the committee which had put the report together. Fans were angry, and being St. Pauli, there was the very real possibility that a motion could be tabled at the forthcoming AGM to have Dr Stenger removed from his post. To many, it was inconceivable that a member of the club's board could have played any part in such proposals. However, the club acted swiftly. They called a meeting with the Supervisory Board, the AFM, the Fanclubsprecherrat, the Standing Fan Committee (Ständiger Fanausschuss), the fan-delegate representatives and the Fanladen, resulting in a statement issued on the club website on 18 October, a day after Union Berlin, rejecting the majority of the report's proposals. It was stated that as there was no firm evidence of an increase in football-related violence, the proposals were unnecessary. It was also stated that vice president Stenger had resigned from the committee responsible for producing the 'Safe Stadium Experience' report.

Unlike Union Berlin's comprehensive response, the club's statement was short and to the point. There was one other crucial difference – it was issued by the club alone. Union's statement had unilateral support from supporters' groups. It was clear that, in St. Pauli's case, there was still a considerable distance between the club's opinion and that of various fan groups. The Ständiger Fanausschuss issued their own much more combative statement. It stated that: 'The planned actions of the DFL are, for us, nothing more than a declaration of war against all organised fans in German football stadiums.' They added that the opinions of the St. Pauli fan scene were very much in line with those of Union Berlin and its supporters, before stating that the club would not reach an agreement to publish a similar joint statement with St. Pauli fan groups.

While there was dismay at this lack of unity between club and fans, it was not totally surprising, and to an extent threatened to open old wounds, with the club and its fan base seemingly moving in different directions. However, football fans across Germany were united in their disdain for the authorities, and at the Ruhr derby between Dortmund and Schalke, the weekend after Union Berlin's and St. Pauli's statements, the Dortmund fans held up a banner praising the two clubs for publicly opposing the proposals.

There had been talk about the 'Safe Stadium Experience' among the fans I'd met at the Dresden game and opposition to the report was unanimous, especially keenly felt by fellow UK-based fans, all of whom have witnessed first hand the commercialisation and gentrification of the British game. By the time we'd returned home (to begin the process of planning our next trip) the opposition to the report had gathered considerable momentum. Many clubs had followed Union Berlin and St. Pauli's lead and expressed their opposition to the report.

At the beginning of November, a Fan Summit was held in Berlin, bringing together various fan groups, club officials and representatives from the DFB and DFL to discuss the report. Fan representatives from over 49 clubs in the top three tiers of German football attended. Andreas Rettig from the DFL stated: 'I understand the criticism of the fans', continuing: 'It (the report) is not set in stone.'

St. Pauli's Sven Brux spoke at the summit, and warned of a spiral of action and reaction between fans and the authorities. He counselled against the (very British) scenario of fans being ostracised and paying €50 at ticket to go to games. Brux also called for a complete reorganisation of the controversial stadium bans and suggested that the police and ultra groups needed to be more reflective and not act in unilateral solidarity.

He concluded: 'The security concept must be thrown in the bin. It would be best to start over again. To press the reset button.'

Sven Brux's presentation drew loud applause, a measure of the respect with which he's held as a founding father of the German fan scene and the common sense he spoke. The summit continued into the early evening, with a statement being issued at its conclusion. It called for the inclusion of supporters in the decision-making process and rejected the DFB/DFL's imposed time frame of 12 December 2012 for finalising the 'Safe Stadium Experience'.

On the same day, an internet petition was launched entitled: 'I Feel Safe'. The website stated sarcastically: 'Reportedly anarchy and violence reign in German football, visiting a stadium has become a dangerous adventure,' before going on to say that visiting a football stadium now is far safer than it was ten or 20 years ago. The petition quickly attracted signatures from all over Germany and beyond, as supporters looked to counter the sensationalist claims made in the media and by the authorities. In the run-up to 12 December 2012, fans of all clubs quickly united behind the '12:12 Ohne Stimme Keine Stimmung' ('No Voice, No Atmosphere') campaign. This led to an eerie silence descending on stadiums across the country for the first 12 minutes and 12 seconds of games, giving the authorities, broadcasters and sponsors an idea of what the game would be like if fans continue to be persecuted. It was a powerful form of protest, although for fans from the UK, the silence was scarily similar to the atmosphere at most grounds these days. In a way that was the point.

Across Europe, the Bundesliga is lauded for its atmosphere and affordable ticket prices, yet the authorities seem hell-bent on following the Premiership model. After all, money talks. On 12.12.12 in Frankfurt the 'Safe Stadium' paper was passed by member clubs, despite five clubs, including Union Berlin and FC St. Pauli, voting for a delay so fans could be consulted. Whether, as widely feared, it turns out to be the death knell for fan culture in Germany remains to be seen. What is certain is that some of the measures passed in the paper are at best draconian and at worst unconstitutional.

The full body searches as used before the game between Bayern Münich and Eintracht Frankfurt were a serious development along with the potential to reduce away fans' ticket allocation to five per cent for games deemed to be 'high-risk'. At least, Union Berlin's flat refusal to sign up to the first draft of the paper prompted several concessions, but the impact on German fan culture could still be immense. The DFL and DFB have taken a lot of flak for their proposals, although there is a school of thought that they were stuck between a rock and a hard place, having their arm twisted by the Interior Ministry, who in turn were responding to tabloid hysteria. The government wanted to be seen as cracking down on something that had been totally blown out of proportion by a sensationalist media. Hammering football fans could also be seen as a quick win for the government. In Germany, just as in England, the authorities are keen to clamp down on the old-school, working-class football fan. And running alongside this narrative is the desire of the television companies, sponsors and advertisers (and some clubs too) to rid the game of troublesome ultras and their ilk, replacing them with a more lucrative, middle-class fan base with more money to spend on their products and services. It is the gentrification of football, pure and simple. Building brand loyalty at the expense of communities. Consumers not fans.

With safety concerns at the top of the agenda, FC St. Pauli v Dynamo Dresden was the first game I'd been to that had been deemed 'high-risk' by the authorities, yet I'd felt totally safe. Both sets of supporters had been loud and created impressive choreos, but at no point had I felt remotely under threat. Despite the police stance, there was never really any risk of trouble; even the banning of beer inside the stadium seemed a nonsense as it was readily available outside the ground. However, I do appreciate that I've not yet travelled to a potentially dodgy away fixture such as Hansa Rostock. I have seen that this can be a risky business with fans being attacked pretty indiscriminately. And when I do travel away, I take the sensible precaution of not wearing my colours until I'm safely inside the guest block. FC St. Pauli may be many people's 'second club' but on my travels to relatively safe places like Aachen or Dusseldorf I'm aware that there's always the risk of bumping into some right-wing hools. For me, being a St. Pauli fan isn't – as it is for some – a fashion statement, it is a political statement.

I started this book searching for something in which to believe: a football club that embodied my political beliefs and a fan scene that represented everything I had loved about football growing up, but that had been taken away from me through the corporatisation of the modern game. I found St. Pauli and fell in love all over again. If I'm honest, as I finish writing, my biggest emotion is fear. Fear that history will repeat itself and that the club I found and with which I fell in love and the atmosphere at German football for which I'm prepared to travel hundreds of miles, by train or plane, will be taken from me. But then I speak to the fellow St. Pauli fans I've met on my trips to the

Millerntor, to the fantastic people at the Fanladen, to Ultrà Sankt Pauli; I read reports on the internet and I feel a passion and determination among German football fans that I'd never felt even at the height of the fanzine movement in the late 1980s in the UK, and I think *we're* not going to give up *our* fan culture without a fight. And I realise that I'm speaking in the first person. I am not some interested third party. I am part of this fan scene and, as such, I'm going to do everything I can to help preserve it.

A year on, in October half-term of 2013, I find myself back on the Südkurve at the Millerntor for a Friday night game against SV Sandhausen. A dour game finishes 0-0, but as I've increasingly come to realise over the years, the actual football matters very little when visiting St. Pauli. This trip really isn't about the football, it's about joining the fans and residents of St. Pauli in support of Hamburg's Lampedusa refugees. The refugees had fled Libya following the unrest in 2011 and had been housed on the Italian island of Lampedusa. After the closure of the Lampedusa camp, 300 or so refugees arrived in Hamburg. After a period in which many lived on the streets, the local church and various social housing projects provided the refugees with somewhere to sleep. However, as the months progressed, the Hamburg authorities began to come down hard on the refugees. Police harassment of the refugees reached a peak during October 2013, and prompted confrontations on the streets with those protesting against the treatment of the refugees. It was against this backdrop of nightly disturbances that we assembled on Millerntorplatz for the solidarity demonstration in support of the Lampedusa refugees. Thanks to some good work by our friends Claudia and Hannah we manage to get hold of some Astra to keep the spirits up on the march and hook back up with the 14 (FOURTEEN!) members of Yorkshire St. Pauli who were over for the trip and had organised a fund-raising evening for Lampedusa in the Jolly Roger the night before – and our old friend Dave from Swearing at Motorists, who lifts everyone's spirits as he sings a rakish version of *Flying Pizza* down the phone to my friend Shaun back in the UK. In the dark of the Millerntorplatz, Claudia makes sure we all put the number of the organisers' solicitor into our phones just in case there's any trouble with the police. As the march sets off, it is impossible to gauge its scale, but right from the start it is clear that the police have decided to take a change of tack and opt for a lower profile. After nights of clashes between protestors and the police, it is a welcome change and probably a result of this being an 'official' i.e. registered protest. We wind our way slowly through the streets singing and chatting. The rain holds off and everyone appears in good spirits. At some point the march turns left onto the Reeperbahn and it is only then that we get an idea of its scale. Craning our necks from the central reservation we can see that there are what look like thousands of people ahead of us. We knew there are a fair few behind us too as the rest of the Yorkshire delegation had radioed in and were at least ten minutes further back. It is a great feeling to know that so many St. Pauli fans and residents have come out to support the refugees. There's still a way to go before reaching the church where some of the Lampedusa refugees are sheltering. We get there eventually, the whole march taking just under two hours. From here the protestors mill about for a bit before dissipating into the night. There isn't even a hint of trouble. I'm not even sure I saw a single police officer on the duration of the march. Estimates say that between 8,000 and 10,000 people were on the streets, making it one of the biggest demonstrations since the days of the Hafenstraße. It is certainly a remarkable show of solidarity, one that hopefully sends a strong message to the Hamburg Senate. If they don't sit up and take notice, and the police don't change their unjust racial profiling of the refugees then the opposition will only intensify. After the march, we say our goodbyes to those not staying at our hotel and head back to the bar.

We are up early the next morning, as we are down to attend the International Refugee Summit taking place at the new Fanräume at the Millerntor. However, before that there's Yorkshire St. Pauli's kick-about to take part in. Dave meet us, reasonably promptly, at 10.30am, on the Reeperbahn and leads us to a small caged asphalt pitch, made more treacherous by a cunning mixture of autumn leaves and broken glass. But hey, we're from Yorkshire (well, I'm not, strictly speaking) and are made of sterner stuff and before we know it we've split into teams and are under way. At this point, it is fair to say that the best player on the pitch was some 12-year-old local kid wearing a Ginczek shirt. At one point this lad sells Scott (who was in nets) an amazing dummy and slots the ball into the empty net. It draws an impromptu round of applause. By the end of the game, he's become YSP's all-time leading goalscorer – by some considerable margin.

The Refugee Summit kicks off at 2pm, going head-to-head with the club shop clearance sale (think Harrods January Sale only with everything available exclusively in brown). The more worthy of these two events includes speakers from USP, United Glasgow, Lampedusa refugees themselves and, of course, Yorkshire St. Pauli's very own Scott Stubbs talking on behalf of Leeds-based refugee charity PAFRAS. It's a well-attended event with the speakers filling in lots of detail about the refugee situation in Hamburg and elsewhere in Europe.

With the presentations over, it is time to head over to the 3G pitches behind the Nordkurve for a game of football between United Glasgow FC and the Lampedusa refugees. Being one player short – many of United Glasgow's regular players are drawn from those seeking asylum in the UK and therefore don't have the necessary 'status' to travel, which really brings it home that, sadly, governments take a very different slant on the 'no person is illegal' mantra – I am able to bag a place at right-back, a position I'd not played in since secondary school. Just playing on the pitches in the shadow of the Millerntor ticks off another of my St. Pauli ambitions, but to do it in support of such a worthy cause makes the occasion even more special. For that, I am especially grateful to the Glasgow guys for giving an international debut to an ageing journeyman, who really struggles not to constantly wander into midfield. It is amazing to play against so many good players too; many of the refugees had played to quite a high level in Africa, and this is evident as they race into a 2-0 lead after just ten minutes. But (Millerntor) roared on by a healthy crowd, United Glasgow fight their way back into the game and claw it back to 2-2 by half-time. The second half sees the teams mixed up a bit and Glasgow run out 4-2 winners. But, like so much in St. Pauli, today's game isn't about the result.

It's a strange one. Football is the vehicle upon which so much of the St. Pauli experience hangs, yet once you are here, the football part seems so insignificant. It's about people giving a toss about each other. About showing that we care, that governments and their policies are wrong. It's not about nations or borders, it's about 10,000 people marching together or 22 people from different backgrounds and cultures coming together through football to show that they appreciate each other. It's bloody powerful and I'm proud to play a tiny part in it.

Sometimes, I struggle to explain to people exactly why I travel over to Germany three or four times a year to watch St. Pauli. This weekend is why. I also sometimes mentally work my way through the list of the 92 League clubs in the UK thinking: is there a club where, after a game, 10,000 fans would join a march in support of a cause that is actually nothing to do with their football team and everything to do with fairness, equality and improving the lives of those less fortunate than them? I simply can't think of one. That's why I love St. Pauli. Of course, as we have seen, this incredible idealistic and compassionate fan scene isn't without its faults and fissures and it would be both naïve and plain wrong to paint it as some kind of footballing utopia, but it's probably as close as we are going to get.

In the space of six years, FC St. Pauli has become part of me and conversely I've become part of them, a bit part player for sure, but I am incredibly proud to be involved with such an amazing set of passionate, principled football fans. In some small way, this book forms some of my contribution. I hope it has both debunked and reinforced certain elements that combine to make up the 'Mythos of St. Pauli', but above all I hope it inspires other like-minded fans to visit the Millerntor – to sample an atmosphere and culture that simply has to be preserved, because it is too valuable to be consumed.

At the start I reproduced the lyrics from Swearing at Motorists' *St. Pauli 'Til I Die*. I hope beyond all hope that this is the case. However, rewind 20 years and it would never have entered my head that one day, in the not so distant future, I would not be a Watford season ticket holder. Things change. I was lucky to find St. Pauli. I chose them not for their football, but for the unique culture that has grown around the club. As a kid starting to follow Watford, it was the players and the team that I owed my loyalty to; now – here in Hamburg – it is the fans. I will be a fan of St. Pauli, if not until the day I die, then for as long as those like-minded individuals continue to stand on the Südkurve, Nordkurve or the Gegengerade. And if the worst comes to the worst, I will follow them wherever they go next. Football without the fans is nothing. The same goes for St. Pauli. As Dave Doughman so brilliantly penned in the above song: '*They're* not a team, *we* are a club.' I'd go one step further and say, '*We* are a community': a community I am proud to be a part of. Long may that continue.

FORZA SANKT PAULI!

ACKNOWLEDGEMENTS

THE LIST OF people I need to thank for their help and support with this book is pretty extensive. I'm also sure I'll end up forgetting people. Apologies in advance.

First and foremost, I am indebted to the folk at Fanladen St. Pauli;without them I wouldn't have got tickets for the games I have witnessed at the Millerntor and without that experience, I'd never have fallen in love with the club, the culture and the district. Thank you in particular: Heiko, Stefan and Justus.

Sönke Goldbeck and Christoph Nagel deserve a particular mention for gently pointing out the factual inaccuracies in my initial drafts and offering valuable insight, suggestions for improvements and support throughout the entire editing process.

Sven Brux and Stefan Schatz provided me with great, in-depth interviews about the Fanladen past and present. Martin from Ultrà Sankt Pauli provided a fascinating insight into USP and the same could be said of the representatives from Sozialromantiker Sankt Pauli who gave up their time for interview. I also need to thank Ian Joy for writing the foreword and for taking the time to chat to me from the other side of the world; your status as an FCSP legend is richly deserved.

The FC St. Pauli UK Messageboard has been a lifeline for keeping up to date with the goings on at the Millerntor and through it I have met up with some incredible people. The Yorkshire St. Pauli fan club have raised the bar in recent years, with Scott Stubbs deserving a particular mention for the help and support he has provided. Social media has made it possible to feel a part of the active fan-scene even when I'm miles from the Millerntor. It has also been a pleasure to regularly communicate with FC St. Pauli legend Michél Mazingu-Dinzey on Twitter. I also need to thank Dave Doughman from Swearing at Motorists, who in a two-minute song, *St. Pauli 'Til I Die*. summarised succinctly what I have tried to say in hundreds of pages.

The dearth of English language material written about FC St. Pauli has caused me to rely quite heavily on a selection of books and articles. I have often quoted at length from these works, but hope that I have stayed the right side of outright plagiarism (that was never my intention). To this end, I need to extend thanks to Chris Sanderson for his incredible dissertation, *'Nie wieder Faschismus, Nie wieder Krieg, Nie wieder 3.Liga!' A Social History of FC St. Pauli, 1986–1991* – a work that I returned to again and again throughout the course of writing this book. Other works by René Martens, Christoph Nagel, Michael Pahl, Ulrich Hesse-Lichtenburger and Keith Lowe made piecing together the history of the club and district an interesting and enjoyable process.

Then there are the countless websites and blogs that I spent hours poring over, running them through Google Translate in the hope of finding nuggets of information about the present-day goings-on at the club. Again, there are too many to mention them all, but KleinerTod's FC St. Pauli Blog has provided me with detailed reports on the goings-on both on and off the pitch at the Millerntor – it is simply brilliant.

Finally, family, friends and colleagues deserve a special mention. Special thanks to Kathryn, Bessy and Charlotte. To Shaun, my best friend, who has been through a rough few years, but has constantly amazed me with his good humour and friendship. And to everyone I've met on various trips to the Millerntor; your warmth and kindness are incredible. Here's a bit of a list in no particular order: Mark and Claudia for spilling beer and taking photos of Deniz Naki respectively, Malte, Lotti, Christian, Nicole, Vanessa, Dom, Luke G, Tommi, Tom Leak, Mick, Thomas Kozinowski, Laura Reinkens, Gary and Katharine, Baptista Silanes Poderoso, Chris Stride, Chris Webster, Spoon, the Port Vale and London lot. *Forza Sankt Pauli!*

SELECT BIBLIOGRAPHY

Backes, Gregor, *Mit Deutschem Sportgruss, Heil Hitler': Der FC St. Pauli im Nationalsozialismus,* Hoffmann und Campe, 2010

Fanladen St. Pauli, *15 Jahre Fanladen St. Pauli, 20 Jahre Politik Im Stadion,* Fanladen St. Pauli, 2005

Hesse-Lichtenberger, Ulrich, *Tor! The Story of German Football,* WSC Books, 2002

Jefferies, Matthew, *Hamburg – A Cultural & Literary History,* Signal Books, 2011

Katzenber, Susanne and Tamm, Olaf, *Millerntor: Das alte Stadion,* Braus, 2012

Khun, Gabriel, *Soccer vs. the State,* PM Press, 2011

Lowe, Keith, *Inferno – The Devastation of Hamburg, 1943,* Penguin Books, 2007

Martens, René, *Niemand Siegt Am Millerntor,* Verlag Die Werkstatt, 2008

Martens, René, *Wunder Gibt Es Immer Wieder, Die Geschichte Des FC St. Pauli,* Verlag Die Werkstatt, 2007

Nagel, Christoph and Pahl, Michael, *FC St. Pauli. Das Buch,* Hoffman und Campe, 2009

Perryman, Mark, *Hooligan Wars: Causes and Effects of Football Violence,* Mainstream, 2002

Sanderson, Chris, *'Nie wieder Faschismus, Nie wieder Krieg, Nie wieder 3. Liga!' A Social History of FC St. Pauli, 1986–1991,* University of Warwick, 2009

The following articles and web-links also provided valuable information:
11 Freunde, http://www.11freunde.de
A-Infos, Autonomia and the Origin of the Black Bloc, http://www.
  ainfos.ca/01/jun/ainfos00170.html
AFM, http://www.fcstpauli-afm.de
Afroh photography, http://afroh.de
BAFF, http://www.stpauli-fanladen.de
Ballesterer, A Dispute Between Neighbours, http://www.ballesterer.at/
  heft/weitere-artikel/streit-unter-nachbarn.html
Basch Fanzine, http://basch-fanzine.de
Berlin Fan Sumit November 2012, http://www.textilvergehen.
  de/2012/11/01/fangipfel-in-berlin-november-2012
*Bundesliga Fanatic, How meatballs and sausages got St. Pauli to the
  top by Niklas Wildhagen,* http://bundesligafanatic.com/how-
  meatballs-and-sausages-got-st-pauli-to-the-top
CNN, Punks, prostitutes and St. Pauli: Inside soccer's coolest club,
  http://edition.cnn.com/2010/SPORT/football/08/18/football.
  st.pauli.punks/index.html
Empire St. Pauli, http://www.empire-stpauli.de
FanladenSt. Pauli, http://www.stpauli-fanladen.de
Fanräume im Millertorstadion, http://www.stpauli-fanladen.de
FC St. Pauli, Club History, http://www.fcstpauli.com/home/verein/
  historie/vereinsgeschichte
FCSP Athens South End Scum, Meet Ultrà Sankt Pauli, http://
  fcspsouthendscum.wordpress.com/2012/02/07/interview-meet-
  ultra-sankt-pauli
FCUM A.D., Do The Right Thing, http://fcumad.tumblr.com/
  post/21659291695/do-the-right-thing-or-st-pauli-3-v-0-fc-
  hansa, *Yes We Have No Bananas,* http://fcumad.tumblr.com/
  post/13248776308/yes-we-have-no-bananas-hansa-rostock
Fussballdaten.de, http://www.fussballdaten.de
Hamburger Morgenpost, I Invented the Skull Cult, http://
  www.mopo.de/news/st--pauli-ich-erfand-den-totenkopf-
  kult,5066732,5150494.html, *Halls Rampage at the
  "Schweinske Cup",* http://www.mopo.de/st-pauli/hallen-
  randale-beim--schweinske-cup--st--pauli-greift-die-polizei-
  an,5067040,11410468.html, *Schweinske Cup Disaster,*

Bibliography

http://www.mopo.de/st-pauli/schweinske-cup-desaster-
-innensenator---polizei-nicht-ausgangspunkt-der-
krawalle-,5067040,11414032.html

Kleinertod's FC St. Pauli Blog, Rumstehterroristen, http://
kleinertod.wordpress.com/2012/04/23/rumstehterroristen-
fcsp-nahezu-ohne-hansa-rostock-im-gefahrengebiet, *Passion in
the Stands, Suffering on the Pitch*, http://kleinertod.wordpress.
com/2012/09/26/leidenschaft-auf-den-rangen-leiden-auf-dem-
platz-fcsp-heimniederlage-gegen-aalen

Magischer FC, http://www.magischerfc.de

Sank Pauli Mafia, http://sanktpaulimafia.blogsport.de

Sozialromantiker Sankt Pauli, http://www.sozialromantiker-stpauli.
de

St. Pauli Forum, http://www.stpauli-forum.de

St. PauliUK Messageboard, http://stpaulifansuk.forumup.co.uk

Stefan Groenveld Photography, http://www.stefangroenveld.de

Taz.de, The Long Shadow of the Past, http://www.taz.de

Ten Meters Without A Head, Chronology of the Hafenstraße,
http://www.nadir.org/nadir/archiv/Haeuserkampf/Hafenstrasse/
story.html

*The Quietus, At The End Of The Grosse Freiheit: The Beatles In
Hamburg*, http://thequietus.com/articles/04982-the-beatles-
hamburg

The Thunder Independent Celtic Fanzine, http://the-thunder.com

Übersteiger-Blog, http://blog.uebersteiger.de

Ultrà Sankt Pauli, http://usp.stpaulifans.de

Yorkshire St. Pauli, http://yorkshirestpauli.com

'A club like no other deserves a Museum like no other' is the motto of 1910 – Museum for FC St. Pauli e.V. This fan-founded society aims to realise a unique place celebrating (and reflecting on) the past and future of the club – including a permanent (and ever-changing) exhibition and professional archive facilities. It is the biggest voluntary project ever started in the club's history.

More information: www.1910-museum.de

Printed in Dunstable, United Kingdom